Wes Collins reveals patterns of centeredness in various aspects of the Mam language, not only in the lexicon as expected, but in the use of spatial deixis and discourse structure as well. As a linguistic anthropologist, Collins' goal is to describe centeredness in the language in a way that makes sense to the native speakers: "Without grounding centeredness in the daily lives and speech of the Mam, we run the risk of proving something to ourselves while not shedding any light whatsoever on local custom and categorization."

Collins contributes greatly to the age-old discussion about the relationship between language and culture, claiming that centeredness is not only a great cultural value for the Mayan peoples of Guatemala but a grammatical theme in their languages as well. He establishes the connections between the use of linguistic centeredness–illustrated in the morphology, syntax, and discourse structure of Mam–and speakers' living out of that centeredness in their architecture, dress, health system, religion, and self-awareness. This book is written in a clear, logical manner and brings forward new information that both anthropologists and linguists alike will appreciate.

Charlotte Schaengold, *Ph.D., Professor of Linguistics and Anthropology, Northern Kentucky University*

Collins' discussion of health and wellness in the Mam community is especially careful to integrate historical evidence of cultural contact, ethnographic details of community variation, and on-the-ground observation of specific individual examples of the on-going accommodation of multiple strands of knowledge and experience to form a coherent understanding of the world.

Laura Martin, *Ph.D., Professor Emerita (Modern Languages and Anthropology), Cleveland State University; co-author of Culture in Clinical Care*

I wish this book had been available to me a half-century ago when I first began trying to learn Agta, an unwritten language in the Philippines. I highly recommend it as a basic how-to guide to ethnography for university courses in linguistic anthropology. Author Collins is an SIL linguistic anthropologist who has spent the past 30-plus years working among the Maya-Mam. In this book he pulls together what he has learned. Collins also ties germane theories to his thesis, such as ethnography as a method, the Sapir-Whorf hypothesis, emics and etics, worldview, and Collins's own notion of "centeredness" as an operating principle of the Maya-Mam people. He does not avoid controversial issues, such as the racist philosophy of Mam as a "lesser language," Mam as an endangered language today, whether culture drives language, whether the introduction of Christianity is an attack on Mayan religion, etc. I highly recommend to linguistic anthropologists who plan to do research in indigenous communities today that they read this book first!

Linguisitcs in light of anthropology is how languages should be studied; anthropology in light of linguistics is how culture should be studied.

Thomas N. Headland, *Ph.D., Fellow, American Anthropological Association; and Senior Anthropology Consultant, SIL International*

The Heart of the Matter

Seeking the Center in Maya-Mam
Language and Culture

SIL International®
Publications in Ethnography

44

The Publications in Ethnography series focuses on cultural studies of minority peoples of various parts of the world. While most volumes are authored by members of SIL International® who have done ethnographic research in a minority language, suitable works by others will also occasionally form part of the series.

Series Editor

Mike Cahill

Volume Editors

Joyce Park

Managing Editor

Bonnie Brown

Production Staff

Lois Gourley, Composition Supervisor
Judy Benjamin, Compositor
Barbara Alber, Cover Design

Cover Photo

Cover photograph by Natasha Schmale
Used by permission of the photographer and the two Mam greeters

The Heart of the Matter

Seeking the Center in Maya-Mam Language and Culture

Wesley M. Collins

Foreword by Brian D. Joseph

SIL International®
Dallas, Texas

© 2015 by SIL International®
Library of Congress Catalog No: 2015946650
ISBN: 978-1-55671-375-0
ISSN: 0-0895-9897

Printed in the United States of America

No part of this publication may be reproduced, stored in a retrieval system, or transmitted in any form or by any means—electronic, mechanical, photocopy, recording, or otherwise—without the express permission of SIL International®. However, short passages, generally understood to be within the limits of fair use, may be quoted without written permission.

Copies of this and other publications of SIL International® may be obtained through distributors such as Amazon, Barnes & Noble, other worldwide distributors and, for select volumes, www.sil.org/resources/publications:

SIL International Publications
7500 W. Camp Wisdom Road
Dallas, Texas 75236-5629 USA

General inquiry: publications_intl@sil.org
Pending order inquiry: sales_intl@sil.org
www.sil.org/resources/publications

Contents

Foreword ix
Preface: What to Expect xiii
1 Getting Started: The View from a Distance 1
   1.1 The heart of the matter: Centeredness as a cultural and
       grammatical theme 1
       1.1.1 Linguistic relativity and the Sapir-Whorf Hypothesis 4
   1.2 How might we show that language and culture are cut from
       the same cloth? 20
       1.2.1 A future for linguistic anthropology 25
   1.3 Methodology employed 27
       1.3.1 Ethnographic methods 27
       1.3.2 Linguistic methods and models 34
   1.4 Analysis of the data 36
   1.5 Who cares? 37
2 Some Context for Better Understanding this Book 41
   2.1 The occasion for research 41
   2.2 Some comments on the Mam 46
       2.2.1 Socio-economic situation 46
       2.2.2 Educational situation 51
       2.2.3 Religious situation 52

	2.2.4 Sociolinguistic situation 54
2.3	Some comments on the Mam language 57
2.4	Mam as an endangered language and efforts at revitalization 60
2.5	What's new in this book? 63

3 Centeredness as Cultural Theme 65
3.1 Introduction 65
3.2 Health as an instantiation of centeredness. 65
3.3 From *space* to *place*: On the meaning of building 72
  3.3.1 Timo's town 76
  3.3.2 Timo's homestead 80
3.4 Religion as a search for centeredness 85
  3.4.1 Centeredness and the *Popol Vuh* 88
  3.4.2 Entering inwardness; Mayan Protestantism 93
3.5 Conclusion 97

4 Centeredness as Cultural Practice 101
4.1 Why ethnography? 101
4.2 Introduction to thick description 104
4.3 Attaining *b'a'n* 107
4.4 Conclusion 131

5 Grammatical Aspects of Centeredness 133
5.1 Introduction 133
5.2 The centeredness of spatial deixis 138
5.3 Mam intransitive verbs of direction 139
5.4 Directional auxiliaries 146
  5.4.1 Directionals and deictic centeredness 150
5.5 Complex directionals 153
5.6 Extended use of *-x* and *-tz* 155
  5.6.1 A narrative context for directional suffixes 156
  5.6.2 *-x* in context 157
  5.6.3 *-tz* in context 159
5.7 The discourse function of *-tz* and *-x* 160
  5.7.1 A discourse function for *-tz* 162
  5.7.2 A possible discourse function for *-x* 164
5.8 Relational nouns as an instantiation of centeredness 166
5.9 Conclusion 168

6 Conclusion 171
6.1 What we've seen 171
6.2 Where do we go from here? 176
6.3 So why the commotion? 177

Appendix A: Text	181
Appendix B: List of Abbreviations	187
Appendix C: Notes on Orthography	189
References	191
Index	199

Foreword

Being asked to write a foreword to a book can be a dangerous enterprise, as one is therefore forever associated with the work, whatever its merits or demerits may be. In this case, however, it is truly an honor to be able to be associated with this book, as author Dr. Wesley Collins has put together a meritorious volume that is both scholarly and interesting, as well as highly readable, a combination unfortunately all too infrequent in academia.

Dr. Collins examines certain aspects of the life and language of the Maya-Mam, speakers, numbering some 500,000 in all, of a Mayan language in the area in and around Comitancillo, Guatemala. Starting with the premise that the Maya-Mam have a focus in their lives on the "center" and on "centeredness," Dr. Collins explores the ways this notion is manifest in both the culture the Maya-Mam live in and in the language which, as he says on p. 60, is available to the Maya-Mam for "the dual tasks of conceptualizing their world and enabling them to operate in it." Centeredness is related to deixis, a basic, and crucial, notion that deals with how we orient ourselves in the world, relative to things and to people.

Author Collins sees centeredness as playing a key role in the Maya-Mam sense of well-being, city planning, the layout of their homes, and other aspects of Maya-Mam physical culture, as well as intangible cultural constructs such as religion, but also—and this is crucial to his argumentation and to his being take seriously as within linguistic anthropology (or anthropological linguistics, terms he sees as largely interchangeable (p. 3)—in the organizational structure of the grammar of their language. The existence of a link between culture and language informs his work from the very start, and pervades the discussion throughout the six chapters of the book. Collins says in Chapter 1 that his "frame or touch point will be this dual notion of grammatical and cultural theme...that there is some kind of relationship or influence between the language that people speak and the culture that they live out on a day-to-day basis," and closes the book in Chapter 6 with the wish that he has "satisfied the hermeneutic approach to the problem" of whether "language and culture are interconstitutive in a measurable, empirical way" by showing that he has been able to interpret "data in a patterned way, consistent with how the Mam themselves view the world, how they see their place in it, their description of it, and their practice within it."

Importantly, Collins is not simply giving impressions gained from thirty-some-odd years experience with the Mam; rather, he builds a solid case for his premise by examining details of Maya-Mam culture in Chapter 3, the structure of a sector of the lexicon in Chapter 4, and in Chapter 5 the formation and meaning of a closed class of intransitive verbs of motion and a set of preposition-like "relational nouns" that serve as deictic orientation markers. In each case, he demonstrates the relevance of "a reference location or deictic center" (p. 169), and thereby gives the anthropological linguist (or linguistic anthropologist) grist for his/her mill. Collins speaks with the authority of one who has "lived Mayan," so to speak, and experienced Mam in a way that few outsiders ever do.

He is not afraid to take on controversy, e.g. regarding the interplay of centeredness and religion (both indigenous and Christian), and his reference throughout to the Sapir-Whorf Hypothesis concerning the relationship between thought and language, a notion which has been controversial from its first articulation in the first half of the 20th century. This willingness to address the provocative is good, for we are not given simply a whitewashed treatment of a feature here or a feature there, but rather we are treated to a deep delving into what makes Maya-Mam culture tick, so to speak.

Linguists may be disappointed that there is only one chapter that is fully language-oriented (centered on language, we might say), with a discussion of how centeredness manifests itself in the grammar. However there is sensitivity to language and structure throughout the book, and no chapter is devoid of linguistic material.

What consequences emerge from Dr. Collins's work? What lessons can we learn? What conclusions can we draw? The answers lie in the direction of the study of the interaction between humans and their world, and thus there are consequences for the Sapir-Whorf Hypothesis, for linguistic determinism, and for the examination of language in the world.

With all this said, I invite the reader to see for him/herself and to move to this most interesting book itself, which should, after all, be the true "center" of attention.

Brian D. Joseph
Distinguished University Professor of Linguistics, and
The Kenneth E. Naylor Professor of South Slavic Languages and Linguistics
The Ohio State University
10 June 2014

Preface: What to Expect

This book is about the Maya-Mam people of Guatemala. It's also about linguistic anthropology, ethnography, cultural and linguistic research, the etic-emic distinction, history, architecture, pattern, health, religion, research methods, scholarship, and lots of people who have studied the Maya.

With a menu so varied, the metaphorical question might arise, "How does one go about eating an elephant?" The answer is, of course, "One bite at a time." That's how complex problems get solved.

That's my plan here.

First off, there's a lot about the Mam (pronounced "mom") that I won't talk about at all. We will narrow our field to the notion of "the center" and how this idea shows up and plays itself out in many divergent areas, both cultural and linguistic.

The format of the book goes along with what the old preacher said to his young disciple when queried about how to go about outlining his sermons. "First, you tell the congregation what it is that you intend to tell them. Then you tell them. Then you tell them what it was you just told them."

Repetition is good pedagogical technique, one which I will make use of here, which is another take on what it takes to eat the proverbial elephant—perseverance over time.

In the first chapter I will introduce our theme in quite a bit of detail, not just as an introductory teaser. In terms of our sermon metaphor, I tell you what it is that I intend to tell you throughout the rest of the book. The basic notion is this: the idea of seeking the center—sometimes physically, sometimes metaphysically—is both a goal and an operating principle of the Maya-Mam people. We will come to see it as a common theme in Mayan architecture, in health and the cause and diagnosis of illness, in religious thought, and in the myriad decisions and observations of the practice of daily life. The astute reader will notice that sometimes I talk about the Maya-Mam, or just the Mam, and sometimes, more generally, about the Maya. The Mam constitute a branch of the Maya, descendants of the great Central American civilization that was occupying their own land when the Spanish came to stake claim to it for the Crown some 500-plus years ago. Much of what I say will resonate beyond the Mam alone as a group to the larger Mayan civilization and its many descendant groups which today speak some thirty languages in Central America and southern Mexico. The term "Maya-Mam" is synonymous with Mam. It just helps people recognize who the Mam really are. They are Maya.

We will also look at Mam language data that seem to reflect in interesting fashion the same theme of centrality or centeredness. The crux of the grammar of centeredness is inherent in the notion of deixis, a grammatical concept that puts the speaker in the center of the entire universe, where everything that happens or might happen is figured from the location and moment of speech of the one who is speaking. All languages do this to some degree, but Mam does it in spades. Virtually every natively spoken utterance in Mam alludes to location and movement in some way, and these ideas are tied to a grammatical "center stake" that interprets speech in terms of just such a center. Indeed, it isn't simply an occasional cultural and linguistic fact that seems to make sense in terms of a center. Rather, the pattern of such a notion seems to show up everywhere, throughout both the culture and the grammar.

We'll attack this issue on a number of fronts. In chapter one we'll lay out some definitions from the linguistic/anthropological literature and we'll see that others have observed much of what I will be telling you. I will talk about a number of these scholars and their observations because of Newton's famous quote about "standing on ye shoulders of giants." Ethnographers never work in a vacuum, and anything we've been able to glean comes in part from the contribution of others. Even the granddaddy of modern ethnography, Bronislaw Malinowski, in his groundbreaking book *Argonauts of the western Pacific...* (1922), tipped his hat to a few scholars, missionaries, and sea-captains who had observed and studied (and published) before him. One of the great things about working among the Maya is that there has been a lot of fieldwork done across the area and through the years. And even though Maya-Mam is underrepresented in the scholarly literature, these cultural principles that I suggest go "way back" and therefore have a presence in other Mayan groups and even beyond. So the giants should be acknowledged.

In chapter two we will look at some of the social context of the Mam, their work and schools, their lives vis-à-vis the dominant Spanish-speaking culture that surrounds them, and their economic and religious lives. We'll hit these topics more fully later in the book, but in chapter two we'll see some of the complexity of the social, linguistic, and religious milieu that these people face.

Mam is endangered, as are all Mayan languages. This doesn't mean that the languages and cultures are on the verge of collapse, but that a perfect storm of factors—education, university studies, the internet, political power, national and international trade, travel, economic achievement, among other issues—all depend on success in Spanish. This puts a lot of pressure on Mam families to simply chuck their native language and "move forward" by means of Spanish. But much is lost when language and culture are abandoned. Questions of this nature used to be largely theoretical, but now virtually all Mam men and women face them to one degree or another.

In chapter three we will look specifically at three areas where centeredness seems fairly straightforward: in architecture and space, in the discussion of health and illness, and in religious notions, both Mayan and Christian. This last topic is controversial—on both sides of the aisle. First, to suggest that there may be cultural issues that would make Christianity an interesting option for rural Maya-Mam might be seen as an attack on Mayan religion. On the other hand, Christians don't like to think of their faith in terms of merely cultural "fit" and sociological tendencies. I suppose I'll hear it from both sides, but I think the discussion will be fascinating. We will look at religion—both traditional, as evidenced in the content of the *Popol Vuh*, the sacred book of the Mayan and in the writings of a number of scholars about present day traditional religion—and Protestant, as discussed in the words of Mam Protestants themselves.

We will consider how the traditional Maya look at health and illness in terms of a center space of health and wellbeing. Related to this, we will look briefly into the Hot-Cold Syndrome and see it as an instantiation of our theme of centeredness.

We will also discuss what is often called architectonics—how people create meaning in the spaces that they occupy, or, as Setha Low and Denise Lawrence-Zúñiga (2003:185) suggest, how people transform physical "space" into meaningful "place." In this section, I discuss how both the Mam homestead and the layout of the central plaza in pre- and post-colonial Guatemala exist as a template and also as a reflection of the Maya-Mam world and worldview.

Chapter four is the heart of the book. It is written in a very different style from the other chapters. Chapter four is both a primer on ethnography and an ethnographic product as well. Ethnography has been criticized as being more about the researcher than the researched. You'll be able to make your own decision when you read chapter four, but I think the style itself will make its point, that centeredness doesn't show up only in the big spaces of Mayan culture, but in the smallest nooks and crannies as well. We will deal with centeredness as cultural practice. I discuss, in ethnographic style, why I chose ethnography as both a process and product for the discussion of centeredness in daily life, and I maintain a meta-dialogue with you, gentle reader, about both the content of the chapter as well as the value of ethnography as scholarly practice. This chapter discusses several events that I participated in, one by invitation, and one definitely *not* by invitation; I tie the events together in terms of a search for centeredness. In this chapter, I also discuss how the Mam themselves (both consciously and unconsciously) talk about centeredness as a structured and structuring enterprise.

I consider ethnography to be the most accessible of scholarly pursuits. Indeed, one of its primary tenets is to entertain. The trick is to keep the entertaining within the broader context of what the author is trying to get across. So if the names and arguments feel dry in the early pages of this book, bear with me long enough to dig into chapter four as a general and practical presentation of these same facts, but in ethnographic form.

Chapter five deals with centeredness as a grammatical theme. This will be the most esoteric part of the book, but linguistics is about language, and language is inherently fascinating, the greatest of human abilities. I will do my best to pass on to you some of that fascination. I discuss a small class of twelve Mam intransitive verbs of motion and a corresponding set of directional auxiliaries and how these depend on a deictic center whether it be a speaker, an "other," or an arbitrary point in space, as part of their lexical (semantic or "dictionary") meaning. We'll talk a lot more on this notion of deixis in chapters one and five. We'll then look at several directional suffixes and discuss how the meaning of both the directionals and the suffixes become less grounded in physical movement—and thereby become more abstract—while still maintaining a sense of center or norm. Next I discuss these same suffixes as grammaticalized discourse deictics that signal discourse material as being either old or new. In terms of discourse structure and centeredness, I also suggest in chapters four and five that the use of couplets in ritual rhetoric in Mam and other Mayan languages is iconic of our principle of centeredness and the sense of dualism that other writers, particularly Gary Gossen (1986:6), have mentioned. Finally, I cite Thomas Godfrey (1981) and Nora England (1983) in regard to Mam relational nouns (the *head* of the trail, the *foot* of the mountain), and I discuss these, too, in terms of Mam centeredness and the body in space. If some of these linguistic terms are unknown to you, be patient; I plan to unlock them as we go along.

In our sermon metaphor, chapters three through five are the content of what it is I want to tell you. Chapter six is a recapitulation of what it is I've told you if you read the book from beginning to end. In chapter six, I tie together the notion of an overlap of cultural and grammatical theme and use it as a heuristic or teaching strategy for commenting further on the relationship between language and culture, and I make a few suggestions about what seem to be good areas for further research.

Language and culture are among the most basic elements of our lives. Thinking about the relationship between the two is one of the privileges and joys our humanity affords us.

I am a college professor by trade; I love teaching. I want to tell you in this book what the Maya-Mam people are like, at least in part. But at the same time, I'd like you to learn about ethnography—what it is and why we use it and why it is the favored tool of linguistic anthropologists. Diving into practical anthropology, we will also learn about etic and emic layers of analysis. And we will consider some of the proponents of the Sapir-Whorf Hypothesis and we'll see why, after seventy-five years, anthropologists are still enchanted by the notion of linguistic relativity, the notion that one's native language itself has an influence on how speakers of that language think about the world. We'll also look at the nature of proof in the humanities and consider what kind of facts we should seek in order to affirm what we say about culture and values. Finally we will test the waters, if not the depths, of theoretical linguistics and see what, if any, overlap there might be among grammatical and cultural notions.

This book started out as a dissertation, "presented in partial fulfillment of the requirements for the degree Doctor of Philosophy in the graduate school of the Ohio State University," as they say. During the process of transforming a dissertation into what I hope becomes a much-more-popular monograph, I changed the style of the book, and much of its content. I dropped a seventy-page chapter and assigned some of that content to other chapters, I did further research beyond the 2005 date of the dissertation's publication, and I worked the discussion over into a more reader-friendly format and style, which I hope is interesting, thoughtful, and compelling. Perhaps that is a lot to hope for. You will be on the panel of judges. When I wrote the dissertation, I needed to sufficiently convince a committee of four that my thoughts were coherent to my premise, and that the premise was valid—that the search for the center explains a lot about the Maya-Mam. Now the book is "on the market" and it is subject to a whole new set of pressures and judgments.

If you prefer dissertations to more accessible formats, you can still download the original dissertation for free at: http://rave.ohiolink.edu/etdc/view?acc_num=osu1123170540.

I do forewarn you, though, that this new book is a lot more fun than the previous one.

Pleasant reading!

1

Getting Started: The View from a Distance

1.1 The heart of the matter: Centeredness as a cultural and grammatical theme

My friend, Eugenio,[1] came to my house one Saturday morning and told me that he and I shared a problem. I asked him what our problem was, and he said that our families were "off center." He didn't actually articulate this shared problem…he gestured it. He said that our families were like this, at which point he extended his arms to each side of his body and tilted his head to the left, lowering his left arm while raising his right, like a child imitating a zooming airplane. When I asked him what he was talking about, he said that neither he nor I had *jun qxel,* a replacement. I queried further, to which he replied that we each had a wife and daughters (my wife and I had two daughters at the time; he and his wife had three), but neither of us had any sons to "take our place" in the world after we were gone. He went on to describe how typical and full families have a father, a mother,

---

[1] In this book, most Mam people's names and some identifying details have been changed.

the daughters, and the sons. A family without either sons or daughters, or a mother or a father is like a dog with only three legs, he explained. It just can't function properly without all four elements.

I didn't realize it at the time, but now I believe that Eugenio was offering me an unasked-for glimpse into the way he and his people conceive of the world—where life is a series of relationships that require constant care in order to achieve and maintain an elusive balance or centeredness: physically, mentally, socially, and spiritually—and also, where the cosmos is understood as the place where balance or, more specifically, centeredness, is the primary and normative good. In addition, each person's place in the universe is an individualized "center" from which all other movement is described grammatically and culturally, physically and metaphysically. This notion of centeredness is a pervasive cultural value in Mam dealings with each other—an organizing principle of daily life—and it is basic to the way they conceive of the present world as well as the world to come.

In this book, I suggest that this sense of centeredness is what Laura Martin (1977) and Nora England (1978:226) call both a cultural and a grammatical theme. Culturally, the idea of seeking centeredness is pervasive in how the Mam conceive of relationships, how they define their presence in the world, how they construct their homes, their cornfields, and their towns, how they understand health and illness, how they discipline their children, how they bury their dead, how they deal with their spiritual lives and how they think of life beyond the grave. These perhaps sound like very divergent and disparate issues, but I show in this study that each of these is conceived in some sort of relationship to a real or metaphorical center space of 'comfort, peace, goodness, and wellbeing', or *b'a'n*. I suggest that this seeking of centeredness in all its varied applications is indeed a single pursuit, a cultural theme, an idea that extends beyond observation of atomistic facts to the underlying and integrating notion that gives these facts their spark of cultural life.

At the same time that centeredness operates on a cultural level, England (1978) defines grammatical themes as "the underlying organizational principles of a language linking structure with semantics." Semantics is about meaning, which is culturally understood (for example, the difference of meaning between a purposeful wink and an involuntary twitch of the eye depends almost entirely on one's culture: its shared gestures and the physical context). Structure is about grammar and how linguistic units relate to

1.1 The heart of the matter: Centeredness as a cultural and grammatical theme

other units and how they combine to form still larger units. Languages tend to highlight, or "privilege," certain issues or themes that are instantiated not only in the lexicon, the list of words in a language, but throughout the grammar of a language—in the morphology (the make-up of words), the syntax (the make-up of sentences), and the discourse structure as well.

In this study, my bottom-line goal is to tell you what the Mam people are like. Such a goal, of course, is a lofty and large one, so there needs to be some way to constrain or restrict it. I don't by any measure claim to know everything about these fascinating people or their language, so how much can I really tell you? And is what I have to say valid?

I'll keep those questions on the back burner as we plow through the data and observations that I present and as we consider a general interpretation of these data. I will try to privilege not what I have to say about Mam culture, but what the Mam themselves have to say about it, both by their actions and their contemplation. Bronislaw Malinowski, the father of ethnographic scholarship, said that the goal of such study is "to grasp the native's point of *view,* his relation to life, to realize *his* vision of *his* world (1922:25, emphasis and masculine pronouns in the original). He wrote this over one hundred years ago, but it's still a good reference point for the meaning and purpose of any purported ethnographic account.

When one writes a book, she or he needs a track to run on, particularly if the work isn't simply a chronological narrative where the passage of time can be the thread that holds the book together. Rather, there needs to be a foil or frame of some kind either against which or upon which to lay out an argument. Ethnography itself isn't an argument at all, but a methodology, one which will be fully unleashed in chapter four, although I'll talk about it quite a bit as anthropological practice later in this chapter. My frame or touch point will be this dual notion of grammatical and cultural theme. This idea, if not the exact vocabulary, crops up often in the linguistic-anthropological literature, the idea that there is some kind of relationship or influence between the language that people speak and the culture that they live out on a day-to-day basis. If you think about it for a moment, anthropology is about culture, and linguistics is about language; so it isn't much of a stretch to consider that linguistic anthropology (or anthropological linguistics) would deal with just such a relationship, that is, that between language and culture. But it's hard to nail down just what that relationship might be. Does language cause a certain kind of culture—or vice versa?

Or are both views true? Or is the relationship one of influence or shading, rather than causation? Are our thoughts constrained in some way or limited by the language that we natively speak? Are so-called "primitive" cultures primitive because they are held back by a primitive language? Or is it the case that a primitive culture doesn't make any intellectual or otherwise provocative demands on the native language, so everything and everyone just sort of passively sits as time goes by? Perhaps you can see the possibility of a racist philosophy here, that speakers of the world's "great" languages are destined to rule over the speakers of the "lesser" languages. Indeed, by such an account, the supposed lesser languages don't permit the thinking needed for world dominion. Suffice it to say, some have used such notions as a justification to stigmatize or to steamroll over others, but racists can use anything as a tool against anyone and we will not pursue such misguided philosophies; rather, we will delight in cultural diversity in the words of the eighteenth century German writer Johann Herder (cited in Schlesinger 1991:13), who celebrated linguistic and cultural diversity with these words:

> Let the nations learn from one another, and let one continue where the other left off...every nation has its center of felicity in itself alone, as every sphere has its center of gravity.... Is not the good distributed through the whole world? It is divided into a thousand forms, transformed, an eternal Proteus!—in every region of the world and in every century.

1.1.1 Linguistic relativity and the Sapir-Whorf Hypothesis

For the record, the person most associated historically with the idea of a causal link between language and culture is Benjamin Whorf and the articulation of said link (whatever it might be) is usually known as or affiliated with the Sapir-Whorf Hypothesis (SWH). The idea behind Sapir-Whorf, is that the language that one natively speaks predisposes that person to certain understandings about the world. Harry Hoijer, Sapir-Whorf's chief apologist, describes the hypothesis like this: "language functions, not simply as a device for reporting experience, but also, and more significantly, as a way of defining experience for its speakers" (1954:93).

Although in this first chapter I will talk a good bit about the Sapir-Whorf Hypothesis (SWH), this book really is not about the hypothesis per se, but I mention it because it is well known even beyond anthropological circles, and it will

1.1 The heart of the matter: Centeredness as a cultural and grammatical theme

be the frame upon which we rest the dual notion of cultural and grammatical theme. In other words, even if SWH ends up not being all that interesting, it won't condemn the present study, since my goal is not to convince you of the validity of the hypothesis but to tell you what the Maya-Mam people are like. I hope to do that using a number of anthropological and linguistic touch points, one of which is the SWH. That said, I think my observations will rise or fall on their own, not on what you end up thinking about the ideas of Sapir and Whorf. On this issue, Franz Boas, the father of American anthropology (although born in Germany!), says in his famous introduction to the *Handbook of American Indian languages*:

> ...language seems to be one of the most instructive fields of inquiry in an investigation of the formation of the fundamental ethnic ideas. The great advantage that linguistics offers in this respect is the fact that, on the whole, the categories which are formed always remain unconscious, and that for this reason the processes which lead to their formation can be followed... (Boas 1911:70)

He means that the invisible qualities of culture can be externalized via language. Boas was Edward Sapir's good friend and faithful mentor. Whorf studied under Sapir along with a group of other well-known early anthropologists, including Morris Swadesh, Margaret Meade, Mary Haas, and George Trager (among others).[2]

Much more recently, Lera Boroditsky, Lauren Schmidt, and Webb Phillips (2003) cite an interesting experiment that supports Sapir-Whorf. In the experiment, fluent bilinguals (German-English in one group and Spanish-English in the other, who were native speakers of German and Spanish, respectively) were asked to supply adjectives (in English) describing English words which were chosen for being of contrasting grammatical gender in the two native languages. The word "bridge," for example, was described by native Spanish-speaking bilinguals with more masculine-like adjectives such as *strong, big, foreboding, scary,* etc. The word for 'bridge' *puente* in Spanish, is grammatically masculine. German speakers described the exact same bridge as *pleasant, unifying* and *graceful*. In German, the word for 'bridge' *Brücke* is feminine. Why would this contrast of modifiers exist? It does indeed appear that grammatical gender, which is randomly assigned by those languages that have it, significantly influences how one perceives the world.[3]

---

[2] I studied anthropology at *the* Ohio State University under Dr. Amy Zaharlick, who was a student of Trager, who, with Whorf, was a student of Sapir, who cut his linguistic-anthropological teeth under Boas. What goes around comes around.

[3] See http://www-psych.stanford.edu/~lera/papers/ for more of Boroditsky's work on this subject.

Just how strong or how influential the link is, is the subject of much discussion, and since the SWH is really more of an observation than a hypothesis, there is plenty of support for it, if not hard proof, although the Boroditsky experiment is pretty convincing. I will talk about this further below and throughout the book. The reason I'm pounding on the idea here is that it is the natural backdrop for our dual notions of cultural and grammatical theme, the interplay of language and culture. These are "old ideas," but they aren't really dated. Sapir-Whorf is still debated in lively fashion in universities around the country and beyond. Bestselling linguistics author Steven Pinker, no friend of Sapir-Whorf, thought enough of the notion to try to convince people of its naïveté in his book, *The language instinct: How the mind creates language* (1994:55–82). I was unconvinced.

Other scholars have discussed the same notion under different terminology. In Sapir-Whorf nomenclature it is called *linguistic relativity*. Mayanist Gary Gossen (1986) discusses the cultural part of our theme as a *symbol cluster,* that a variety of cultural observations can be generalized as variants of the same symbol or cultural value. Anna Wierzbicka (1997) speaks of *key words* as being a link between language and culture, that culture is articulated in words or, even more subtly, in grammar, while at the same time, it is language that is a most powerful means of cultural assimilation (for both insiders and outsiders). Language and culture are two sides of the same coin. Ken Hale[4] (1986) presents our notion in what he calls "World View-1" and "World View-2" (which I will elaborate on directly), and Nick Enfield has a recent edited volume titled *Ethnosyntax* (2002), which is a transparent marking of some sort of integration between culture (ethno) and grammar (syntax). So there is still a lot of interest in our theme, Pinker notwithstanding. We'll see quite a few more authors who display more than a passing interest in it. Whorf was somewhat eccentric, even back in the day, but he was much appreciated and highly regarded by his colleagues some seventy-five years ago, and he continues to be oft-cited today—even by his detractors.

Both Martin and England use these related ideas of cultural and grammatical theme as a discovery procedure for discussing the broader relationship of language to culture. Indeed, Dell Hymes, an early pillar of linguistic anthropology, says, "Cultural values and beliefs are in part constitutive

---

[4] Ken Hale (d. 2001) was a renowned field linguist at M.I.T. My syntax professor at Ohio State, Peter Culicover, also of M.I.T. vintage, told me that once he heard Hale muttering under his breath as Hale was poring over a notebook of data he had elicited from an Amerindian speaker, "I'm going to learn to speak this language if it takes me all week."

1.1 The heart of the matter: Centeredness as a cultural and grammatical theme

of linguistic reality" (1966:116). In other words, a language will encode cultural factors that are salient to its speakers. So, the discovery of such factors suggests areas where we can successfully look to elicit culturally meaningful linguistic data. At the same time, as we discover relationships among the formal structures of a language—say, how the grammar marks honorifics, ambiguity, and indirection in Japanese—we can assume that these may reflect important cultural thematic material, as they certainly do in Japanese.[5]

To pursue these twin notions of cultural and grammatical theme, in addition to Whorf we will consider Hale's claim (1986) that all cultures have two worldviews, what he labels World View-1 (what I'm calling, following Martin and England, cultural theme) and, not surprisingly, World View-2 (grammatical theme). According to Hale, World View-1 is more philosophical than grammatical. Indeed, he says that it is learned apart from language and that it is independent of a language's grammar. It is acquired by participating in a group's cultural ways—even if one does not necessarily speak the native language. For example, Charlotte Schaengold reports for Navajo: "Some Navajo families seem to maintain Navajo cultural norms without fluent use of the Navajo language. The proper respect for the elderly and clan relationships with other Navajos can apparently be maintained without the Navajo language itself" (2004:18). Even without the critical cultural formation that language provides and guides, cultural norms nonetheless flow out of, or emerge from, the behavior, observations, and choices of members of a society even when members no longer speak the language.

To achieve World View-1, then, one need not be a fully fluent native speaker of the language in question. Hale additionally claims that some details of such a worldview are not even necessarily shared by all who are native speakers of the language, because of different levels of sophistication and access to the events and esoteric knowledge that point to what the world is like. Certain areas of cultural knowledge are inaccessible to men, for example, or to women or to youth or to the otherwise uninitiated. This is an important caveat. It is worth stating that worldview is not a monolithic concept that all cultural insiders are essentially tied to and from which they are unable to escape. Rather, worldview as per Hale's World View-1 is a propensity and tendency to see and understand the

---

[5] Honorifics are words like *tú* and *usted* in Spanish that mark social distinction. Japanese and many other languages have very complex societal "rules" governing the use of such terms.

world in particular ways, promoting and privileging certain understandings of how the world works.

Nevertheless, World View-1, though largely independent of language by Hale's reckoning, is not distinct from language. Its relation to language is not based on the grammar but on meaning. World View-1 is elaborated in the lexicon, for example, in the now-mythic, yea cultic, status of the supposed dozens (or scores or even hundreds!) of "Inuit words for snow" (see Martin 1986 for a far more realistic and investigative view of this arctic notion), where a culture's ways and concerns are coded in the words used to speak of issues significant to the members of a specific culture. The meanings are "out there" in the eyes and minds of beholders, even when the language itself starts to slip away and gets replaced by a majority "monster" language like English or Spanish. We might consider this phenomenon similarly to that of a deaf child growing up in a hearing society. Although she doesn't have the benefit of the assimilative power of spoken language, this does not mean that she is not an active and comprehending member of the society as she assimilates the culture in ways beyond spoken language itself. So language lays down a template of meaning in the world, and World View-1 picks up and understands much of the template, even without fluency in the language. Navajo youth honor their grandparents in cultural ritual and respect even without Navajo fluency. Of course, if form follows function, even these cultural rituals may be lost as young people shift their language usage toward English where the new language doesn't support time-honored traditions.

Still, language is complex because the world is complex. A language must have the resources (grammatical, phonological, and semantic) to express all that is culturally significant to its speakers. But even when speakers begin to shift their language use to a second language (L2), the real-life complexity of their first-language (L1) world is still out there for them to participate in and to describe (Hale's World View-1), albeit now less convincingly, and probably less ably, in an L2. I say "less ably" on the assumption that the language that best describes a series of integrated cultural phenomena (like the respect shown to Navajo elders as mentioned above) would necessarily be the native language of the people to whom these phenomena are personal, meaningful, and pervasive—like snow and related categories to the Inuit.

On the other hand, Hale's World View-2 is necessarily and automatically shared by all native speakers as a by-product of learning to speak natively

1.1 The heart of the matter: Centeredness as a cultural and grammatical theme

one's heart language. This is very different from World View-1, which is only loosely tied to language, and it means that World View-2 is shared communally because the group's native language is shared communally. World View-2 has an intimate relationship to the grammar far beyond the mere accumulation of entries into a cultural dictionary. Hale's notion of World View-2 is as that part of culture that we absorb in the learning of the grammatical distinctions and requirements made in our native languages, like Boroditsky's German and Spanish friends as they learned about bridges as either grammatically masculine or feminine. A bridge is a bridge, but culture always rubs off.

World View-2 deals not with the simple naming of cultural phenomena (not that this is necessarily all that simple), nor with the content of history or ritual, but rather in the way the grammar privileges certain recurrent themes that are instantiated in various grammatical structures or on different grammatical levels, say the morphology and syntax.[6] Hale claims that World View-2 is necessarily shared by all L1 C1 (native language and native culture) members of the society since these broad themes are acquired in the very process of learning one's first language. It is clearly not autonomous of the grammar but rather is co-referential with it in that the internalizing of these grammatical categories is how World View-2 is acquired.

Anna Wierzbicka shows to some degree how this works out in English. She concedes that clearly, words carry cultural meaning, but, she says, "certain meanings are so important to communities of speakers that they become not just lexicalized (linked with individual words, WMC) but grammaticalized, that is, embodied in the language's deep structural patterns" (2002:162).

She talks about the legacy of English in the world and the parallel practice of democracy in many English-speaking countries, particularly in the United States. She says that as industry developed in the US, the need to get people to do things and follow orders became increasingly important. In the meantime, the growth of democracy taught citizens that just as their individual votes were worth as much as the individual votes of the wealthy, so their dignity and equality are commensurate with that of others. So at

---

[6] Naming cultural phenomena is not always a simple matter. In the July 2012 *National Geographic Magazine,* Russ Rymer reports (p. 66) that in Tuvan, a Russian minority language, the word *ezenggileer* means "to sing with the rhythms of riding a horse." That such a notion would be lexicalized as a single word in a language gives an indication of the importance of horses—and music—among its speakers.

the same time that grammatical imperatives would seem the way to communicate orders, Wierzbicka suggests that other strategies needed to be adapted that reflect the day-to-day ideology of democracy. "The cultural emphasis on personal autonomy, characteristic of the modern Anglo society...is no doubt closely related to the expansion of causative constructions in modern English" (2002:166).

She says that, compared to other languages, English is loaded with watered-down imperative constructions. Instead of just telling someone to do something, which, on occasion, we do in fact do, Wierzbicka says that "the growing avoidance of the straight imperative, is an unparalleled phenomenon in modern American English" (2002:167). She cites constructions like *would you do something, could you do something, that someone should do something, to have someone do something, to persuade them do it, to get someone to do it,* along with a number of "let" constructions: *"Let's think of a better solution," "Let's not do that,"* etc. Additionally, there are all kinds of indirect strategies such as asking a question *("Can you pass the guacamole?")* rather than simply and blatantly demanding that the guacamole be passed—or the use of just the bare noun in *"Guacamole, please,"* where the presence of "please" shows us that the use of the noun is really and truly an imperative, although it doesn't carry the same social heaviness of a straight-up, demanding imperative. This, latter "bare noun" strategy parallels the situation where a friend comes to the door and buzzes you. You answer, "Yes?" "It's John," he says. Here the imperative is simply a name, and you interpret the pragmatics of the situation to let John in. "It's John" operates as a veiled imperative. The so-called whimperatives (a term derived from wh-imperative—not from "wimpy" imperatives)—are imperatives that masquerade as questions (questions are often called wh-structures in linguistics since so many question words (in English) begin with *wh-: when why, who, where,* etc.). These whimperatives are also called stealth imperatives by Steven Pinker (2007), which are structures with imperative force that don't "look like" imperatives. Some examples of whimperative are: "Why don't we do it like this?" "If you would be so kind," "So, when do you plan to finish your homework?"

To these constructions I add a few additional ones. Recently I had a plumber and an HVAC technician (heating, ventilation and air conditioning) come to our home to give us some advice. The plumber said, "A fellow could cut this off here and 'tee' into the main line over there." The other

1.1 The heart of the matter: Centeredness as a cultural and grammatical theme   11

said, "You might could consider not doing anything until fall." These are clearly muted imperatives, on par with *one could...* and *one might...*, which are perhaps used more extensively. In any event, there are a lot of options in English for telling people what to do, without really telling them. It's the linguistic analog of the iron fist in the velvet glove.

Wierzbicka goes to all this trouble in order to show some kind of relationship between culture and grammar, not necessarily causation, which is very hard to prove (although, like Boroditsky, she makes a strong case). But she does show at the very least a clear pattern both in the grammatical data and the cultural, observations. Not only are there lots of grammatical options for indirect imperatives in English, but the number of constructions seems to be growing, as I reported regarding my own observations from my very own basement in Ohio. Wierzbicka claims that not only are there many more constructions of this sort in English when compared to other languages across the board (not just European languages), but that their usage in English is very high as well. She points out that such grammatical options (and their actual use in day-to-day discourse) tell us something about the culture of people that use these grammatical strategies, in this case, the importance of respecting others' esteem by not being obviously and blatantly demanding.

Saying that the egalitarianism of US culture is behind the use of these constructions may seem like common sense, but such a pronouncement is fraught with peril. Perhaps it is the other way around, that language precedes culture, and we have grown egalitarian because of the abundance of expressions we have to express such a notion. The use of she/he, for example, is an attempt to provide some gender equality in academic writing, along with a sentence like "A person should consider their own best interests," where we sacrifice grammaticality for the hope of greater inclusion. Here we're trying to affect culture with language. Causation is hard to prove, and it's most likely that it goes both ways, at least in practice, so I won't be dogmatic. But we will certainly shoot for patterns among the data presented here.

We can see the possibility of using such cultural features as discovery procedures to search for corresponding grammatical features that encode these culturally key concepts. At the same time, if we observe lots of grammatical material related to a common theme, this certainly gives us cause to search for corresponding cultural aspects of such grammatical themes.

Some concepts are coded subconsciously and automatically (grammatically) in a given language, while others must be articulated more analytically, in more piecemeal fashion, laying out for hearers just how a situation is to be understood. This reflects what the well-known linguist Charles Hockett said: "Languages differ not so much as to what can be said in them, but rather as to what it is *relatively easy* to say (because of its grammatical coding)" (1954:122, emphasis in original, parenthetical comment, WMC).

In terms of causation—that culture "causes" language to be a certain way—Hale says, "It seems to me to be a matter of luck, a chance happening when a neat correspondence between World View-1 and a principle of grammar...is met with" (1986:237). Nevertheless, he says that part of our work as language and culture specialists is to search for just such correlations between World View-1 and World View-2. What is particularly difficult about finding or purporting any "neat correspondence" between language and culture is that it is extremely challenging to figure out any way to prove that there is causation involved, that language would cause a certain kind of cultural behavior, or a certain type of culture would cause the grammatical codification of a certain grammatical theme. There are so many variables. Humans are complex.

Understanding causation has always been a goal in the human sciences, but being empirical about plumbing the depths of causation has been an ongoing challenge. Wierzbicka (1997) cuts through some of the haze here. She suggests that languages that have a word for 'orange marmalade' certainly have a cultural product by that name. It is not the case that language creates the product. Rather, culture members create or discover something that becomes meaningful to them and they need a way to talk about it. Culture comes first, then language. Language serves culture. Nevertheless, language then becomes the major tool that a culture uses to replicate itself, from its deepest values to its sweetest fruit concoctions. As Wierzbicka (1997:1) claims, "there is a very close link between the life of a society and the lexicon of the language spoken by it." She agrees with Sapir and quotes him: "Vocabulary is a very sensitive index of the culture of a people" (cited in Mandelbaum 1949:27). Again, she quotes Sapir, "Language is a symbolic guide to culture" (ibid.:162). In other words, there is a connection, perhaps causal, but certainly considerable, between language and culture.

As mentioned previously, this notion of a relationship or influence between the language that people speak and the daily life that they live is a

1.1 The heart of the matter: Centeredness as a cultural and grammatical theme

notion usually attributed to Benjamin Whorf and his mentor, Edward Sapir, and is known as the Sapir-Whorf Hypothesis.

Whorf claimed:

> ...each language is not merely a reproducing instrument for voicing ideas but rather is itself the shaper of ideas, the program and guide for the individual's mental activity, for his analysis of impressions, for his synthesis of his mental stock in trade.... We dissect nature along lines laid down by our native languages. The categories and types that we isolate from the world of phenomena we do not find there because they stare every observer in the face; on the contrary, the world is presented in a kaleidoscopic flux of impressions which has to be organized by our minds—and this means largely by the linguistic systems of our minds. (1940, reprinted in Carroll 1956: 212–213)

The "categories and types" that he mentions here are cultural constructs that depend on the interaction of language and culture for their meaning. To affirm this idea, we need only consider Geertz's discussion of the difference between a wink and a twitch, a difference I mentioned a few pages ago. Geertz says that the wink construct is the "speck of behavior" (the action itself) together with the meaning behind it, what he calls "a fleck of culture" (1973:6). Meaning is culture based. There is nothing about the physical act of the wink/twitch in and of itself that makes it meaningful. Indeed, one might easily assume that there are cultures where what we consider to be a volitional wink is utterly meaningless and therefore ignored as cultural detritus. It is rather the history of experiences with such behavior and the cultural contract or underlying agreement of those who have so interpreted it in the past that gives it meaning. The etics of behavior—what the camera sees (the physical twitch)—are important to us as outsiders trying to understand what is going on, but it is the emics—the meaning, the interpretation by locals (the wink, and all that it might mean)—that speaks to the relationship between language and culture. Whatever else we might say about the relationship, it is my position that the link between language and culture—or in the present case, between grammatical and cultural theme—is meaning based. I think Whorf would have agreed.[7] He got this partly from his own study and observation and certainly in part from his mentor and teacher, Edward Sapir. In perhaps Sapir's most oft-cited quote, he says:

---

[7] Whorf's analysis of the Hopi data, upon which he based his theory, has been challenged and debunked, but the SWH has had lots of other support, and appears to be alive and well.

> Though language is not ordinarily thought of as of essential interest to the students of social science, it powerfully conditions all our thinking about social processes and problems. Human beings do not live in the objective world alone, nor alone in the world of social activity as ordinarily understood, but are very much at the mercy of the particular language which has become the medium of expression for their society. It is quite an illusion to imagine that one adjusts to reality essentially without the use of language and that language is merely an incidental means of solving specific problems of communication or reflection. The fact of the matter is that the "real world" is to a large extent unconsciously built up on the language habits of the group. No two languages are ever sufficiently similar to be considered as representing the same social reality. The worlds in which different societies live are distinct worlds, not merely the same world with different labels attached. (cited in Mandelbaum 1949:162)

Harry Hoijer is the scholar perhaps most responsible for the post-World War II revived interest in the Sapir-Whorf Hypothesis after the two men's early deaths, Sapir at 55 in 1939 and Whorf at only 44 years of age in 1941. In fact, it is most likely Hoijer who first coined the term the Sapir-Whorf Hypothesis. Hoijer's definition of the SWH is the observation that "language functions, not simply as a device for reporting experience, but also, and more significantly, as a way of defining experience for its speakers" (1954). Two readings of Whorf are possible. The first is that language determines the way we think about things, or, more subtly, that it determines the thoughts that are available to us. The second reading is that our language merely influences how we think. These two positions have come to be known as the strong version and the weak version of the SWH, respectively.[8] And although both Sapir and Whorf are on record with statements that could be construed as deterministic, they often mitigated these strong statements in print and most certainly held the milder view, that of influence and not determinism. The SWH is often thought of in terms of how language potentially constrains thought, but from the outset, Hoijer saw it in more general terms—how language and culture interact.

Hoijer and Mayanist Robert Redfield organized a conference in 1953 at the University of Chicago that brought together some of the leading linguists and anthropologists in the country with the idea of laying out just what was meant by the SWH, and how it can be sustained through

---

[8] For a helpful overview of linguistic relativity, and particularly its strong and weak versions, see Schlesinger (1991).

linguistic analysis and cultural observation. Hoijer's subsequent publication of the proceedings of that conference (1954:93) includes not only the papers presented, but the gist of the ensuing discussions as well. It is an outstanding resource for understanding the SWH in terms of how Sapir and Whorf's friends and contemporaries understood it, and in these articles, we can see that they were trying to feed linguistic and cultural data "up" to a more general level in order to develop a larger encompassing theory of the interaction of language and culture. Nonetheless, even Whorf's friends and colleagues found it difficult to pinpoint exactly what Whorf meant by linguistic relativity. Still, in the papers and discussions, several points were recurrent. First, that whatever one could say about the relationship between language structure and cultural experience in the world, it needs to be backed up by nonlinguistic, that is, cultural material. Formulating hypotheses about such a relationship on the basis of linguistic data and then using further linguistic data to prove these hypotheses is circular and trivial. Hoijer suggests that any connection between language and culture will come "from a totality of categories cutting across lexical, morphological, and syntactical materials plus the impresses of these upon other behavior which is nonlinguistic" (1954:129). The categories he mentions are what we're calling grammatical themes, while the nonlinguistic behavior reflects our cultural themes.

In his discussion, Hoijer lays out a research agenda for establishing the value of the Sapir-Whorf Hypothesis for cross-cultural understanding and to "develop the hypothesis" (1954:102). It's interesting that he didn't see the hypothesis as something to be proved or disproved, but rather, as a discovery procedure to be developed. As in all scientific endeavor, his basic research question is in essence, "What is going on here?" His call for research has no clinical, laboratory component (although many such experiments have been carried out such as those by John Lucy (1992) and Lera Boroditsky, Lauren Schmidt, and Webb Phillips (2003), which I think are very convincing). Rather, Hoijer's call is mostly related to the gathering of nonlinguistic, cultural information that would enable cross-cultural comparison of similar and dissimilar languages with similar and dissimilar cultures, in order to understand not only "what is going on" in specific cultures, but to provide empirical data for the cross-cultural comparison of how language and culture interrelate at a higher level. This book is in part a belated response to Hoijer's plea.

In this book, I suggest that we look at the relationship between language and culture in terms of local interpretation. This removes—albeit only partially—the investigator from the analytical process by asking how the people themselves view such a relationship between how their grammar works and what are some of the salient values of the culture that they live out on a daily basis. How is such a grammatical theme instantiated in the culture and vice versa, how is such a central cultural theme instantiated in the grammar, and how does an outsider mount evidence to endorse such an integral interpretation? To do this, I suggest that we adopt an interpretive model of analysis based not on empirical (physically measureable) findings, but on interpretive reflection.

The Finnish linguist Esa Itkonen (1978) claims that proof in the human sciences is different in a number of ways from proof in the natural sciences. He says that proof (and data) for the more "human" sciences is hermeneutic, interpretive rather than positivistic, where the term "positivistic" implies logical or mathematical preciseness and measureable proof. This is not meant to be an apology for anthropology, but an admission that what we're looking for is not spread out over the measurable spaces between and among cultural players. Rather, we're looking for what things mean to locals.

A hermeneutic approach is basic to Clifford Geertz's interpretive anthropology, an understanding of culture that privileges local action as well as local understanding and explanation. Nevertheless, for Geertz, although the local view is privileged, it isn't presented in isolation, nor does it trump all outsider observation. Just because we may be outsiders, it doesn't follow that we can make no valid observations about another culture. Rather, Geertz models an ethnographic technique where he observes culture as a participant, one involved (even embroiled) in the very cultural and linguistic notions he is attempting to understand and explain. At the same time, he relates this participation and these formal linguistic notions to similar situations in our own culture and language. In this way, he tries to make the strange familiar by showing how an event as gruesome to Western eyes and minds as a cockfight (1973:412–453) is basically an instantiation of the issues of prestige, leadership, dominance, and respect—things that we understand very well within our own cultural trappings. At the same time, by focusing on the common occurrences of daily life in almost microscopic detail, Geertz also succeeds in making the familiar seem strange by showing us that we are largely unaware of many of the intricate details of things

1.1 The heart of the matter: Centeredness as a cultural and grammatical theme

that we think and do each day. Anthropologists call this idea of making the strange familiar (or vice versa) *strangemaking*. I detail this ethnographic technique in chapter four and discuss how an emic (insider) analysis of cultural values overlays an etic (outsider) account of "what the camera sees." We will try to see beyond the reach of the camera's lens.

This etic-emic distinction in anthropology is attributed to Ken Pike, who first applied the difference between phonetics and phonemics from the field of linguistics, to culture. For a thorough discussion of these terms, especially as used by anthropologists, see Headland, Pike, and Harris (1990).

Geertz explains that the difference can be encapsulated in the difference between a wink and a twitch, a comparison we've mentioned several times already, but which gives us a good touch point for discussion. Although the mechanics of the two movements are identical, one is full of cultural meaning (the wink), whereas the other is simply a response to a bug in your eye. In ethnography, it is local meaning—the wink—that is of greatest interest, not the twitch. The reason we're concerned about the etic perspective at all is that, as outsiders, we can't know ahead of time what will end up mattering and what won't. For example, there is a common rural Guatemalan gesture where you bend your index finger and swipe it lightly across your nose. It seems to be merely the classic response to an itchy nose, but it isn't. It actually means "nothing happened." So I could say something like, "I went to Carlos's house to get what he owes me, but [gesture]," which would mean Carlos didn't cough up the ten bucks he has owed me for two years. If I had made no observation of the etic swipe of the nose—what the video camera itself would have duly recorded—I would have almost certainly missed this, interpreting it to mean the same thing in the new culture as it does in my own culture, merely a response to an itch, and I would never have learned that there is something behind the swipe: real, cultural, meaning. So being attuned to the etic perspective keeps us open to what might shake out as meaningful and emic upon further cogitation.

For Geertz, the goal of ethnography is not a recapitulation of everything etic, as the empirical behaviorist would want it—think B.F. Skinner—but rather an understanding in the hermeneutic sense of interpreting behavior as it is locally meaningful. Dealing with culture and the human sciences is less about logic in the strict sense of the physical scientist and more readily about meaning, interpretation, or validation—showing pattern, if not necessarily cause.

Of course, since culture is so often expressed linguistically, and since language can only be fully understood in extended cultural context, the teasing apart of the linguistic and cultural aspects of these themes—especially when they coincide—may not be at all straightforward, but, repeating England, "Where these themes overlap [culturally and linguistically, WMC] will be found powerful elements of the world view of a people" (1978:226). This makes sense, since we would expect a language to code most adequately and extensively those factors most important to the speakers of that language, or, as John DuBois so quotably puts it: "grammars code best what speakers do most" (1985:363). This coincides with Dell Hymes's observation that not only does our native language affect how we conceive of the world (linguistic relativity as per Benjamin Whorf), but also culture—how we look at the world and participate in it—has a profound effect on our native language, by effectively coding or "packaging" those elements and themes that are most salient to us as cultural insiders (1966).

I propose that the Maya-Mam theme of centeredness is just such a powerful cultural and grammatical element, one which reflects, affirms and, indeed, constructs this Maya-Mam worldview. As one speaks Mam, the worldview that is represented and reflected by the language is confirmed and established. Indeed, it emerges in the very act of speaking. Action in the world, of which speaking is a prime example, is both the outflow or product of the worldview which engenders it, as well as the prime building block used to establish that very worldview. This is at the root of what Pierre Bourdieu calls the habitus, the idea that as language actively structures cultural reality, at the same time, it is itself structured by that reality (1990:52). In the same way, I consider centeredness among the Mam as both a template of how the world works (that which is seen as a structured whole) as well as a goal to achieve personal peace and communal accord (that which helps structure our behavior). Mayanist Evon Vogt of Harvard (d. 2004) says that this idea of the Mayan sense of centeredness "symbolizes the essence of social order, civilized behavior" (1976:33)—whether out in the hamlets with their clusters of house compounds or in the ceremonial center with the "houses for the saints" with the "navel of the earth" at its center. This is in opposition to the "undomesticated domain populated by wild plants, wild animals and demons" (ibid.), where civilizing centeredness is unknown.

It is this sense of order, equilibrium, fairness, and harmony that typifies the world as it should be: centered—not extreme, nor unbalanced nor skewed. At the same time, the world is rarely so nicely organized, so centeredness becomes a goal to work toward and a cultural value that comprises that which is ultimately *b'a'n,* good and meaningful. I will continue to spell this out as we look at data from a variety of contexts.

So the distinction between what Hale calls World View-1 and World View-2 is not as neat as the finite numbers may have intimated: first one, then the other. Rather, the two are "interconstitutive, through overlap and interplay between people's cultural practices and preoccupations and the grammatical structures they habitually employ" (Enfield: 2002).

To understand another culture, it isn't enough to simply note their practices, even less so the physical coordinates and measurements of the bodies that "do" those practices. Rather, such understanding is built up in community and over time. It includes the perspective and practice of history, both the acquisition and augmentation of cultural knowledge, as well as how that knowledge has been appropriately expressed throughout reported history. This sense of "that's how things are and how they have always been" lays down extremely powerful cultural norms for regulating and interpreting behavior. Language gives us a powerful tool for understanding and interpreting these norms.

Of course, we can only hope to approximate, rather than attain, a truly local or emic analysis of culture—particularly a culture other than our own—but to strive to do so leads us into an analysis of the practices and cultural knowledge of a people, both of which can be expressed in language. This is what Geertz means when he says that culture is public—it is "out there" where it can be seen, discovered, learned, taught, acted out, and interpreted. It isn't magic. It's real—if not fully material. In this study, I am assuming that both grammatical and cultural themes are indeed public, "out there" and discoverable in the world as it is understood by the Maya-Mam.

My goal in this study is to establish the Maya-Mam integrating value of centeredness as a cultural and grammatical theme, and to posit the relevance of such a theme to our understanding of the relationship between language and culture. I show that the particular overlap of the cultural and grammatical theme of centeredness is specific to Maya-Mam and basic to the Mam conception of the world. As such, this notion supports the concept of linguistic relativity, according to which language affects culture (language is a force for structuring the world). But it also shows that culture affects language (language is a construct built up by the articulation of our understanding of the world and how it works).

1.2 How might we show that language and culture are cut from the same cloth?

What kinds of evidence would we consider adequate to such an enterprise? First, England and Martin agree that grammatical and cultural themes need to be verified independently. In other words, grammatical themes should emerge from the formal analysis of naturally occurring texts in addition to the meanings and distribution of individual lexical items (words and affixes). And they should operate both across and within levels of the linguistic hierarchy—lexical, morphological (the make-up of words), and syntactic (the make-up of sentences), as well as in discourse.[9] I suggest that deictic centeredness as a formal grammatical theme operates on just these levels of Mam grammar. We will talk more about deixis a little later and also in chapter five, but for now we will let a few examples stand for the whole.

The difference between the verbs *bring* and *take* is a deictic distinction; the topic of discussion is called deixis. When someone *brings* something, it comes toward or to the speaker. When someone *takes* something, it goes away from the speaker or from where the speaker was when he or she articulated the phrase. The speaker occupies a "center space" from which the orientation of this kind of motion (toward or away from the speaker) is determined. The words *here* and *there* and *this* and *that* also define a deictic center space from which location is measured. *Here* and *this* are near me as the speaker (this book that I have here in my hand). *There* and *that* code things that are not near to the speaker, at least when compared to *here* and *this* (that cat over there). This can get complicated as we will see later.

We will find the notion of the deictic center or *origo* to be extremely productive in Mam grammar.

In addition, the meanings of lexical items should be construed within an overarching semantic domain which is meaningful to locals. This is possible by comparing and contrasting both use and meaning of words and affixes as they occur in daily practice, grounding centeredness in the daily

---

[9] The notion of discourse in linguistics is basically related to the study of structure, order, and meaning beyond the sentence.

lives and speech of the Mam. Centeredness is indeed "a big-ticket item" among the Mam.

Likewise, to posit centeredness as a cultural theme requires independent, nonlinguistic, or paralinguistic verification across a number of cultural areas—religion, daily life, construction, the use of space, health and illness etiology, etc. This is just what Hoijer, Hymes, Hale, Martin, England, and Enfield are asking for—establishing cultural and grammatical themes independently of each other and then comparing them for similarities and overlap. Still, any generalizations that we reach must be cross-checked with cultural insiders to prevent the "eye of the beholder" effect, where things seem perfectly clear to an outside researcher but remain opaque to locals. Of course, pattern unrecognized is still pattern, but my claim is that grammatical and cultural themes converge in local meaning, so pattern, though crucial, isn't enough. We seek local interpretation in order to show meaningful linkage between linguistic and cultural material.

Enfield, like Hale, cautions against the overzealous positing of causal, non-arbitrary links between linguistic and nonlinguistic phenomena, yet he claims that "exploratory attempts at explanation can be extremely valuable" (2002:24) in that they give us an idea where to look for strong arguments supporting these links. He suggests that these arguments may well be psychological in nature, wrapped up in the meaning assigned by native speakers to linguistic and cultural phenomena. To that end, "it is well worth exploring the idea that a language's morphosyntactic resources are related to the cultural knowledge, attitudes, and practices of its speakers" (idem). So, although we're skating on thin ice when we posit that language causes certain cultural responses or that culture is behind certain grammatical structures, this is just the vocation that Enfield and Hale call us to.

As mentioned above, Itkonen claims that proof in anthropology, sociology, history, and other human sciences is different in a number of ways from proof in the natural sciences. First, for the natural sciences, "Since each centimeter or second is identical with each other centimeter or second, the differences and similarities between (physical) things and events can be ascertained in a precise and perfectly general way" (1978:25, parenthetical comment his). In the human sciences, on the other hand, such measurement is either impossible or trivial. Cultural phenomena such as values, contentment, faith, and honor, are not readily reducible to numbers and precise calculation. Of course, there are physical, spatio-temporal coordinates to cultural phenomena, but to reduce the phenomena themselves to the location where they take place and to the measured movements of bodies in space, though not unimportant, is to a large degree orthogonal—or at best minimally relevant—to what it is that cultural anthropologists are trying to find out. Second, whereas positivistic proof requires the precise measurement of calculable phenomena—observable "objects" in space and time—the human sciences strive not to measure but to understand or interpret observations not reducible to such calculable phenomena: things like attitudes, cultural values, and worldview. Third, a positivist scientist attempts to stand outside of the universe of measurement and the things to be measured, and in this way, to be truly "objective," whereas social scientists "investigate something which they themselves, qua scientists, are part of" (ibid.:30).

Itkonen says that proof (and data) for the more "human" sciences is hermeneutic, rather than positivistic. He defines this by suggesting that "it might be said that hermeneutics acquires its data through understanding meanings, intentions, values, norms, or rules, and the hermeneutic analysis consists in reflection upon what has been understood" (ibid.:20). This gives rise to a fourth and final Itkonen observation: whereas the methodology of positivistic science is well established, hermeneutic methodology has no standard discovery procedure. It is eclectic, participatory, and interpretive.

With this in mind, how do we go about "proving" that centeredness is a cultural and grammatical theme in Mam?

1. First, we don't do away with careful observation. Rather, we contextualize it. Itkonen reminds us that meaning exists only in social context. So, instead of trying to extract ourselves from social context, linguistic anthropologists embrace it. This is quintessential participant observation, the hallmark of ethnographic description (see section 4.1 below). The ethnographer is part of the context—not a fly on the wall—and, as such, needs to be described and discussed just as any other fact of the context. Some feel that this kind of reorienting of context around the researcher is useless and tangential navel gazing. Like anything else, it can get out of hand, but by committing to a focus on those being researched, the researcher is normally only manifested as a grounds against which more central figures play out their roles. The focus of good ethnography, while not denying the researcher's presence, is not about the researcher.

1.2 How might we show that language and culture are cut from the same cloth? 23

2. We look for historical continuities. Frenchman Émile Durkheim, the father of modern sociology, says, "The determining cause of a social fact should be sought among the social facts preceding it" (1988:244). Since I claim that centeredness is a "social fact," in the tradition of Durkheim, that is, a pervasive, culture-wide phenomenon, it should be manifested through time, as well as across social sub-groups within the culture. These facts don't just pop up fully grown like Aphrodite from the sea foam. They take time to spread—more broadly and more deeply. And despite differences of gender, social class, education, home region, religion, and economic standing, there are nevertheless issues that supersede these differences in uniting members of a culture group. These include language, values, and worldview, continuities which can be uniting principles even in the face of extensive social variation.

3. We seek patterns in the data that we observe, both linguistic and cultural; the more disparate and atomistic the data, the more helpful an encompassing theory "within which the observations find a natural place" (Chafe 1994:21). And, as we've discussed already, the patterns should be independently verified (chapter three); yet, at the same time, we should be able to unite them under the common notion of centeredness. Hymes says that a basic practice of anthropological study is "the showing of a pattern, fashion of speaking, or style among a number of traits" (1966:117). This is the goal of my study—to explain how such diverse observations as religious choice, the constructed world, the perception of health and illness, daily language use, and aspects of the formal grammar of Mam are all instantiations of a single theme.

This kind of analysis is based on triangulation, a term used by ethnographers to indicate that conclusions are drawn from a variety of sources based on disparate observations across different aspects of the culture, in order to draw inferences that are integrated across the observations and commensurate with native opinion. Something that we observe just once really doesn't tell us anything. If we see it a second time, perhaps it is a coincidence. But if it happens three times or even more, there may well be a pattern emerging.

4. Itkonen says that the people themselves must be able to understand and accept the description arrived at in our research (1978). This is what Amy Zaharlick, in a personal communication, calls the "Aha! factor." When locals appropriately understand the data and the explanation, they should

agree that the analysis is realistic and that it reflects how they view the world. The fact that locals would say, "You know, this is really the way we think about things," is itself data and therefore subject to analysis.

5. When someone acts outside cultural norms we can expect some kind of critical reaction from the group. Culture includes learned and shared patterns of behavior. These cultural norms aren't deterministic—people can decide to comply or not to. Nevertheless, these norms exert tremendous pressure on individuals in the culture to conform. As Durkheim (1988:240) says, because society "surpasses the individual in time as well as in space, it is in a position to impose upon him ways of acting and thinking which it has consecrated with its prestige." As we have said, culture is built up over time and its influence is spread over entire areas of habitation. It is practiced by family, friends, and pretty much everyone—and has been for a long time. A cultural value becomes salient via its absence, and ignoring these norms exacts a price. I discuss this in chapter three in terms of Timo's patio. When centeredness was considered compromised (ignored or flouted), something had to be done.

6. Finally, assuming that our theme of centeredness is as pervasive and explanatory as I've suggested, we would expect it to be manifested in many ways in the daily life of the Mam.

In chapters three, four, and five I attempt to "prove" or affirm my premise via this six-fold rubric. The careful reader will see that the first three points of the rubric are methodological in nature—the priority of participant observation, the search for continuity from the past, and the identification of patterns of behavior. The second three points are predictive, something we should expect from any theory worth its salt. Our rubric predicts that the Mam will generally agree to the notion of the center as an organizing and influential principle of life, that either the flouting or ignoring of this principle leads to strong response and that the instantiation of centeredness will be pervasive and varied in Mam behavior. These six points will provide us with a track to run on.

I consider chapter four the heart of the book. In it I show how centeredness is a part of daily life among the Mam. I look at a marriage proposal and an agreement protocol where I was personally (and innocently, I might add) involved in offending a man's wife, and I discuss how centeredness comes into play in each event and, also, how the two events coalesce around the notion of a commitment to reciprocal action, which I claim is an analogue of a search for metaphorical center space among disputants. I also discuss the language of centeredness, how the Mam themselves talk about daily life in terms of our theme and what vocabulary they use to do so. Most of this is based on lexical items taken from discussions in which I played a participatory role, although the longer discussion of -*k'u'j* 'stomach' terms stems from Scotchmer's (1978) unpublished componential analysis of such terms and my resultant ethnographic interview session with a number of Mam men based on Scotchmer's findings, and confirmed in local conversations.

1.2.1 A future for linguistic anthropology

As sociolinguistics has become a well-respected branch of linguistics by showing the relevance of social context to language choice and structure, so I believe that anthropological linguistics merits the same respect from the broader linguistic field, as we see how relevant cultural context is to language. My hope is that this study will be a step in that direction, presenting linguistic and anthropological data together in order to show the critical importance of both in our quest to understand another culture and the language that culture members speak.

As sociolinguistics looks at variety within language, based on differing social contexts (when language varies or correlates with gender, age, socioeconomic class, geographic region, education, vocation, etc.), so linguistic anthropology seeks to understand the commonalities that all culture members share despite social and linguistic variation. In this sense, I consider culture to provide a "context for contexts." In other words, despite language variation based on the variables mentioned above—along with other potential factors[10]—people within the larger culture still largely agree on linguistic code and worldview, powerful factors that allow for successful communication and basic agreement about how the world works despite observable differences within the larger group. I suggest that it is these cultural themes that hold across social and even linguistic contexts, as well as across time, that help solidify and account for social practice, "the behavior of whole cultural groups" (Martin 1977:366), despite the distinctions of class, gender, education, and geographic region.

---

[10] For a fascinating discussion of these "potential factors," see Dodsworth 2005, an Ohio State dissertation.

An academic book should put its claims in a larger context. A study of great beaches shouldn't limit itself to observations about the chemical composition of the sand. So I will keep coming back to the bigger picture. We've already talked quite a bit about linguistic anthropology, specifically the Sapir-Whorf Hypothesis and the corresponding notions of cultural and grammatical theme. We've heard the voices of a number of heavy hitters, all of whom have at one time or another considered linguistic relativity with kind eyes. Boas, Malinowski, Sapir, Whorf, Hoijer, Hockett, Pike, Hymes, Bourdieu, Geertz, Gossen, Hale, Zaharlick, England, Martin, Wierzbicka, Boroditsky, Enfield, and others have become colleagues and mentors in our quest for understanding the heartbeat of Maya-Mam culture.

These people are modern linguists, which means that we all are interested in the commonalities of languages around the world. It is truly astounding that, despite the obvious differences among the world's languages in terms of their sounds and meanings and structures, nonetheless there is a tremendous amount of similarity and even "universality" among them. This look at the forest rather than the trees is Chomsky's major contribution to modern linguistics, indeed, it virtually defines modern linguistics. But in our quest for the universal, we must not overlook the beauty and reality of linguistic and cultural diversity. Although languages seem to be cut from the same cognitive cloth, the variety of that cloth is also astounding and worthy of study. This is the purview of linguistic anthropology, trying to keep both the universal and the particular in focus.

In addition to these "heavy hitters" we've also heard from my friend Eugenio about the power of the center for orienting behavior and for providing a template for understanding how the world is supposed to work. We will hear from many others, since ethnography is a multi-voiced and many-layered discipline. My hope is that the mix of scholarship with the earthiness of data and observations drawn from the real lives of real people will enrich us, both intellectually and humanly. And you, gentle reader, will decide for yourself if I have cleared the high bar of good ethnography which requires hearty entertainment, solid teaching, accurate reporting, and integrated analysis.

This is what good ethnography is about. We'll be working this out together through the rest of the book.

1.3 Methodology employed

This study combines various methodologies drawn from linguistics and linguistic anthropology, ethnography, and discourse analysis. It is a mix of the scholarship of others and my own research. My contribution is largely in the arrangement and interpretation of the data, although much of the linguistic data is a result of my own investigation. I have corroborated among Central Mam speakers all the data that I have included from others and I have, to my thinking, made the data from other sources "my own," in the sense that I've attempted to find analogues in the speech and culture of Comitecos (people from Comitancillo, where Central Mam is spoken) concomitant with the data of others that I have cited in the cultural fields of architectonics, health and illness, religion and conversion, and in daily life and speech.

1.3.1 Ethnographic methods

My life among the Mam has been largely as a participant observer, although not exactly as an ethnographer. When my wife and I moved to Comitancillo in 1980 I had had a single graduate cultural anthropology course, although I had fairly extensive SIL training in second language acquisition (which had a strong cultural component).[11] I also had my recent Spanish acquisition experience to aid me in approaching a third language. Our language-learning program was socially, not academically, based. It was basically learning by wandering around and getting involved in activities and conversations wherever and whenever possible. This has ended up being the main strength within my ethnographic contribution via this book, since good ethnography is based on native-language participation.

In 1980 not a lot had been published about Mam beyond a few dissertations. These were especially helpful for providing some advance notice of what to look for. Yet today, although much more is available about the language, including a great deal written by the Mam themselves, England still maintains, in a personal communication, that Mam is extremely underrepresented in the scholarly literature.

---

[11] SIL International, previously known as the Summer Institute of Linguistics, is a Christian linguistic organization committed to language development among the ethnic minority languages of the world, to bilingual education, and to Bible translation.

My Mam language-learning experience centered around a "route" that I walked several times a week, meeting people in store fronts and visiting in homes or in the plaza, or in the lines of people waiting to get into the municipal buildings to pay a fee or see the mayor. In these different contexts, I recited a short, memorized monologue with the dozens of people willing to listen to a gringo stumble over their language.

Later that day, after evaluating my performance and dealing with any questions that arose, I would learn another short monologue and repeat the process. At the end of each week, I would review my progress, write up any interesting cultural or linguistic observations, and plan for the following week.

This route-based system of language learning was founded on the work of Tom and Betty Sue Brewster, a married team of language-acquisition gurus who taught that learning a language is as natural as having a baby. Rather than turning the experience over to the language schools and "experts," they proclaimed that we should embrace the naturalness of the language acquisition situation and learn a language socially rather than formally.[12] This made sense to us since there were no schools in Comitancillo for learning Mam, nor were there any Mam-101 instructors, nor texts of any kind.

While we were still in Guatemala City, before moving to Comitancillo, both my wife, Nancy, and I walked Spanish language-learning "routes" each day. I found that, after moving to Comitancillo, memorizing Mam monologues was much more challenging than learning Spanish routines. I was unable to learn enough overnight to warrant another foray into the community the following day. I usually made these visits of several hours in length two or three times a week.

An acquaintance (and eventually an employee), Gilberto, worked several hours with me each afternoon, helping me construct grammatically correct monologues that would answer questions people had about my wife and me and our newborn daughter. Where were we from? Were our parents living? Why did we have just one child? Why had we come to Comitancillo? What was life like in the United States? Did I have a real job? Did we eat tortillas?

When Gilberto and I had prepared a short monologue (usually just three or four sentences), he would record it three times in its entirety on a cassette

---

[12] The Brewsters were indeed naturalists. Just a few months before arriving in Guatemala City to help lead a two-month Spanish-learning workshop, Betty Sue had given birth to their first and only child, attended by a midwife and by husband Tom, who was quadriplegic (d. 1985).

1.3 Methodology employed

recorder. I would listen to this recording over and over, often putting it on an everlasting tape loop, and I would try to match Gilberto's rate of speech and his intonation by speaking the monologue together with the advancing tape. Then he would record it again, going through the text a phrase at a time, leaving a short dead space after each phrase so I could repeat it after him. Then he would tape another exercise, building the phrases up to full sentences for repetition, eventually to the point where I could say the entire text verbatim and at normal speed. I would often listen to these tapes and recite my text hundreds of times before trying it out on people in town. Gilberto would also note sounds that were difficult for me to produce and we would create taped exercises to focus on those sounds. We would also develop exercises to help me learn verb tense and aspect, person marking and new vocabulary. So although I claim that I learned language socially rather than academically (there being no schools to attend or adequate programmed materials to work through), there was still a strong formal component to my methodology,[13] much of which Gilberto and I developed as we went along. The difference in the Brewsters' system and a more typically formal one is based on the Brewsters' insistence on self direction, a very strong social component, and learning things as needed rather than according to a predetermined scope and sequence. After some six months dedicated to learning Spanish in the streets of Guatemala City, I spent almost two years concentrating pretty much full time on learning to speak Mam. Although I've never been mistaken for a native speaker, I was usually/often able to understand what was going on around me, and word spread about my language ability, which was usually overstated in the telling. In a way, this is a sad situation. Since there have been so few outsiders who have made even a stab at learning to speak this wonderful language, any that do become hot news. People often ask me how long it took me to "learn Mam." I usually tell them quite truthfully, "I'm still learning," which is certainly true. It did indeed take all of two years before I felt comfortable speaking Mam even in limited contexts.

The social and formal components of my language-learning experience were bolstered by the technical work of translation. This is where I learned much about Mam language and culture as I worked with native speakers to try to understand together with them Biblical content and the best way to get this content across in Mam. Using Mam as the medium of

---

[13] For a fuller discussion of this methodology, see Brewster and Brewster 1976.

communication and participation has been crucial to any insight I've been able to put forth in this study.

Good ethnography is based on just such participant observation. Participation implies a degree of language ability such that the researcher can share in the practice of daily life without constantly referring to the mechanics of speech. Speaking ability comes to be assumed and is used as an avenue through which deeper understandings are achieved.

Ethnography is both a methodology and a product. It offers explanations in terms of multiple voices, and it highlights views not often publicized. Basically, it tries to answer the question, What is it like to be a member of this culture and a speaker of this language?

Ethnography is a broad, interdisciplinary methodology. Yet, despite its all-comers eclecticism, there are some basic elements that hold true of all ethnographic inquiry, as suggested by Martyn Hammersly and Paul Atkinson (1986). It is based on participant observation. It denies even the possibility of being the so-called fly on the wall that is privy to everything that happens and which enables one to make "valid" judgments about its meaning. Ethnographers admit that the observer's paradox is real (Labov 1972, especially chapter eight). This paradox, also known as the thermometer effect, constantly badgers the analyst. If you want to know the temperature of a glass of water, you stick a thermometer in the water and wait for a reading. But the thermometer being in the water affects the temperature, and the reading is therefore suspect. So the presence of an anthropologist affects the context such that what she or he has to say about it is itself suspect. We basically want to observe what the people are like when they are not being observed. If that sounds like an impossibility, you get the picture.

The solution to this conundrum is not to try to extract oneself from the situation, to "rise above it," or to hide a tape recorder or video camera under one's sombrero (which, by the way, is unacceptable to any reputable university social science department). Rather, effective analysts participate (in varying degrees) in the very events that they describe. The goal is to understand the emic categories of the people being studied. With this in mind, ethnography is long-term. One can't simply ask people, "So, what are your emic categories?" These are uncovered over many months and years of inquiry—both formal and informal—and observation. Ethnography assumes that research is done in the native language as much as possible, and that it is based on firsthand observation. In addition, the search for emic

1.3 Methodology employed

categories makes those studied the experts, since they know what things mean, and we don't. So an ethnographer's role is one of a learner, and she learns naturalistically, that is, in social context via relationships with native speakers—they who are the holders of the emic categories and are the ultimate goal of the research. This characteristic of the researcher-as-participant is what ethnographers mean when they say that they themselves are the research instrument. Members of the group being studied answer questions for the ethnographer; they give advice, teach, and learn skills, share meals, and help solve problems in ways that include the researcher in the local life of the group. In such a context, ethnographic researchers plumb their own thoughts and responses to how they are included (or not) in the local scene and they study the language and practices of inclusion and exclusion. In this way, ethnography is reactive and iterative. Questions are never fully answered. Rather, more and more data are brought to bear on how an issue is to be understood in different ways under different circumstances. In this way, researchers can write not about some objectified/sterile sense of what behaviors are exhibited by group members, but they can talk of life in context from the point of view of the cultural insider. That is our goal.

Ethnography is holistic. Ethnographers start with some cultural detail—for example, a cockfight (Geertz 1973:412–453) or a short proverb (Becker 1996:142–159)—and begin to explore it. In the exploration, more and more context is brought to bear upon its interpretation. Questions are asked. Contrasts are sought. Both Geertz and Becker expand the scope of their original topics to include much larger issues of local life, language and thought, Geertz beginning with culture, Becker beginning with language. And yet both end up in a similar place, a thickly described slice of local life with adequate perspective to show us how that slice fits into the larger life of the group.[14]

The product of effective participant observation is thick description (Geertz 1973), where a researcher looks first at what seems to be going on, at which point he or she begins to add layers of further description by discussing language use, linguistic and cultural categories, local interpretations of events, and further relevant detail. It is this multi-layering that makes the description "thick." This contrasts with "thin" description

---

[14] For a succinct and helpful discussion of the common characteristics of ethnography in whatever field it is practiced, see Zaharlick 1992.

which merely states the physical facts, the etic layer with no interpetation. Thick description is reflective as well as recursive, going back over details again and again, and thinking about them from different perspectives and answering new and further research questions until all emic moisture is wrung out of both real-time observation and further discussion with actual participants. This emic wringing Geertz calls "interpretive anthropology," where the explication of worldview is plumbed, along with how this worldview is realized in linguistic and cultural practice.

Thick description not only extracts the emic from the etic (or the meaningful from the mundane), but it also explains the use of language in culturally accepted and socially expected ways. In essence, thick description is an amalgam of how both cultural insiders and participant observers view a social situation and its relevant context, and it is the technique I use to plumb the idea of centeredness as a cultural theme. What makes Geertz particularly appropriate here is his integration of linguistic and cultural data encompassing two points of view. Both are important. The first has to do with what the data themselves show, the story that Geertz sees. The second point of view emerges from Geertz's own language and culture, who he is as a person and not just as a scholar. This helps him to relate closely with his audience, and they see the "foreign" story through his eyes, whereby it loses much of its foreignness. This would not be possible if Geertz were to stick with just one side of the story. For example, in his article on Balinese cockfights (1973:412–451) Geertz shows that an ethnographer must look at what he calls the microscopic details of a single event (the etic layer), while also addressing the broader issues of how those details fit into the larger picture of cultural/linguistic life by comparing them with others in contrastive life situations and texts. It is this layering of analysis that is the essence of thick description, which includes ethnolinguistic techniques for probing semantic categories, seeking information and asking questions around topics like kinship, work, religion, or, as in the present case, centeredness and balance.

Geertz's emic study gives us a powerful ethnographic model to emulate. For Geertz, ethnographic participant observation is different from a simple parade of anecdotes in that it is purposeful, integrated, holistic, contextualized, and centered not only on the researcher's rendition of what is happening, but on local analysis as well. The ethnographic report based on participant observation is not merely the retelling of anecdotes. Anecdotes are flat—told from a single point of view. They are also streamlined—trying to make a single point. An ethnographer, rather, tells the story from many angles—her own, both personally and professionally, as well as from that of the speakers/doers themselves. The ethnographic story is layered and nuanced.

One's point of view is not readily reducible to proofs and numbers. In the same way, any connection between language and culture is not so much something subject to measurement as it is to interpretation. Cultural studies don't enable us necessarily to predict cultural phenomena, but rather to understand them. A Geertzian interpretation, as mentioned above, has both etic (the description) and emic (the meaning) components.

As mentioned earlier, the researcher supports his or her construal of events by triangulation, where generalizations are pursued across the variety of observations, which may or may not seem to be related on the surface, but at a deeper level may be instantiations of the same theme. My goal in this study is in one sense, as Hymes (1966:117) says, to seek not proof, but pattern. But beyond Hymes, we are seeking local interpretation of this pattern. Pattern alone is not enough. Where language and culture come together is in the minds of native speakers. So it is this emic perspective—local meaning—that I'm seeking in this study. How is centeredness, as realized in cultural and grammatical theme, conceived and reflected in talk among the Mam themselves?

What I try to do then, as an ethnographer, is attempt to live the life of a Maya-Mam—at least to a limited degree. What I hope to discover is whether what ends up in my own head and behavior as I endeavor to live that life, corresponds to the way that the Mam themselves think and act. My goal is for them to say, when we talk about my findings: *Tzuyxpetzin tu'n*. 'Yep, you got it'.

These ethnographic methods together with their respective ethnographic products give us a clear goal to shoot for.[15] I hope to emulate in chapter four the fine work of Hymes, Geertz, Becker, and Duranti (whom we'll meet later). In that chapter we will look in depth, and in ethnographic style, at a Mam agreement ritual.

---

[15] Of the many good ethnographies that have been published (including Geertz and Becker mentioned above), see especially Duranti 1992, for a solid example of ethnography as both a process and a product, where he brings together linguistic and cultural practice in terms of Samoan ceremonial greetings. A related (and abridged) account of a Samonan *fono* appears in Duranti 1997.

1.3.2 Linguistic methods and models

Linguistically, I follow Charles Fillmore and John Lyons in terms of my discussion of deixis. We talked about this (if not about Fillmore and Lyons) a number of pages back. Deixis projects from a traditional "egocentric" idea of the deictic center. Actually, deictic notions aren't limited to *here* and *there,* although these will be the most relevant in our study since it is spatial relations that particularly concern us. Regarding the fuller notion of deixis, Fillmore says: "I carry around with me, everywhere I go, my own private world. The spatial centre of this world is my location (here)...the temporal centre of this world is the passing moment of my consciousness (now)...the social centre of this world is me" (1998:40–41) (1998:40–42, parenthetical glosses, WMC). The speaker—ego—is the center point from which all deictic notions (person, place, and time) are determined. By virtually all accounts, deixis is quintessentially egocentric, based on where the speaker is at the moment of utterance. This deictic center serves like a surveyor's monument stake, a binding starting point from which all deictic measurements are calculated. This deictic center anchors the meaning of the words *you* and *me, this* and *that, now* and *then.* These words don't have an exact denotation like the word *dog* or *joy* or *Ralph,* things we can point to. Indeed, the term "deictic" means to point or indicate. The meaning of deictic terms is determined contextually. When I am speaking, the words *I* and *me* refer to me. But when the conversation swings and you are speaking, your use of *I* and *me* refers to you, not me. The same holds for *here* and *there. Here* is close to me and *there* is away from me; but when you wrest the floor from me and you are doing the talking, *here* is close to you and *there* is away from you—perhaps close to me. Which is which depends on who is speaking, and to whom. As complicated as this seems to be, deictics are among the early lexical forms that children acquire, albeit not without some confusion.

The present study is not specifically about deixis, at least not directly; rather it deals with the formal, grammatical apparatus the Mam use that relates to and is defined by centeredness, of which the idea of a deictic center is the prime formal example.

I also talk in chapter five about a field of linguistics called discourse analysis. The basic question here is, What makes a text a unified whole as opposed to a simple gluing together of unrelated sentences? A classic work in the field was done by M. A. K. Halliday and Ruqaiya Hasan (1976), where

1.3 Methodology employed

they identify what they call *ties* between what comes earlier in a text and what comes later, like pronouns and their antecedents, and related vocabulary that moves a text forward as it unfolds. The study of discourse has tended to have two emphases. One deals with the mechanics of discourse, how the grammar of a language links what comes next to what has come before. The other downplays the grammar of discourse[16] for a number of reasons and is more interested in the connected ideas themselves, how the story or the arguments flow from one proposition to the next.

I subscribe to a more holistic approach. I think the mechanics of discourse are fascinating and important. At the same time, grammar is the slave of meaning, and meaning is really what the use of spoken (or written) discourse is about, the flow of ideas. This dual idea of "what discourse means" and "how discourse works" is best exemplified, I think, by Sanders, Spooren, and Noordman (1992, and more so Sanders and Spooren 2001), for which see the bibliography.

You don't need to be a linguist to understand the grammar that we will be talking about under the broader issue of grammatical theme, but for those of you who are linguists, I'd like to give you a fair indication of where I'm coming from.

Studying texts is an age-old strategy of language learning and analysis. It works more slowly but far more efficiently than just memorizing vocabulary, which is the easiest thing to learn in a foreign language. Over the years I have taped dozens and dozens of texts—all with the permission and cooperation of the speakers. Although perhaps more natural, texts recorded on the sly represent unethical and disrespectful practice, and data from such are disallowed in serious academic research.

Many of the texts that I have recorded have arisen out of questions I had about how or why people do things. For example, I've asked a number of people to tell me how one goes about building a house. This has given me a variety of different perspectives based on whether the speaker was a man or woman, a girl or boy. Far from finding that people were nervous about recording, I have found most of my Mam friends and many strangers to be

---

[16] Chomsky, the father of modern linguistics, doesn't even consider discourse studies to be part of linguistics, but sees them instead as more related to rhetoric or behavior studies. He claims that grammar begins with morphemes (roots and affixes) and ends with sentences. On this view, anything beyond the sentence is less science and more interpretation. The notion that how people actually talk would be considered not a part of linguistics has flummoxed discourse analysts for decades. Certainly, discourse study isn't as "neat" as the study of phrases and sentences, but it is every bit as fascinating and important.

animated before a microphone and happy to record their language. I also have an inventory of interviews recorded by Gilberto who was putting together a booklet on the cultural and religious history of Comitancillo. He interviewed several speakers over sixty years old and helped transcribe these texts. Although they've not been published, they have been part of the input I've had as a language learner, and they inform my comments on Mam discourse in chapter five.

In terms of lexical meaning, I worked through with five Comitecos the details of David Scotchmer's unpublished manuscript (1978) on -*k'u'j* terms and I have added additional lexical material beyond his findings. Just to whet your appetite, the word *tk'u'j* literally means 'his/her stomach' or 'essence', and it shows up in phrases throughout the language, coding such meanings as 'to covet', 'to be bored', 'to love', 'to remember', 'to forget', 'to lust', 'to envy', 'to exhort', 'to encourage', 'to foresee', to vacillate', 'to have compassion', 'to withstand', and many, many more, as we will see in chapter four.

In my discussion of how the grammatical and cultural themes relate to the ongoing debate of any connection between language and culture, I concur with Bourdieu, the French philosopher and sociologist, who claims that they mutually inform. Language is part of the *habitus,* the history, values, and ethos of a group of people, that both structures and informs culture and is structured and informed by it. So language and culture are hard to tease apart. Language is culture's main contribution to a people and to the world, while at the same time, it is culture that influences so strongly what it is that people need to talk about. Repeating Enfield, the two notions are "interconstitutive." I will discuss this at some length in chapter five.

1.4 Analysis of the data

Chapter four deals with Mam daily life and the vocabulary of centeredness. It is written from a Geertzian ethnographic perspective that highlights the beauty and wisdom and meaning of daily practice among the Mam. It is a chapter in which I am personally and inextricably involved as a protagonist and, later, a supplicant. In this, I follow Geertz and Becker, whose insight into Balinese and Burmese cultures respectively, were based on their embroiled participation in actual cultural events, not simply the reporting of these events from a perspective supposedly "outside" of them.

This would indeed be impossible. Even hiding on the dark side of a one-way glass window, we would not really be able to observe and understand what people are like when they are not being observed.

The meta-dialogue that I maintain with the reader in chapter four is a characteristic of the "product" of ethnography. In this meta-dialogue I also discuss how I analyzed the data—conferring with other Mam not involved in the actual events about the specifics of cultural practice and discourse—and reflecting on the etic "camera view' of my situation and the emic "insider view" of what was happening. In this, I try to emulate Geertz and Becker, who, I suggest, are masters of the genre.

Much of the analysis of the cultural data that I've cited in this study is a recasting of the data in terms of centeredness and a bringing to bear of my own observations and experience from Comitancillo.

Similarly, much of my linguistic analysis comes from England (1983) and Godfrey (1981), again recast in terms of a deictic center.

In the end, what I try to do in this study is look at disparate phenomena in both the culture of the Mam (health and illness etiology, the constructed world, religion, and daily practice) and the language of the Mam (in the lexicon, the morphosyntax, and in narrative discourse) and show links between them that are salient to Mam speakers and helpful to us as outsiders in understanding Mam cultural life.

1.5 Who cares?

This book is aimed at several different groups, although authors are continually reminded by their editors to write to a specific audience. The most basic audience in my mind consists of people interested in language and culture beyond simply signing up for a cruise to an exotic destination. And since you are still reading, my first audience is you and people of similar persuasion. I assume that you, kind reader, are a college grad and fascinated by both the universal aspects as well as the captivating diversity of the world's minority languages and cultures. After all, you've stuck with the book this far and I think it only gets more interesting as we move forward.

Although the book is aimed at you, I think there also will be interest among people who "do language and culture" professionally, that is, linguists and anthropologists. So, as I've streamlined the discussion from when this work was a somewhat esoteric dissertation, I've attempted in all ways to maintain its integrity and seriousness. To this audience, I offer what I believe to be a larger view of context than social context alone. For example, Dell Hymes's model of speech variation (1974) is appropriately sociolinguistic—that language choice is in part determined by the participants involved, the goals of the speaker(s), the setting, and other social factors, all of which are critical to understanding and explaining speech variation. What a model based on the overlap of cultural and grammatical theme brings to the table is what I have previously called "a context for contexts." In other words, culture is the bigger picture within which sociolinguistic variation and social context operate. Culture includes the language, the unifying values, and the worldview of a people, an overarching context which is largely shared and agreed upon, despite social and personal differences.

A subset of this second group would be the Mayanists, those who study the languages and cultures of the five million-plus Maya still living in southern Mexico, Guatemala, and Belize (or who have emigrated north). Linguistic and cultural data on the Mam is limited, so I believe this study will be welcomed for its data, if not its analysis. Since deeply held values have a history, it is not surprising that the Mam cultural value of seeking the center shows up in Mayan cultures and is articulated via Mayan languages throughout Mesoamerica. Indeed, some sense of the center may be a "regional feature" that carries beyond the Maya themselves to other groups.

An additional group would be those interested in acquiring a second language and culture. To this group, I suggest that the complementary ideas of cultural and grammatical theme present us with a discovery procedure for second language and culture acquisition in the sense that pervasive cultural categories and values are likely to have a linguistic counterpart. As mentioned above, Hymes says, "Cultural values and beliefs are in part constitutive of linguistic reality" (1966:116). The discovery of comparable cultural factors will point out areas of cultural salience where we can look for elaborated vocabulary (dozens of words for "to carry," for example). Or, looking at it the other way around, where there is a pile-up of grammatical features or options of similar meaning, as we saw with Wierzbicka's comments about English "watered-down" imperatives, we can perhaps find cultural corollaries that are reflected in the grammar.

1.5 Who cares?

This overlap of cultural and grammatical theme gets at the details of what one must understand when he or she claims to "know" a language, where social and cultural context are as critical as grammatical competence to being a cultural insider.

A final group that may find this book interesting includes those who work in language development, those who, together with their indigenous colleagues, establish strategies for promoting language maintenance and use. Maya-Mam, along with the other thirty-plus Mayan languages, is an endangered language, and efforts at cultural and linguistic revitalization should take into account the linguistic system within its broad cultural context. Language and culture comprise a system of life, thought, and practice that are worthy of our investment and support.

2

Some Context for Better Understanding this Book

2.1 The occasion for research

Data for this book were gathered over the span of the thirty-plus years that I've been associated with the Mam of Comitancillo, Guatemala, an important town in the Central dialect area in the department of San Marcos (see maps 2.1 and 2.2). The municipal area of Comitancillo includes over 65,000 people, 98% of whom are L1 speakers of Mam according to the most recently published census information (1994). Central Mam speakers also live in San Lorenzo, Tejutla, and parts of Concepción Tutuapa and San Miguel Ixtahuacán, all in the department of San Marcos.

Map 2.1. Central America; adapted by Barbara Alber. Used with permission.

© d-maps.com. http://d-maps.com/carte.php?num_car=1389&lang=en
The boundaries shown on this map do not imply official endorsement or acceptance.

Nancy (and eventually our three children) and I lived in Comitancillo from 1980–1983, and again from 1985–1993. In other years (1984 and 1994–1998), we lived in Guatemala City, but still made frequent trips to Comitancillo and continued to work in Mam-related projects under the aegis of the Summer Institute of Linguistics.

2.1 *The occasion for research* 43

Map 2.2. Principal divisions in the Mam area; adapted by Craig Banghart from England (1983). Used with permission.

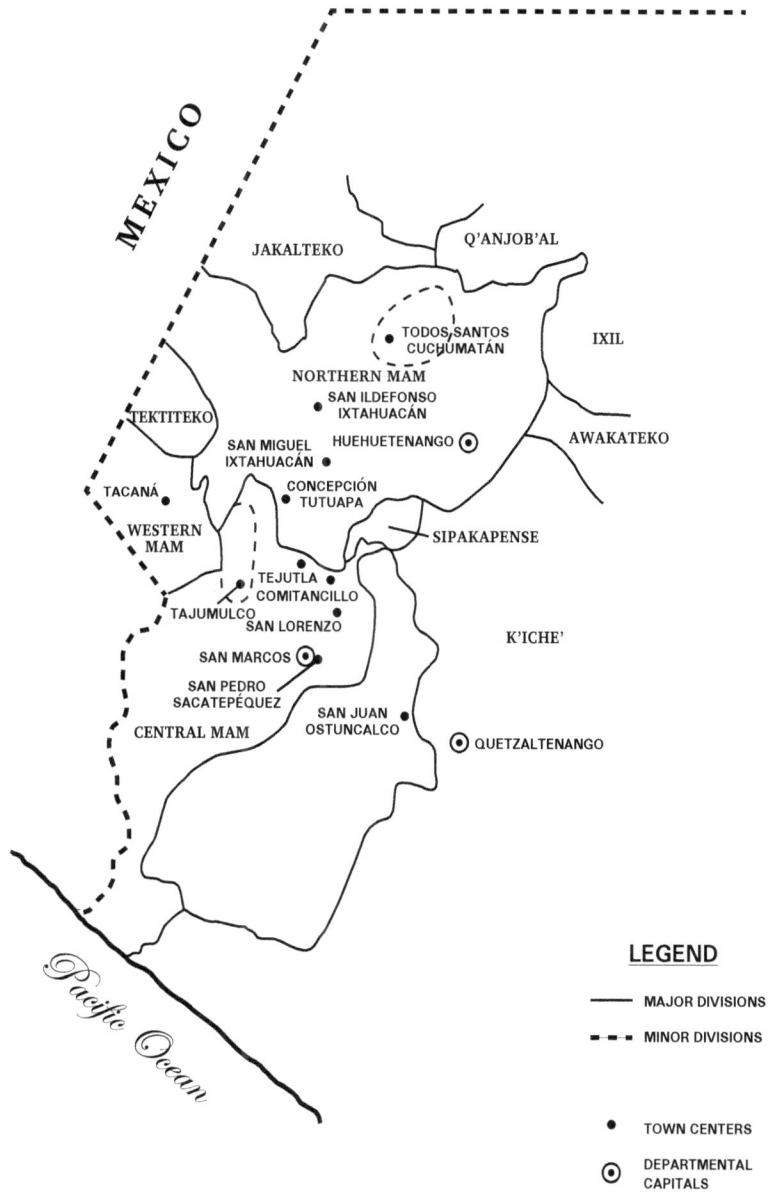

Nancy is a registered nurse and ran an informal clinic in our patio where she dealt with ten to twenty patients a day. Much of the information in chapter three about the hot-cold syndrome is from her vantage point as one who discussed with locals illness and treatment from a Mam perspective.

Both Nancy and I arrived in Guatemala City in August 1979 with master's degrees in applied linguistics from the University of Texas at Arlington. Our university training was a practical orientation to syntax, morphology, and phonology and it dealt largely with the nuts and bolts of language analysis. We also had very basic training in translation, literacy, anthropology, and community development. While in Guatemala City we studied Spanish and walked the streets of the capital using what Spanish we were "mastering" from day to day. As I mentioned earlier (section 1.3.1), our language-learning mentors were Tom and Elizabeth Brewster, who refined a method for learning a language socially rather than academically (see their book *Language acquisition made practical* [1976]). We took no formal classes in Spanish but learned it in daily interactions with friends and acquaintances in the streets, markets, restaurants, theaters, buses of Guatemala City, and in the homes and shops of Guatemalans.

Nancy was seven months pregnant with our first child when we arrived in Guatemala. This fact gave us no end of material for discussion with our new friends, and we were warmly received by locals who realized that our firstborn would be not only a *gringa,* but a Guatemalan as well. We spent six months in full time Spanish language learning as well as in learning to be parents. In both contexts, it was a new world.

Nancy and I were originally invited to Comitancillo by the leadership of the local Evangelical church of the Central American Mission in order to help with literacy and to survey the need for Bible translation. In response to this request, we moved to a rented house in Comitancillo in May 1980 just as the rainy season was beginning. We spent our first two years in language learning. Our Spanish was not very good at the time, but we were able to use it haltingly to get a grip on Mam, a language which we now speak fairly well. Although I speak Spanish better than Mam, I am able to do most of my work in Mam. I was happy to hear Eugenio say to me several years ago, *Ay tu'n tyolin noqx casi normal* 'you sound almost normal'. I took this as Eugenio's shot at a compliment. I talk a bit more about my language-learning experience in sections 1.3.1 and 1.3.2 on methodology.

I worked among a cadre of Mam men and an occasional woman as a literacy worker and Bible translator. As mentioned above, the Central Mam

2.1 The occasion for research

New Testament was published in 1998, with a second edition (in a slightly revised alphabet) in 2002. I continue to have the highest regard for the Christian Scriptures and their message of hope, which I believe is both cross-culturally relevant and highly respectful of cultural and linguistic diversity.

I also cooperated with local school teachers and administrators to help fund and publish a series of primers that were used for several years in Comitancillo schools and in volunteer literacy programs sponsored by area churches. I worked with Mam educators to help train authors and to publish literature in the Central dialect of Mam. I had a hand in upwards of thirty different Mam-authored titles published since the early eighties, although recently there has been a growing number of independent publications by local authors in addition to a host of new titles, particularly educational materials, published by PRONEBI (Programa Nacional de Educación Bilingüe), the national bilingual education program, and made available to all Mam schools.[1]

In addition, I worked with a number of Mam men and women in establishing (with generous support from the United States) a half dozen *microempresas* 'small businesses' and several local institutions including a municipal library and a Christian and educational training institute. Comitancillo has proved to be a wonderful place to work. Both men and women, young and old, take pride in the local language and culture, while also wanting to learn new things. It is a place with a worldview strongly rooted in the past, but which also provides flexibility and applicability in the present. People are comfortable with their Mayanness. I hope and trust that our own work and presence in Comitancillo over the years has made a small contribution to the ethnic health of these fascinating people.

The Central Mam New Testament was dedicated in 1999. In 2000 I began my doctorate in linguistics at *the* Ohio State University; I graduated in 2005. This book is a rewrite of my dissertation aimed at a wider public. I hope it gives you some idea of the joy we've had in sharing life with the Mam.

---

[1] Pan-Mam literature must deal with extensive regional variation. For a discussion on the standardization of written Mam, see England 1996.

2.2 Some comments on the Mam

Mam is a Mayan group of some 500,000 people in Guatemala's Western Highlands and in some areas of southwestern coastal Guatemala, and parts of the state of Chiapas in southeastern Mexico. The Mam homeland is in the Guatemalan departments of Huehuetenango, San Marcos, and western Quetzaltenango, while the further reaches of the language area beyond the traditional homeland are due to recent migrations caused by the lack of day-labor opportunities and affordable land in the traditional highland home of the Mam. There are Mam colonizers in the far northwest of Guatemala near Barillas, and more and more Mam are migrating (some legally, but most illegally) to the United States. Most of these live near Los Angeles, Chicago, and West Palm Beach, while others are involved in meatpacking and seasonal harvesting mostly in the South.

2.2.1 Socio-economic situation

In their home area, Mam men practice slash-and-burn agriculture, growing a single crop of corn per year. They also plant black beans that vine up the corn stalks, and squash, which grows up and down the rows between the corn plants. Most families also have a few animals: chickens and turkeys, a few sheep, and maybe a horse or mule to help carry loads. More rarely, there may be a pig or two and one or two cows. These larger animals normally aren't butchered for household meat, since rural refrigeration is rare. Rather, they are raised to be sold for cash in order to purchase needed household and personal items. Most families also have several dogs for protection and sometimes a cat to help guard stored corn from thieving rats and mice.

Work outside the home is considered a man's realm: preparing the fields, cutting trees for firewood, hauling loads to and from town, minor construction projects, and traveling to the large urban areas.

A Mayan family normally needs at least an acre or so of land to grow sufficient corn to feed the family and their animals for a year. Most families don't have that much land, so many are forced to seek wage labor in the lowlands in order to earn the money required to buy the corn that their families need to subsist. In the past, the Maya were required by vague and racist "vagrancy laws" to work as laborers on the lowland plantations, picking coffee and cotton and harvesting sugar cane. Although no longer obligated by law to work in the lowlands, the exigencies of their economic plight are such that hundreds of thousands of Maya do so nonetheless, living for months each year in extremely unhealthy conditions, both physically and socially. Sometimes entire families "go to the coast" to work, leaving their animals and lands in the care of others who stay behind. Often just the men and older sons go, leaving the women to care for the highland homestead. The work is very arduous and the daytime temperatures are extreme, but many families have no other option than to work in the lowlands in order to eat. Lowland diseases, particularly malaria and hot-climate parasites, differ from sicknesses back in their home villages, and many return after three or four months of labor, sick and having spent much of their earnings on food and medicine. Sexually transmitted diseases are also commonly contracted while away from home for long periods of time. Wages on the lowland plantations have traditionally been set by the government (often in collusion with the wealthy landowners), so that Guatemalan-grown products would be competitive in the world commodity markets. Today, Mayan laborers may make from six to ten dollars a day working long hours.

It is rare for Mam women to work outside the home (except in those families where clothes are washed at the river), although some have become school teachers, or storekeepers in the family *tiendas,* and many offer goods for sale at the weekly local market. My impression is that the majority of the women who sell at the market do so more for the social benefit and not for the profit margin, although some women have clear entrepreneurial skills. Women are responsible for all work within the home: grinding the corn and cooking, starting and stoking the fire, cleaning and organizing the home, washing clothes (either at the river or on a concrete *pila* at home), and caring for the children. Many women weave on a backstrap loom, making the traditional belts for which Comitancillo is renowned. Daughters help their mothers with women's chores as soon as they are able. It is common for a four-year-old girl to carry around on her back a younger sibling wrapped securely in a shawl.

Although men's and women's roles are largely gender specific, two activities in particular seem to belong to both men and women, and their location as to either outside the home or inside is somewhat ambiguous. Husking and shelling corn is a kind of transition step from outside to inside. It is the physical shift of the corn from the fields and drying area (often on top of the roof, where the men have done the work of hauling corn in from the fields and distributed it on the roof to be sun-dried) to the kitchen, where it is transformed into *wab'j* 'tortillas' or 'tamalitos'[2] by the women. This places corn husking and shelling in the ambiguous position of being both outside and inside the home—both men's and women's realms—and it is something in which both men and women participate—usually together with the children. Indeed, it is a festive occasion. In similar fashion, men cut the trees, split the firewood into transportable logs, and haul it to the homestead. Here again, both men and women may split it further as the logs are outside the door ready to come in and be added to the fire. If my comment on the ambiguity of the outside/inside distinction of corn husking and shelling is correct, the secondary splitting of firewood may be another task where the normally clear line of gender roles is a bit fuzzy. And this secondary firewood splitting is indeed performed by both men and women either in the cookhouse proper or just outside the doorway.

It is extremely common for women to bear their first child a year after marriage and to experience six to ten pregnancies or more over the span of their childbearing years. Marriage is by agreement between families, normally at the urging of the young couple, although occasionally a new wife will not know her husband until her wedding day, the arrangements having been made by the groom or his intercessor and the bride's father. I discuss some details of a traditional marriage proposal in chapter four.

Although couples practicing birth control are increasing in number, they constitute a decided minority. It is not unusual that a woman and her older daughters may be pregnant at the same time. Most families have lost a child or more to dysentery or illnesses caused by parasites. Despite high infant mortality, the pressure on limited available land is acute and many have moved to the larger Guatemalan cities or to the United States in search of work. They often locate in urban areas with others of their home area, where language and many customs can be maintained, at least to some degree.

Most Mam families that can, save by investing in real goods: land (which is at a premium in Comitancillo), construction,[3] animals (which involve risk,

---

[2] *Tamalitos* are made of the same corn dough as tortillas, but instead of being patted thin and put on the *comal,* a thin clay plate, to cook, they are wrapped in large leaves, usually banana or oak, and steamed.

[3] Historically, homes were built of adobe, with baked clay tile roofs and dirt floors. Lately, more homes, especially multi-level homes, are built of light-weight cement block (reinforced with iron and concrete) and corrugated metal roofing. Modern floors are usually covered with a thin layer of concrete.

2.2 Some comments on the Mam

of course), and inventory to be sold at the market, in the small *tiendas*, or in larger stores in town. There is a local banking cooperative that holds money at interest for people who want high liquidity. Two of the national banks have established branches in Comitancillo. This idea has been met with mixed emotions. People are proud that their little town generates enough movement of money to be noticed by the banking system. But they are also concerned about people like Willie Sutton, the notorious American bank robber, who purportedly answered the question as to why he robbed banks by saying, "Because that's where the money is." Although Comitancillo continues to grow economically and educationally, many people miss "the good old days" of just a few buses, a handful of small cottage industries, no police or army (and therefore no guns), no strangers, and no armed thieves. Those days are gone.

A number of individuals also lend money at interest. The Mam loan money to each other at ten percent interest or more per month. The usual scenario, if a man were to borrow the equivalent of a thousand dollars on the first of March, is that he'd return on the first of each ensuing month and pay one hundred dollars to his creditor. On the following first of March, one year after the loan was made, and after paying $1,200 in interest in monthly installments, he would pay back the principal of $1,000 in a lump sum. Understandably, many Mam have become very prosperous, lending in this way, while the borrowers have suffered.

The Comitancillo market has become a major highland business venue. Upwards of 10,000 people come each Sunday to buy, sell, trade, and catch up on local news. Trucks come from several hours away bringing merchants and their wares. Roads have been much improved over the last twenty years, and many mountain roads are now paved. Today, one can find fruit and vegetables (both local and from all over the country), shoes, clothing (both traditional and Western style), animals, local meat, fresh fish, kitchen appliances, radios, televisions, and on and on. The Comitancillo Sunday market has traditionally been part of a Highland *solar market system* where each of four or five area towns would host a market on different days of the week. In this way, merchants could rotate through the area making needed products available to a large buying public. Over the last few years, what has traditionally been a secondary market day in Comitancillo—Wednesday—has become busy as well. In fact, a number of merchants keep market stalls hopping throughout the week, offering goods every day. Some merchants still travel the cycle of the solar, weekly, market, but if vendors can maintain sales volume in a single spot, it is much easier than packing everything anew every day and carting it off to the next venue by uncomfortable truck at 5:00 in the morning.

The digital age has come to Comitancillo. There are over a dozen internet cafés throughout the town and several private "academies" that teach computer skills. Cell phones are everywhere, and I occasionally receive calls in Ohio from Mam friends in their village homes, some without running water or electricity, but now with a telecommunications link to the rest of the world.

One certainly wonders how such a strong market economy is able to thrive among people that make at most ten dollars a day (village day-laborers usually make much less working near home than they can on the southern plantations, but with lower expenses as well.) There are two main reasons. First, Comitancillo has become a regional market and transportation center. When my family and I first went to live there in 1980, there were three buses that left the village each morning for San Marcos, the departmental seat, and returned later in the day. Today, there are over twenty different buses that leave throughout the day and go not only to San Marcos, but to Quetzaltenango (Guatemala's *second city*) and Guatemala City. Dozens of trucks are titled to Comitecos. These carry produce, animals, merchandise, and people to destinations throughout the country. So, one source of significant income is local business, either transport or retail sales.

A second source is the money sent back to Guatemala by family members who have gone to the United States. These remittances have created a dual economy in many towns, where dollars trump local currency and inflate prices, particularly the price of land and construction projects. Land and small homes in Comitancillo are now the same price as in many areas of Guatemala City. This has the effect of making people that own land or homes in town into virtual tycoons. Because of access to dollars and the relative devaluing of local currency, more and more people are motivated to travel to the United States in order to get in on the dollar economy, which is increasingly the only viable economy on the local scene as well. Land in town is sold for dollars, not for *quetzales,* the local currency.

Another, albeit unofficial, reason for the influx of cash to the area is the drug trade. Heroin poppies are grown and seed pods are transported in parts of Guatemala's western highlands, especially in areas near the

2.2 Some comments on the Mam

Mexico border where local business connects with the world market. The Comitancillo area is heavily populated and well traveled, so land beyond the eyes of neighbors is not as readily available for growing poppies as it is in Tajumulco and Tacaná, but word on the street is that some of the money pumped into local construction is from sources unknown, which often implies that the source is indeed known, but unspecified.

2.2.2 Educational situation

There are three pre-university levels of education in Guatemala, which are the same in both urban and rural areas. Primary school goes from grade one through grade six. As of 2005, virtually every *aldea* 'hamlet' in Comitancillo has had a public primary school. Most of these schools also offer a pre-primary or "headstart" year of bilingual education aimed at helping Mam children (usually six or seven years old) to learn to read minimally in their own language and to speak a modicum of Spanish before attending first grade. Historically, primary school was taught in Spanish, and children were punished and insulted for speaking their native language. One friend told me that as a child he was once ridiculed for speaking his native language in class and was required by his teacher to sit in the corner with mule ears perched upon his head. Fortunately this has changed for the better. Now bilingual education is part of the curriculum throughout primary school and in many cases beyond. Of course, quality of instruction depends more on the individual teacher than on the stated curriculum, and not all bilingual teachers are committed to bilingual education. I'll discuss this further below.

When students pass their sixth grade proficiency tests, they can enter their *basic education* phase, which lasts three more years. The town of Comitancillo has both public and private schools of basic education and a number of the larger hamlets do as well. At this level, students occasionally have a class in Mayan language and culture, but all other courses are taught in Spanish, usually by Spanish monolingual teachers, although there is a growing number of Mam-Spanish bilinguals who teach as well. Upon graduation from *básico*, students can opt for further studies in a diversified field, usually basic accounting, primary education, or college preparatory. The accounting and education programs last three years and qualify graduates for entry-level jobs in their respective fields. The college preparatory course lasts two years and prepares students for entry into university level studies. Comitancillo has had a teacher-training program at the diversified level, as did several of the larger hamlets. Recently the government has discontinued this diversified primary educaton track since the country has hundreds of thousands of trained teachers for whom there are no available jobs.

Most of the national universities (four well established and a half-dozen nascent) have rural outreach programs to help qualified and interested students get the training and degree they desire. Classes are often in the evenings or on weekends to accommodate students' jobs and responsibilities.

In part because of good international funding, at least initially, three of the universities (San Carlos, Rafael Landívar, and Mariano Gálvez) have maintained programs in applied linguistics for the past fifteen years or more. At Rafael Landívar and Mariano Gálvez, North American linguists were involved as professors during the early years of these programs. I was privileged to be involved in the start-up of the linguistics program at Mariano Gálvez University in the early 80s.

2.2.3 Religious situation

I deal with religion as a search for centeredness in chapter three. The main point I make there is that the Maya are a deeply religious people, while at the same time they have their feet planted firmly in the rich soil. Both traditional religion and conversion to Christianity (in this study I deal more with Protestantism than Catholicism) are seen as an embracing of the Mayan cultural value of centeredness. This is a controversial claim, which I support with data from both historical and present-day sources. The choice of continuing with a traditional understanding of relating to God or the gods, or opting for conversion to another religious system is a very salient issue among the Mam, one discussed on the trails, in the markets, on the buses, and over the airwaves as people host *cultos* 'worship services' in their homes and broadcast the music and sermons to the four winds by means of battery-powered public address systems.

In the Comitancillo area, very few would consider themselves followers of traditional Mayan religion, although the number among Mam youth is growing. Perhaps twenty percent would call themselves *Evangélicos*

'Evangelicals', or 'Protestants', while almost all of the rest would self identify as *Católicos*. Historically, Catholics have been less demanding than *Evangélicos* in regard to calling for repentance from traditional Mayan views and practice, and the church is more syncretistic than the Evangelical churches, at least on the surface, often incorporating traditional ceremonies such as those centered around *Maximón* (whose name is thought to be a blend of *max* 'tobacco' and St. Simon), the cigar-toting icon carried through the streets during Holy Week. Other festivals that blend Mayan and Catholic teaching include May Day celebrations that mark the *day of the cross* and the beginning of the rainy season, New Year ceremonies, and *Day of the Dead* (November 1) rituals. For a fascinating and easy-reading Mayan diary that journals some of the overlap between traditional Mayan and Catholic life, see Sexton 1981.

Many *Evangélicos* are so concerned about syncretism that they avoid the term *Maya* when identifying themselves in Spanish, preferring the term *indígena* 'indigenous', since they believe that things *Mayan* have been co-opted by those who they believe would like to impose traditional religion on all Maya. Of course, the word *syncretism* itself is a loaded term, implying both a lack of theological purity and a non-directed, non-reflective approach to faith. Eugenio Mauer (1993) prefers the term *synthesis*, since he feels that it is not the case that Christianity is grafted onto a pre-Christian base, but rather that modern Mayan religion reflects a situation where the two faith traditions inform each other. By his account, the faith of most Maya today is something new, rather than a blend of pre-invasion and post-invasion traditions. Nonetheless, Mam Evangelicals would have issues with this view as well. They feel that conversion is necessary not only for practitioners of traditional religion, but for Catholics as well. They consider Catholicism to be the extension of traditional Mayan religion, which people are simply born into. They preach that a Christian is something you become, and that it is not merely part of one's cultural heritage. They believe that true Christianity implies a break with and a conversion from their religious past, not just an addition to it, which they understand Catholicism to be. In this study, I will deal almost exclusively with traditional religion and Evangelicalism, not Catholicism. For further discussion on this topic and on the relationship between Catholicism and Evangelicalism in Guatemala, see Scotchmer (1989) and Annis (1987).

Obviously, religious belief continues to be a main area of contention among the Mam.

2.2.4 Sociolinguistic situation

Of course, the three previous subsections in this chapter on socio-economics, education, and religion are all sociolinguistic in that they are relevant to speech choice and variation, but in this section, I'd like to highlight the relationship between Spanish and Mayan languages.

The mixing of Mayan groups—Mam, K'iche', Kaqchikel, Q'anjobal, Pokomchí, and others—on the lowland plantations provides a hothouse environment (no pun intended) for the development of Mayan-influenced dialects of Spanish, where the Maya learn Spanish as their second language largely from other non-native Spanish speakers. These non-prescriptive (Spanish) dialects are stigmatized by the Spanish-speaking majority, and although the Maya fuel much of the Guatemalan economy, their economic contribution, while crucial, is minimized, and their native languages and lifestyle are ridiculed as backward and ill-suited to the modern age. At the same time that the majority Spanish-speaking culture belittles the Maya, Spanish is needed on the plantations by the Maya in order to communicate with farm authorities, in order to travel, and in order to do business at the local lowland markets, not only with native Spanish speakers, but also with other Maya who don't speak one's own language or variety. So the Maya, like so many minority peoples around the world, find themselves pressured to use a language that they speak non-natively, one that historically is the language of their oppressors and colonizers.

While the larger society has considered the Maya to be second-class citizens, tourism has replaced coffee as the leading dollar producer in the Guatemalan economy. Today, in addition to depending on Mayan labor to harvest the nation's major money crops, the Maya are themselves a major reason why the world's travelers are coming to Guatemala. Now, the larger society has a vested interest in the traditions of the Maya. After all, tourism based on Mayan rites and sites, both pre-invasion and present-day, brings in hundreds of millions of dollars and euros each year. Certainly, some that today promote tourism are the same ones who were quick to pronounce judgment on such "sub-development" just a few years before. That the country could be considered a multi-cultural space shared among equals is still a hope unfulfilled.

2.2 Some comments on the Mam

For many years the Guatemalan government has tried to deal with "the Indian problem," an issue oft cited, albeit ill defined, but having generally to do with a low levels of education, lack of basic literacy, rural and urban poverty, lack of a consumer mentality, limited political participation, and the supposed divisiveness of minority languages and cultures. The early vagrancy laws obligated the Maya to provide a number of days of free labor to their community in order to keep area roads level and cleared. These same laws, as mentioned above, also required Indian men to work on the lowland plantations (where they were paid a pittance) in order to bring in the yearly coffee crop, which has historically been Guatemala's largest producer of dollars (recently supplanted by tourism). Men who didn't have their identification cards stamped for completing these work requirements could be jailed for vagrancy. This forced-cheap-labor idea was revisited during *la violencia* with army recruiting schemes set up to coerce locals to "volunteer" their time on civil patrols, groups of poorly armed men (if they were armed at all) which served as a buffer between the army and a well armed insurgency. Even today, the Maya continue to be a part of the motor that keeps the Guatemalan economy humming. As I mentioned above, the Maya fuel a large and important tourist industry. Plus, the big three agricultural exports—coffee, sugar cane, and cotton—are all harvested by hand, and the economic reality of many highland families is such that seasonal work on the lowland plantations is all that keeps them from extreme duress or even starvation.

In addition to the pressure to speak Spanish caused by the communication needs of seasonal plantation work, the media have made tremendous inroads into the Mam area. In Comitancillo, for example, cable TV—twenty-some channels in Spanish, with a few in Portuguese and English—is offered 24 hours a day. Regional and national newspapers—all in Spanish—flood the local market. Many towns boast at least one internet café, a service offered via satellite; computer training is also common, classes where Spanish vocabulary—not Mam—rules. Local government schools are in Spanish, and even bilingual schools, where Mam is supposedly respected and used as a medium of instruction, are seen by many parents, teachers, and students as merely a means to the goal of learning Spanish—a method of "subtractive bilingualism," where Mam is used only as a bridge to Spanish, after which the bridge can be burned.

Funding agencies require project proposals to be written in Spanish; government agencies operate largely in Spanish; bank documents and contracts for the now ubiquitous cell phones are written in Spanish; churches often teach in Spanish and sing Spanish hymns; radio programs and popular music playing on the ever-present boom boxes are blared out in Spanish; and buses, cars, and trucks carry people from the earliest hours of the morning out of the villages into the larger Spanish-speaking world. For the thousands of Maya who emigrate to the cities, or beyond Guatemala's borders to Mexico, the United States, or Canada, their native languages are, in practical terms, just a nostalgic part of the past.

With such a complex of issues related to the viability of Mam and the other Mayan languages, there have been a variety of indigenous responses. Some have abandoned the language altogether assuming that the future would depend on Spanish skills. The large majority has opted for bilingualism in one form or another. In Collins (2005:255) I discuss codeswitching as a linguistic strategy of the masses of dual identification with both the prestige of Spanish and the comfort of Mam. There is a third group of young professionals that considers codeswitching to be a capitulation to Spanish-speaking society. This group favors language purity, speaking both Spanish and Mam well and without inter-linguistic contamination. It is this group that is leading a Mayan revitalization movement, which is an exciting embrace of Mayan culture in the face of five hundred years of denigration and inequality. The Mayan Language Academy is comprised of people from this group, as is the Maya Writers' Association and other Mayan university and community groups.

One of the truly astounding capacities of the Maya is their ability to take what they see as helpful from the larger society without compromising who they are as a proud and viable minority group. Gary Gossen (1986:6) points to a possible explanation. He says: "The principle of complementary dualism has the potential to lead to a revised paradigm for thinking about syncretism in Mesoamerica." He claims that throughout the Mesoamerican region, men have been the assimilators of change and new codes (language, clothing, economic systems, political and military participation, among others), while the women have been the guardians of tradition (indigenous dress, curing knowledge, agricultural ritual, and particularly the use of native languages).

This push-pull dualism is seen, for example, in the contrasting poles of public and private life, male and female roles, and national and ethnic identities, which are not so much in conflict but in healthy and mutually supporting tension. Gossen suggests that this sense of dualism or balance helps explain how the Maya are able to benefit from new technologies and options offered by the West (and which are received to a large extent by those who travel widely—the men), while at the same time, they dig in their heels to resist the destruction of their deeply established life ways (as instantiated by the lives of the stay-at-home women). As Gossen says, "New masters were pragmatically accommodated, yet the integrity of local identity and local knowledge was not shaken" (1986:7).

From this dual perspective comes a unity of Mayan values that looks both forward and back.

This renders intelligible the enigma that has impressed many scholars and casual observers of Indian communities in Mesoamerica: people seem at once to be Mexican or Guatemalan peasants and living shadows of a vanquished pre-Columbian world. Which is the "true" identity? It seems clear that both identities are, simultaneously, true identities, for Mesoamerican ideology accommodates such complementary duality easily. "The public sector voluntarily adapted, or forcibly capitulated to the ideological demands of the more inclusive system, while the domestic sector held fast" (Gossen 1986:6–7).

This idea of cultural continuity within culture change is perhaps the key notion in beginning to understand the complexity of modern Mayan life. They are truly a magnificent, surprising, and multifaceted people. It has been a humbling and wonderful privilege to have known them and worked together with them for these many years.

2.3 Some comments on the Mam language

Mam is a strongly ergative language,[4] and typologically considered to be of unmarked VSO word order (verb followed by the subject, followed by the direct object), although other word orders are common for purposes of topicalization or focus (Aissen 1992). It is most known among linguistic scholars for its directional auxiliary verbs and for grammatical structures containing them, the related directional particles, and full intransitive verbs.

Michael Coe (1999) cites Mam, and its linguistic near-neighbors Teko, Awakateko, and Ixil, as constituting the Mamean branch of Eastern Mayan

---

[4] The term *ergativity* has to do with how subjects and objects are marked in a language's syntax.

which, together with Quichean split off from what were to become, some four thousand years ago, the Western, Yucatecan, and Huastecan daughter branches of Proto-Mayan (figure 2.1).

Dialect divergence among the Mam is pervasive (Godfrey and Collins 1987), stemming in part from the provincial lifestyle of a people who historically have spent little time outside of their home environs. This was most likely also true in the Mayan "city-state" pre-colonial past, where, although there seems to have been extensive contact, trade, alliances and even war among independent groups, Jorge Suárez (1982) suggests that it was the leadership of the city-state along with the material and ceremonial aspects of Mayan culture which were most affected by this contact, leaving the commoners in a far more isolated position.[5] This provincialism was later taken advantage of as a method for controlling the flow of people and ideas during early Spanish occupation of the Maya homeland. This "divide and conquer" strategy was certainly part of what enabled Spain to exert hegemony over a much larger population. Indeed, there is some evidence that the vivid colors and unique patterns and styles of Maya traditional dress were promoted not by the Maya themselves, but by their oppressors, who used the clothing's distinctive features in order to identify someone's home *municipio*[6] and thus monitor the movement of people and political ideas throughout the area (see Altman and West 1992:20–21 for limited discussion).

Godfrey and Collins (1987) posit six significant dialect areas, including Western Mam, or Takaneko, a moribund dialect presently spoken only by bilingual (Spanish-Mam) older adults. Among the significant variants of Mam, England (1990) cites differences in phonology, morphology, syntax, and discourse; so the historical, political, and social distance among the Mam is matched to some extent by diversity of linguistic features as well.

---

[5] For a helpful summary of Mayan provincialism and an interesting discussion of both its repercussions and its possible causes, see Brown 1998.

[6] A *municipio* corresponds to a town and its political environs. It is made up of a *cabecera* (main town of the same name as the entire *municipio*) and a number of hamlets (officially recognized *aldeas* and unchartered *caseríos*). Guatemala is divided into 22 departments. There are altogether 330 *municipios*.

2.3 Some comments on the Mam language

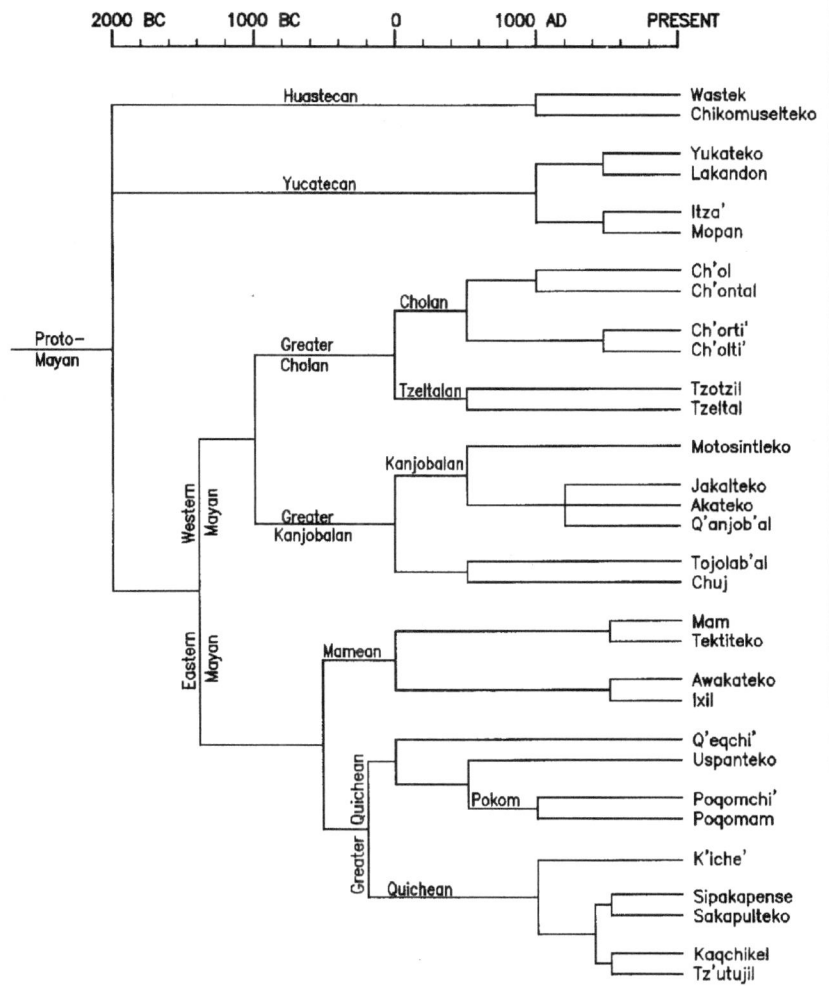

Figure 2.1. Classification and time depth of Mayan languages. Adapted with permission from Michael D. Coe (1999).

Today there is a strong movement to standardize the written form of Mam (as well as other Mayan languages), since it is seen to be a unifying and educationally more realistic strategy than promoting a plethora of individual dialects (see England 1996 for details).

2.4 Mam as an endangered language and efforts at revitalization

There's little doubt as to why Mam is endangered. Indeed, that it survives at all is a tribute to the tenacity of a people apart. There is tremendous pressure to abandon Mam and adopt Spanish from both outside the language group (the government, the schools, the economy, and the larger Guatemalan society); inside (parents who have decided that Spanish will serve them and their children better than Mam); bilingual schoolteachers who buy into subtractive bilingualism; and others who are embarrassed to speak Mam in public. Nevertheless, many people love their language and culture and are committed to keeping them alive both in their hearts and on their tongues.

In some ways, despite the tremendous globalizing pressures mentioned, the wheel is turning. When I first arrived in Guatemala in 1979, I read through SIL's files on Mam, and I found a photocopy of a memo from a large mission organization that stated that they were recommending no further Mam-language ministry because of the pervasive use of Spanish throughout the area, the encroachment of Spanish into the daily lives of Mam speakers, and the likelihood that Mam would fall into disuse within a generation. The memo was dated June 1937. And when my Mam colleagues and I first offered Mam language booklets for sale in the local market in 1981, a number of people were bewildered. "Why are you offering us books in Mam?" they queried. *Nti' tajb'in lo* 'these are worthless'. "We already speak Mam, and look where it's gotten us. If you really wanted to help us you'd help us learn Spanish." Yet today, some seventy-five years after the memo, and over thirty years after my first market encounter, Mam is still spoken natively by hundreds of thousands of people who find it adequate to the dual tasks of conceptualizing their world and enabling them to operate in it, globalizing and homogenizing as that world may be. Indeed, the Mam of Comitancillo are participating in a larger Mayan renaissance that is taking place throughout Central America and southern Mexico, where there is renewed interest in being Maya and maintaining Mayan culture and languages. See particularly the work by Susan Garzon and her colleagues (1998) regarding the scope of and an analysis of this revitalization movement.

Language isn't maintained in a vacuum. Salikoko Mufwene of the University of Chicago points out that in multilingual situations, languages aren't so much abandoned as deliberate action, but rather as "the cumulative consequence of repeated communicative acts" (2002:387). These acts are benefit driven. If a person needs English or Spanish or Mandarin to make a living, it is unlikely that the native language will long be able to withstand these major languages' intrusion into the domain of the home, where the last bastion of resistance can give way to what many speakers feel is the inevitable move toward the modern, globalizing world, and its concomitant handful of languages. In such cases what's left of the local vernacular can perhaps hold on as a specialized language for ceremonial events but spoken only by an esoteric few who keep the language going for a generation or so. Emiliana Cruz (2004) suggests, however, that when the responsibility to maintain a dying language rests with just one individual or a small guild, or a single family, any number of events, such as religious conversion, illness, or physical displacement of some kind can cause the language quickly to cease to exist. When this happens and blame is meted out on the last family or individual who supposedly has let the language slip away, it indicates that the language barely existed even before its final demise. Our hope is that Mam never reaches that point. Ever.

So the larger linguistic and cultural context is always important, and each situation, despite intriguing similarities, is different. In Guatemala, a number of factors have converged to help promote the possibility of language and culture revitalization:

1. The awarding of the 1992 Nobel Peace Prize to Rigoberta Menchú, a Mayan woman, has brought international attention to the plight of Central and South American indigenous groups. Mufwene considers political support the second bulwark of language maintenance (economic feasibility is first).

2. The National Bilingual Education Program has been funded for over twenty years. Well over a million Mayan children have received primary school instruction in their native language. This has heightened interest in native-language literacy and literature production.

3. Three national universities have established applied linguistics programs that have helped train hundreds of Mayan teachers and professionals.

4. In 1991, the Academy of Mayan Languages became an autonomous national institution (for details see England 1998:106). This grass-roots organization provides a forum for Guatemalan Mayan people to discuss and to resolve issues related to Mayan life and particularly Mayan languages. Despite many challenges, the academy has been a focal point for Mayans promoting native language and cultural maintenance.

5. The signing of the Peace Accords in December 1996 has led to (the possibility of) greater respect for human rights, including indigenous rights, throughout the nation, although violence and delinquency continue to be major problems in much of the country.

6. Tourism has become the main motor of the Guatemalan economy replacing coffee as the nation's greatest dollar earner. Tourism officials realize that much of what tourists come to see is Maya-related, so the government and the economy have a vested interest in Maya language and culture maintenance. This doesn't necessarily bode well for the Maya. The Maya can easily be seen as just another resource to exploit, rather than as a cultural group with which to share a multicultural nation-space.

In addition to this national/international context conducive to revitalization, Comitancillo seems especially to be a place where there has been a certain readiness to respond positively within this overarching context. Although open to outsiders, the entire *municipio* is still populated almost exclusively by insiders. One needn't speak Spanish at the market or in most churches; speaking Mam is sufficient. Local government offices have Mam-speaking attendants. Mam books are sold from several local bookstores. A growing number of titles is available that include easy-reading booklets and *fotonovelas* (a kind of reality comic book), the Central Mam New Testament (1998, 2002), a Mam hymnbook (2003) and concordance (2002), a verb dictionary (1991), and a number of educational titles and booklets and several Scripture portions. A Mam local radio station was established in 2002 and other regional Mam stations and programs have existed for over ten years. A monthly newspaper funded by local businesses has been in and out of publication since May 2003. There are bilingual schools throughout the *municipio*, and most Mam teachers are committed to language maintenance and a high view of Mam culture.[7] Mam parents continue to teach Mam to their children as their first language. Although Spanish is highly valued, Mam is as well. So, in spite of the tremendous wearing down effect of Spanish, Mam language and culture continue to be held in high esteem by many locals. There is a support structure for Mayan revitalization; it is more than just wishful thinking on the part of a few. In Mufwene's words, there exists the "concurrent mobilization of the political and economic machineries" (2002: 390) that buttress a context where being Mam and speaking Mam is benefit driven, not only politically and economically, but socially and educationally as well.

---

[7] For a detailed look at teachers' role in Mam revitalization, see Collins 2005.

The benefits aren't just these, however; there is a strong intellectual component as well. Three Mam-speaking professors told me in three different conversations that, as Maya, the way they conceive of the world fits the way the world is. They claimed that thinking of life in terms of complementarity, balance, and centeredness is a fully contemporary and adequate way to think about how the modern world really works; it isn't a primitive way of thought and language that is incapable of coping with the complexity of modern life. The fact that long before Christopher Columbus came to the new world, the Maya developed complex systems for writing, mathematics, and record keeping, and that their astronomers could predict lunar and solar eclipses and the phases of both the moon and Venus, is proof enough of the ability of their language (both then and now) to contain the technical flexibility and depth necessary to discuss and understand extremely sophisticated material. In addition, these professors suggest that the *Popol Vuh*, the sacred book of the Maya, discusses human drama and history in ways that rival Shakespeare and Cervantes for clarity and intensity.

In other words, even regarding modern life, there is a certain "degree of fit" between the model of the world as reflected by Mam language and culture and the real world that the Mam come in contact with both in the village and far beyond it.

2.5 What's new in this book?

In many ways, this book is a reshuffling of the cards. Many of the observations aren't original with me, but I try to see them in a new arrangement. The disparate notions of the hot-cold syndrome, the similar design of Mayan homesteads and cities, and the seeking of a central moral ground in both traditional religion and Christianity, are all, I claim, instantiations of a single theme—centeredness. This theme is reinforced by the language that people use in daily practice both to talk about issues they see as centered (for example, agreement protocols, the disciplining of children, and advice to the wayward) and as components of meaning in terms that they don't necessarily see as impinging on the notion of centeredness (-$k'u'j$ terms, for example, in chapter four), but which, to careful analysis, seem indeed to do so. But our theme is also bolstered by the formal grammatical structures of the language, as the deictic center ascribes a formal sense of center or origo to the lexical meanings of intransitive verbs and to the pragmatic calculation of metaphorical senses of directional auxiliaries, affixes, and discourse particles. I also suggest that the far-reaching notion of dualism in Mayan language and culture is a further instantiation of our theme.

That such a theme (or any other) would be manifested in both the culture and the grammar of a people seems mundane and obvious, yet it is an idea that has inspired linguists and anthropologists for generations. Is there a relationship between the world that one knows (culture) and the language she or he uses to describe and construct that world? To that question I offer no new empirical evidence. But, as per Itkonen (1978), I present what seems to me to be a strong pattern of instantiations and a different kind of proof—a hermeneutic kind—that is more appropriate to the human sciences, where notions like values, faith, and loyalty, though real, are not readily measured. As we've said, Itkonen defines this hermeneutic approach by suggesting that it "acquires its data through understanding meanings, intentions, values, norms, or rules, and...hermeneutic analysis consists in reflection upon what has been understood" (1978:20).

This kind of understanding privileges an approach to culture like Geertz's interpretive anthropology, which is aimed at discovering the emic categories of a group and grounding them in the context of daily practice.

The model that I use to showcase the disparate instantiations of centeredness is one suggested by Martin (1977) and England (1978), where both cultural theme and grammatical theme are established independently and then compared both etically and emically to see if any detected pattern is salient to native speakers, and not just to hopeful researchers.

Through time, many linguistic anthropologists have asked for further studies aimed at shedding light on a possible relationship between language and culture: Hoijer, Hymes, Hale, Martin, England, Enfield, and many others. Showing a clear and unconstrained relationship between language and culture is perhaps not possible, and if anyone makes claims to that effect, he or she is asking for trouble.[8] However, I think it is indeed possible to show an overarching pattern that is salient to native speakers and that includes both cultural and grammatical data. This is my goal in this book.

---

[8] Everett (2005) makes just such a claim, namely, that language (at least Piraha) is driven by culture. His article appears in volume 46 number 24 of *Current Anthropology,* along with a number of articles critical of his research and findings.

3

Centeredness as Cultural Theme

3.1 Introduction

In chapter four we will look at how centeredness is talked about and manifested in the daily life of the Mam. This chapter is a precursor, but with three specific areas of cultural life in view: health and illness, architectonics, and religion. In this chapter, I draw more on the expertise of others, affirming their research with observations of my own, observations which are neither as extensive nor as personal as those discussed in chapter four. There, I take a more holistic and integrated ethnographic approach to both my observations and write-up. Here I look at three areas of culture in a more isolated and analytical way. I conclude with some generalizations about how centeredness is manifested in each of the three areas discussed in this chapter.

3.2 Health as an instantiation of centeredness

As mentioned in chapter one, Redfield reports that, for the Yukateko-Maya, "Health of body and peace of soul depend on the maintenance of conditions of balance" (1941:128). He adds that good health is the "maintenance of that median condition which the native expresses in terms of heat and cold." Helen Neuenswander and Shirley Souder (1977) suggest that the hot-cold syndrome is almost certainly pre-Columbian. It is found throughout the Maya homeland as an explanation of illness etiology (the cause of illness) and as a metric for the treatment of disease. Assuming its pre-invasion presence among the Maya, the notion was clearly abetted by the humoral health and wellness system of the invaders, who got it ultimately from the Greeks. The Hippocratic notion of good health as the balance of humors—earth, air, fire, and water; or dry, cold, hot, and wet respectively—was passed on to the Arabs who lived for a thousand years in the Iberian Peninsula, who then passed the notion on to the Spanish (see Manderson 1987:329 for a discussion of this cultural transmission).

By the time of the Spanish invasion of the New World, the understanding of health as an integrated balance of the humors was widespread in Renaissance Europe (Messer 1981:133) and was exported by health professionals to the New World. The Spanish found ready acceptance of their humoral notion of health which leads us to assume that a similar system was already in place. A further piece of evidence is that the four humors—hot and cold, wet and dry—are still part of the understanding of illness etiology in the Kiche' town of Joyabaj. The wet-dry aspect of the humors has been lost virtually everywhere else in Latin America, while the hot-cold syndrome is pervasive throughout the Maya area and the entire Mesoamerican region (for example, among the Aztecs [Orellana 1987:36] and the Zapotecs [Messer 1981:133–139]). The fact that the wet-dry contrast of the humors has been maintained only in Joyabaj has led Neuenswander and Souder to conjecture that the system had been promoted by a well-respected priest-medic. "Otherwise it seems unlikely that there would still exist in Joyabaj the remnants of a system which has not been reported elsewhere in Mesoamerica" (1977:118). On the other hand, the pervasiveness of the hot-cold syndrome throughout the region leads us to the conclusion that humoral medicine was most likely an overlay to an older, but similar system—a two-way system, not a four-way.

Early anthropological accounts have noted that the hot-cold syndrome has been part of Maya culture since the earliest days of contact with the Spanish. Redfield and Villa Rojas (1962:372) cite reports from the sixteenth century claiming that when the Maya were questioned as to the nature of medicinal plants, most were unable to give an answer

3.2 Health as an instantiation of centeredness

to the exact name except to say that the plants were considered *hot* or *cold*.

Among the Mam who visited Nancy's village clinic, symptoms were explained to her in terms of events considered to be hot (sexual relations, pregnancy, outdoor work, cooking, getting drunk) and cold (working with metal tools, eating certain foods, drinking water or juice, or being caught in heavy rain or high winds). Diseases considered hot by the Maya (malaria, urinary infections, worms, and illnesses caused by sorcery) are considered caused by overexposure to hot, while cold diseases (swelling, measles, rheumatism, anemia, general pain, and *susto* [general sense of fright, stress, and uneasiness]) are caused by overexposure to cold. Symptoms are treated with herbs, teas, medicines, foods, and ceremonies that are meant to counteract the overabundance of hot or cold built up in the ailing body. Cooler medicines and therapeutic foods, are used to combat hot illnesses, while warmer medicines and foods are used to treat cold illnesses, the goal being to bring the body back to a center space of balance and health. This was the specific cultural background of most of the Mam that visited Nancy's clinic, and who talked to us about their concerns for improving their health and for treating various illnesses.

Interestingly, the categorization of foods and medicines as hot or cold doesn't have a whole lot to do with the actual temperature of the items in question, at least not directly. Ellen Messer says that the hot-cold principle "refers to intrinsic quality rather than thermal temperatures of medicines, foods and body conditions" (1981:133). For example, oranges and plantains are considered hot, while lemons and bananas are considered cold. Beef and chicken are hot, while pork, rabbit, and fish are cold. Black beans are hot. Green beans and white beans are cold. Injections of medicine are considered hot, while oral doses of the same medicine are cold.

Neuenswander and Souder (1977:107–108) elucidate the metric by which the Maya determine an element's hotness or coldness. For example, certain items such as cheese and corn gain heat with age. Things that grow in or near water or that grow underground in the damp soil (potatoes, onions, and beets) are colder than those which do not. The meat of domesticated animals (cows, sheep, turkeys) is hot (with the exception of pork), while the meat of animals which historically were hunted (squirrels, rabbits, and (wild) pigs and birds) is cold. Strong or piquant flavors are hot (red chili peppers, coffee, spices, honey, liquor), while bland flavors (rice and most fruits and vegetables) are cold.

With the wide array of food choices and herbal teas available, it isn't hard to find a diet that would move someone with either a hot or a cold disease back toward the center space of good health. Local *curanderos* 'curers' and culturally sensitive healthcare workers respect the assumptions of locals and prescribe foods and medicines appropriately.

Messer points out that hot-cold systems don't float freely in cultures (such systems are common throughout the world, for which see Manderson (1987) and Messer (1981:134) for brief overviews). Rather they are integrated with social and environmental factors that interact with an individual's body. Children are cooler than adults and are therefore subject to difficulties from foods that are cold. Adults normally become hotter with age. Old men with spiritual power are considered hot and can cause illness just by someone getting too close to them. Women who are pregnant or breast feeding are hotter than when they aren't. Weather and time of day also interact with the hot and cold properties of foods and medicines. Messer points out that cool remedies are considered more effective when taken in the cool of the morning, whereas cold ailments are best treated with hot remedies during the heat of the day (1981:137).

My point here is that the hot-cold syndrome is part of a larger picture, one that integrates the conception of wellbeing into the daily practice of life. People go through hotter and cooler periods depending on when and where they work, what and who they come in contact with, what they eat and drink, as well as what are their basic propensities toward hotheadedness (hot) or calm (cold). So the concept of balancing hot and cold factors in life is not simply a matter of treating illness; it is, rather, part of the overall goal of maintaining centeredness in the midst of life's demands.

The hot-cold syndrome is still very strong among the Mam. Most of the people that visit my wife's clinic ask questions about what they should eat and drink—or what they shouldn't—in order not to counteract the hotness or coldness of any medicine or herbal tea or remedies that she prescribes.[1] They assume that injections are hot "because they go straight to the blood," but they routinely ask about the hot and cold properties of pills, vitamins, or drinks, which could go either way. Often patients determine whether Nancy feels their illness is hot or cold based on what she tells them to eat or not eat, to do or not do. A "cold" prescription implies a hot ailment, while

---

[1] See Neuenswander and Souder (1977:104) for a typical conversation of a health care professional and a Mayan patient.

3.2 Health as an instantiation of centeredness

the prescription of an injection of antibiotics and certain "hot" teas implies a cold illness.

In December 1990 I was driving to a nearby market town with three Mam school teachers, Gilberto, Goyo, and Abel. I told them that Nancy and I had discussed some of her patients' concerns about the hotness and coldness of their symptoms and Nancy's prescriptions. I asked them what they knew about the hot-cold syndrome.

There was an uneasy silence. Finally Goyo admitted that some old women *en las aldeas* 'in small rural hamlets' believe that certain illnesses are caused by exposure to heat, and that they have to be treated with remedies considered cold, while cold ailments are treated with hot remedies. They told me that most people nowadays don't believe such things.

I mentioned to them that I was interested in the idea, because I had run several days before in the noonday heat. When I got back home, I took a shower (as I did after running virtually every day). Lately, I told them that I felt weak and lethargic. All three of my friends agreed that it was my own fault. Since I was in the hot sun exerting myself physically I needed to cool down slowly. They asked if I had had a cold drink when I got home. I told them that I probably did, since that was my custom. They told me that my gringo customs were responsible for my being sick. I shouldn't have tried to get back to normal temperature so quickly. These situations are delicate, they told me. I said that I had taken a warm shower, not a cold one, hoping that that would absolve me in their eyes. They said that it didn't matter. A shower is cool by definition, and the shock of being cooled quickly after being so hot was clearly the root of my problem. So, even though the goal is a hot-cold balance in the body, trying to achieve such a balance too quickly is considered bad health practice. Marianna Kunow includes this sense of weakness as a result of *pasmo*, a cover term that includes a number of debilitating illnesses such as "tetanus, eye-twitching and convulsions, infertility in women and post partum diseases" (2003:65). She says that it is a cold ailment, often caused by cooling off too quickly after a hot episode of some kind. In other words, balance alone isn't so much in view as centeredness. If the paradigm were simply a matter of balancing extremes, we might assume that extreme cold would counteract extreme heat, but that isn't how the Mam view it. The goal is "that median condition" (Redfield 1941:128) of centeredness that is calm, peaceful, and moderate, not a measured balance of extremes. Balance, rather, is a strategy for achieving centeredness, which is the ultimate goal.

What interests me particularly about this situation with my three friends is the attempt by these professional young men to keep a foot in both worlds. They are well aware of the modern understanding of health and illness, so they didn't want to tip their hand to me that they still bought into what some might consider old wives' tales. But they've seen their indigenous system work too many times to simply brush it off. As Messer says: "Since people eventually recover from most illnesses, in almost every case they can rationalize that the hot-cold system 'works'" (1981:139). Actually, although I take Messer's quote to be true, I would be a bit more magnanimous about it. The Mam come to their values, as we all do, by cultural transmission and linguistic and cultural practice, but they also see these values confirmed in the real world from day to day. The Mam are observers and survivors in a world where their language and life ways are under assault. Their values are not simply a rationalization of how they've been told that the world works, but even beyond this, they stand as a summary statement of accumulated observations. This is one of the conundrums of modern health care in the developing world. Not only are the values different between West and non-West, but both versions are firmly held and empirically supported. Privately, Abel told me that his mother doesn't accept the notion that illnesses are caused by germs in the dirt. She says that she has had eight children. Each of them has lived the same life, crawling on the same dirt floor of the same home, a floor which the babies share with the cats, dogs, and the occasional diarrheal chicken. They put things in their mouths, suck dirty thumbs, and eat and drink the same food and water as their siblings did before them. Some of them get sick and some don't; some die, some live. There is no cause and effect in her mind that supports the Western view of illness etiology. But illness as imbalance works. She's seen it over and over and over again. Sometimes the details of what caused the departure from center are clear, sometimes they aren't, but "illness as deviation from centeredness" is time-honored and at least as empirically proven in the minds of most Mam as are Western versions of the cause of illness being by means of invisible, malevolent bugs, and the maintenance of good health via nasty chemical intervention.

My professional friends were dealing with the same problem. They know about germs and disinfectants, the need for boiling water, and using latrines, but they've also seen the hot-cold syndrome work. So while they are somewhat apologetic about it, they won't let it go either. When I so blatantly

3.2 Health as an instantiation of centeredness

cast aside good sense by showering too soon after running, values deeply held and even suppressed came bubbling to the surface since centeredness is a part of life and not just a rubric for determining the treatment of illness. Even though the men had just said that the hot-cold syndrome was basically the purview of old women and the uneducated, they commented on my carelessness in showering too soon and thereby risking my health by ignoring the hot-cold syndrome. Apparently, when push came to shove, they couldn't quite let go of the same diagnosis their mothers would have made. These men, though modern professionals, are deeply Mayan as well.

Messer (1981:138) says that it is young motherhood where the hot-cold syndrome is most practically learned and applied. Before she has her own children, a woman lives off the knowledge provided by her own mother. Girls learn early what foods and medicines are hot and cold, but they don't have the practical experience of this knowledge until they begin to watch patterns in the lives of their own children. This experience of seeing a hot-cold etiology work is what validates culture not simply as "a way" to conceive of the world, but as "*the* way." It is reflected in the language, in cultural instantiations (religion, architecture, health, etc.) and in the world itself. Gossen points out that it is the women who are largely responsible for cultural continuity, bringing the past into the present (1986:6–7), and we see here that understanding and using the hot-cold syndrome is one way in which women bring the past forward.

Richardson (1977:80–82) reports a somewhat analogous situation among the Yali of Indonesia in regard to Messer's quote (1981:139) about the inevitability of cultural assumptions "working." As Yali boys go through initiation rites, if there is thunder before the mid-morning ceremony is completed, it stands as an omen that the spirits have rejected one (or more) of the initiates, who will die an early death. Thunder is frequent in those parts, and death by warfare, feud, and disease is common. And people have long memories. If and when a man dies "prematurely," the thunder curse is confirmed. And if it hasn't been confirmed yet, it might be tomorrow or the next day. The cultural viewpoint is once again sustained in the real world. Telling them otherwise is usually futile since they've seen the thunder curse confirmed time after time after time.

This continual confirmation accounts for the resistance to change of cultures around the world even in the face of contact with the modern, globalizing forces that offer so much for the taking. Still, people can't just walk away from that which they've seen confirmed time and time again. Culture provides a filter through which to understand what happens in the world. At the same time, the very notions contained in cultural lore and practice are confirmed by life in the real world. The search for centeredness is the search for how the world works—as we've seen with the maintenance of good health. A centered life is good health practice. We achieve health when we're able to align ourselves with how the world works, punishing extremes. However, not only do we draw cultural knowledge from the world as we understand it, we also get personally involved. As we'll see in section 3.3, the construction of Maya-Mam homesteads and of ancient Mayan cities reflect the notion of centeredness, and provide "ongoing influence in daily life" (Robinson 1989:253). So cultural notions are both in the world and in our heads; this makes them very resistant to change.

3.3 From *space* to *place*: On the meaning of building

I have worked from time to time writing copy as a freelance advertiser. One of my most fascinating projects was creating ads for a plumbing supply company that was planning to introduce a new line of fixtures—Jacuzzi-type bathtubs, designer sinks and toilets, and elegant shower fixtures—to the public. I wrote not about porcelain and flowing water, but about the demands of modern life, the "busyness" of the daily grind, and the need to find small opportunities to get away from it all. Into this picture, I introduced what I called the "architecture of isolation," and I suggested that modern bathroom construction epitomized the need to escape from the constant din of the demands of life. Indeed, modern Western bathrooms often contain luxury accouterments like fireplaces, surround sound, garden views, fountains, built-in bookshelves and planters, even entertainment and internet connections.

Architecture as therapy, architecture as iconicity, architecture as much more than mere function is extremely modern, yet it is not new. From soaring Gothic steeples, literally as well as symbolically reaching toward heaven, to the hogans of the Navajo that emulate the distant mountains, architecture evokes meaning. As evidenced by many years of discussion and debate about the Freedom Tower, which is designed to replace the Twin Towers of the destroyed World Trade Center in New York City, most Americans are far more interested in the significance and symbolic nature

3.3 From space to place: On the meaning of building

of the new structure than they are in its mere utility. Building has meaning far beyond function. Construction reflects not just the needs of the builder, but of the builder's soul as well.

Refocusing from the east coast of the US to Central America, Setha Low says that, "Maya cities were laid out as microcosms, with buildings arranged so as to symbolically equate the architectural center of civic power with the center of the universe," what she calls a "sacred geography" (2000:109), an idea which is reminiscent of many Mayan groups that consider their hometown to be the navel of the earth.

As Low sees the Mayan plaza, so Susan Gillespie (2000) sees the Mayan house as microcosmic of the larger world. She cites Evon Vogt (1969), who called Mayan house construction a manifestation of "structured replication," where the four walls of the house mimic the four cardinal directions in the world. In fact, she sees the Mayan house as part of an "encompassing concentricity," where the house is both "contained and container, but on multiple levels" (2000:158). Just as the house replicates the structure of the world, so the bed and family altar within the house represent the structure of the house with their four pillars or legs and four sides (see figures 3.1 and 3.2). She cites Charles Wisdom (1940:43), who observed: "The square is the only sacred plane, since it has the form of the *milpa* 'corn field' and the altar and has four corners." Similarly, Vogt (1976:11) quotes one of his Maya-Tzotzil friends as saying that the universe is "like a house, like a table" and he concludes that "all preeminent cultural symbols are square."

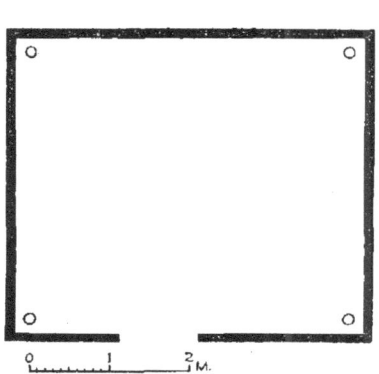 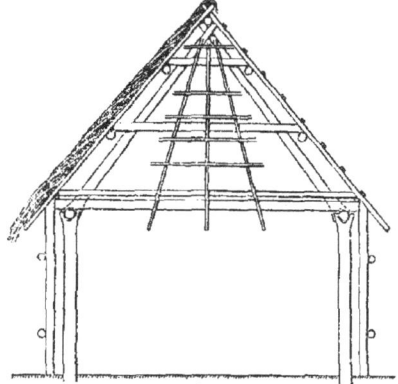

Figure 3.1. Common Mam house, San Sebastián, Huehuetenango; from Robert Wauchope (1938). Used with permission.

David Freidel et al. say:

> We now know that the first act of Creation was to center the world by placing the stones of the cosmic hearth. The second was to raise the sky, establish the sides and corners of the cosmic house that is the sky. The Maya at places like Cerros, Yaxuna, and Zinacantan have been centering the world and creating the four sides ever since. The center could be both grand in scale and execution, or like the navel of a human being, it could be a faint vestigial marker of the remains of the umbilicus that was once connected to an original source of creation and sustenance. It could be created by ritual wherever the Maya needed one. (1993:127)

Freidel et al. include the center as part of the quincuxial cardinal directions, the four sides described by a square center, and a center described by its four sides (see figure 3.2). Hanks (1990:349) says, "Altars, yards, cornfields, the earth, the sky, and the highest atmospheres are described in terms of the five-point cardinal frame (four directions plus the center [WMC])." So in the gods' first act of creation and in the Maya's daily interaction with them, with the land, in the constructed world and with each other, seeking the center was and is both a lofty goal and a practical operating principle of life.

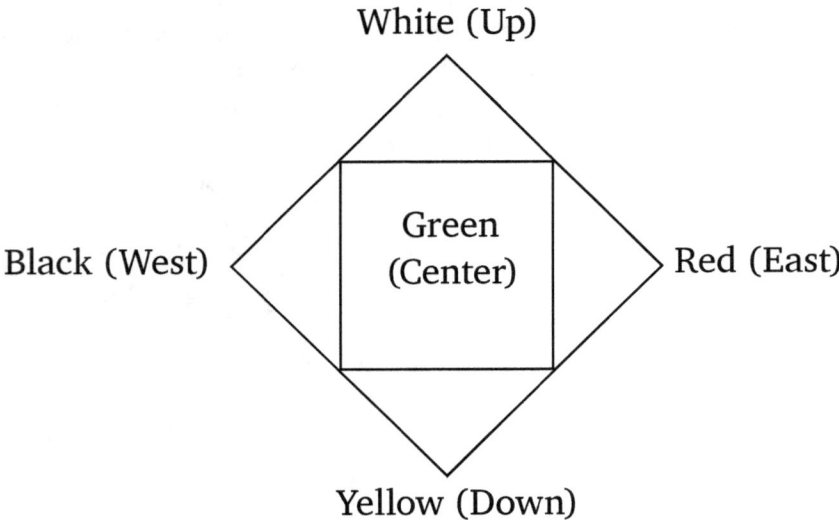

Figure 3.2. God's eye, a quincunx, adapted with permission from Morley (1956).

3.3 From space to place: On the meaning of building

In terms of construction practice and pattern, recent anthropological literature, aside from the archaeologists who continue to describe structures as they existed long ago, has focused on the notions of space and place. In this study, I adopt Low and Lawrence-Zúñiga's distinction that space is general and universal, whereas place is particular and personally meaningful. They say about their work, "We are interested in how people form meaningful relationships with the locales they occupy, how they attach meaning to space, and transform 'space' into 'place'" (2003:13).

Anthropologists identify this distinction as etic vs. emic, a notion we befriended in chapter one. In terms of space and place, we can think of space as general and etic, as what the camera sees, whereas place is space within our grasp and under control, space with cultural meaning (emic).

In this section, I look at two specific places, the Mam home and the town plaza, and suggest that they instantiate the Maya-Mam cultural value of centeredness. I lift the idea pursued here—construction as microcosm—from two sources: Bourdieu (he of the *habitus*; see sections 1.1 and 1.3), who speaks of the Berber home as "a microcosm organized according to the same oppositions that govern all the universe" (2003:136)[2]; and Low, who says of the Maya central plaza: "Maya cities were laid out as microcosms, with buildings arranged so as to symbolically equate the architectural center of civic power with the center of the universe" (2000:109). These two places, the home and the plaza; two microcosms.

Julia Robinson says, "Architecture structures activity and ways of thinking... the ideas manifest in built form have an ongoing influence in daily life" (1989). She goes on to say: "When cultural patterns and built patterns fit, they become a strong mutual reinforcement," that built forms "mirror" cultural values. Henri Lefebvre (1997) gets at this when he says that there is a mutual reinforcement of that which is created and the meaning behind it. Although people live in the practical spaces that they have established for themselves, these created forms can be abstracted away from their common usage and considered in terms of deeper cultural meaning "which will transform it into monumental space: the vase will become holy, the garment ceremonial, the chair a seat of authority" (1997). He means that there is a duality of function in architecture. It is at once useful and practical and at the same time it can become *monumental* and timeless, as cultural meaning is encoded in built form.

---

[2] Although the Berber culture is North African and not Mayan, Bourdieu's point is still valid, that the construction of the house has cultural meaning apart from its basic function of protecting its inhabitants.

3.3.1 Timo's town

The central plaza was a defining feature in the city planning of both Aztec and Mayan pre-invasion towns. Low (2000) suggests that, although the notion of the central plaza was common to the ancient Greeks and Renaissance Italians and French, it was not widespread in Spain. Indeed, she asserts that the concept of the central plaza was picked up, or at least affirmed, in New World centers such as Tenochtitlán (Aztec) and Tikal (Maya), and was subsequently shipped back to Spain where Madrid was "an architectural laboratory of ideas received from Spanish-controlled cities" (2000:94). She claims that the Spanish American plaza "is actually a syncretic urban design form derived from European architectural traditions of medieval *bastides* and the Mesoamerican plaza temple complex and urban plans of the cities that the Spanish encountered during the conquest of the New World" (1997:319).

Only after this syncretic blend of Old and New World plaza construction was accomplished, was the architecture of a civic center passed on to Spanish settlements in Latin America and codified in the 1573 *Orders for Discovery and Settlement* (Low 1997:319). Although the idea that sixteenth-century Spain got the idea for grand plazas from the New World is controversial, archaeological evidence points to the likelihood that early indigenous central plaza areas were built over with Spanish buildings, establishing what today is a common visage—the Catholic church on one side, municipal buildings across from that, and often commercial buildings and private housing (or military headquarters) filling out the four sides. Indeed, as quoted above, Low (1997) cites evidence that at the time of what the Maya call *la invasión*, "Maya cities were laid out as microcosms," where the buildings around a center "place" were iconic of the cultural value of centeredness, where things were ordered, culturally significant, and deeply understood.

She goes on to suggest that the Spanish exerted hegemony over the Maya by appropriating the architecture of centeredness—where the new Spanish central plaza with its concomitant religious, governmental, and commercial interests, subverted and replaced the former Maya center of community and ceremonial life. It may well be that this co-opting of such culturally significant space helped cement Spanish control over both the Maya and Aztec nations. Low suggests that both European and New World

3.3 *From space to place: On the meaning of building* 77

plazas "were designed to display military and market domination." Indeed, "since the spatial relations of plaza to buildings, hierarchy of spaces, and functions of the plaza remain somewhat the same, the symbolism (artistic representation) retains aspects of both cultural histories" (Low 1997:319).

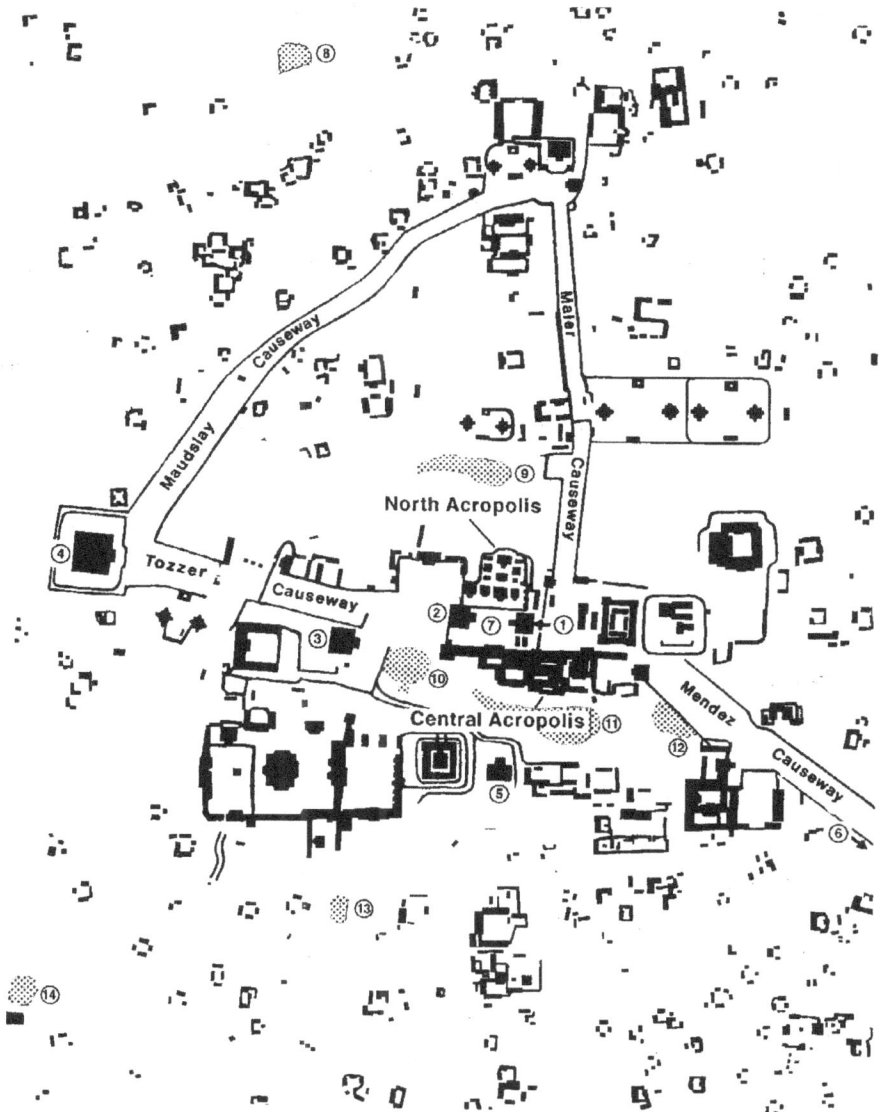

Figure 3.3. Tikal central environs, covering roughly one square mile; from Coe (1999). Used with permission.

The Latin American plaza, then, is a mix of the architectonic vision of both the invaders and the invaded. Despite the fact that the overlay of Spanish dominance is the gold plating of the modern central plaza, the core concept remains very much part of a continuity from the pre-invasion past. Coe (1999:103–104) points out that Tikal, the largest Maya site, may have been home to as many as 90,000 people during its zenith.[3] As the city expanded, new construction was more haphazard than in the Aztec capital of Teotihuacán, which had roads and an apparent plan for urban sprawl, building outward from the central plaza in grid-like fashion. Tikal, on the other hand, had a well devised ceremonial center (see figure 3.4), but as one moved outward from the central constructions, geometric organization lessened and small huts were scattered in "colloidal" fashion toward the outskirts of the site. However, as we look at a general map of the central environs of Tikal (figure 3.3), we're struck with its overall organization from the Great Plaza (number 7) outward to the humblest homes. Since the Maya built these homes on raised rectangular mounds to guard against seasonal flooding, archaeologists have a very good idea what the city construction array was like, even though most of the site's peripheral buildings have been ravaged by time and the weather. For a closer view of the Great Plaza (see figure 3.4). It's interesting that the small homesteads were usually constructed around a central patio (see the homestead sites toward both the top and bottom of figure 3.3). So, what Tikal was—microcosm writ large—the homesteads were, writ small. That is, constructed sites where center spaces (either plazas or patios) were defined by the buildings constructed around them.

---

[3] Coe suggests a number between 10,000 and 90,000. The great variation in number may hinge on the fact that Tikal, like most Mayan towns today, was a ceremonial and commercial center (see Thompson 1966:66ff. for a discussion of Tikal being just such a center). In Comitancillo, for example, some 2,000 actually occupy the official *cabecera municipal* 'municipal seat', while over 60,000+ live in the environs (the *aldeas* and *caseríos* throughout the *municipio*) and consider Comitancillo their ceremonial, political, and commercial center. Some 10,000 people visit the *cabecera* on market day—even more during special fiestas—although the actual *cabecera* population is much smaller.

3.3 *From space to place: On the meaning of building* 79

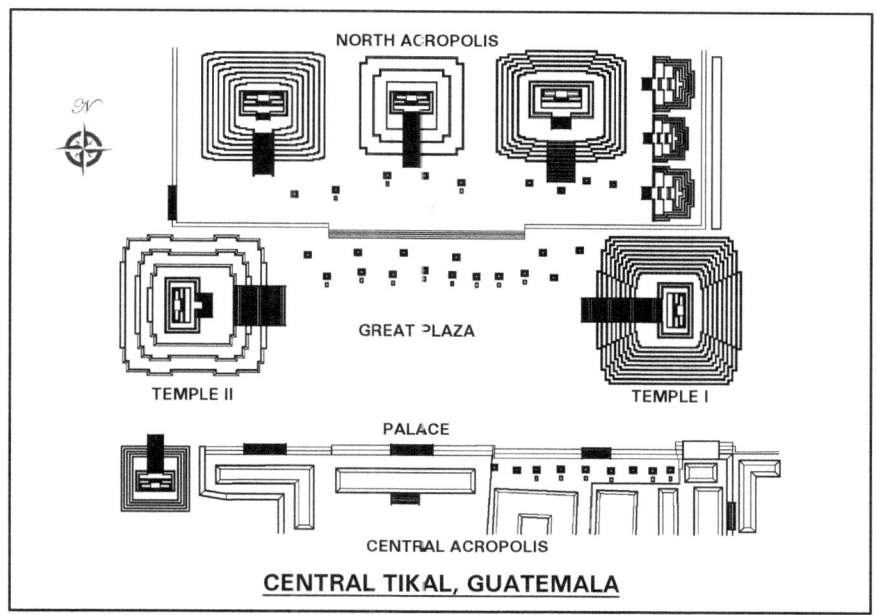

Figure 3.4. Close-up of the Great Plaza at Tikal.
Drawn by Craig Banghart. Used with permission.

Low (1996) suggests that it is the use of space that really defines its cultural function. She shows how the use and meaning of the two main plazas in San José, Costa Rica, are contested. Locals have one view, the government and elite quite another. In the same way, Latin American plazas are a contested space, publicly marked off by the accouterments of Spanish culture, but locally understood as iconic of a deep sense of groundedness and belonging.

We will see that the Tzotzil of Chamula identify their town as the navel of the earth. Similarly, the Mam have told me that the town is the center of the *municipio*[4] and the central plaza is the heart (or stomach) of the town. In Mam, the verb *plasaril* 'to be in the plaza (ostensibly to buy or sell)', is one of only two borrowings I am aware of that verbalizes a place name.[5] Other important place nouns have been borrowed into Mam such as *camposant*

---

[4] A *municipio* includes a central town with all of its rural hamlets and lands. For example, Comitancillo is an "urban" town of some 2,500 people, but the entire *municipio* (also called Comitancillo) has over 60,000 inhabitants scattered over one hundred square miles and including some 50 different hamlets (*aldeas* and *caseríos*). Just as the town has a central plaza, the *aldeas* and *caseríos* usually have a small center area bounded by an official meeting place, a jail, and sometimes a school or cook house.

[5] The word *skwelil* 'to go to school' from Spanish *escuela* 'school' is the only other place name that I know of that has been borrowed into Mam and verbalized.

from Spanish *camposanto* 'cemetery', *yiles (iglesia)* 'church', *municipalidad* 'town civil center', *capital* 'capital', and *Estados Unidos*, 'United States', but none of these has a verbalized form.

I visited my friend Agustín, who was selling rope on market day in the plaza. "What is it that you like about coming here on market day?" I asked him.

"The plaza is one place where I feel totally at ease," he said. *Nimx nniky'a ti'j tkyaqilx, a nb'aj tzalu'n* 'I understand well everything that goes on here'. I know where all the sellers are and where all the different produce is located. I see all my friends. I know everyone and they know me." He went on to say that the plaza seems chaotic with people and animals all over the place and tarps and ropes strung everywhere, but that there is an abiding and joyful unity beneath the surface. He said that the press of humanity at the plaza—the pushing and noises, the smells and activity—is *puro alegr* 'pure happiness', from Spanish *puro alegre*.

I take Agustín's words to be indicative of the contested space of the central plaza. It is at once a government imposition with rules and taxes and vending licenses while at the same time being symbolic of a deep-seated sense of belonging. For Agustín the plaza just feels right. It's not so much that he thinks about the plaza as iconic of the cultural theme of centeredness that he lives day in and day out, but it fits this very view—his view—of how the world works.

As mentioned previously, I discussed this sense of centeredness with a group of six Mam teachers and educational leaders in June 2004 and again in March 2005 and with a group of over twenty teachers and professionals in November 2014. They said that one of the things that helps maintain the historic cultural value of equilibrium and centeredness among their people is that it is a value that works in the modern world. It isn't an "old wives' tale" that is clearly mismatched with the dictates and complexity of modern life. Rather, maintaining balance and seeking moderation and centeredness is as much a moral compass to modern Maya as it was to their pre-invasion ancestors. And the central plaza, although the product of conflicting views of dominance and meaning, still holds for the Mam a sense that things are as they ought to be.

3.3.2 Timo's homestead

As Low (2000) calls the Mayan plaza (both pre-invasion and actual) a microcosm of the whole universe, so Bourdieu, in like manner, calls the Berber home "a microcosm organized according to the same oppositions

3.3 *From space to place: On the meaning of building*   81

that govern all the universe" (2003:136). I suggest we can say the same thing about the Mam home. In the modern world, the home is one of the places where the Mam can connect to the timeless. Friends have told me that just as the plaza is the center of town, so the patio is the physical center of the homestead. The emotional center of the home is the cook house, and the center of the cook house is the hearth where families gather to eat and talk, just as Mayan families have done for millennia. Gillespie (2000:139) says of the Mayan home, "One who is seated in his house is in his place, representing a microcenter," the place where one is grounded and where he or she belongs.

I've known Timo since 1980. The first time I visited him at home was 1983. He had just moved from a nearby hamlet to a piece of property he'd bought in an *aldea* 'hamlet' of San Lorenzo, the town immediately south of Comitancillo. Before actually moving to the property, he built two small adobe structures, each approximately twenty feet long and twelve feet wide (figure 3.5).

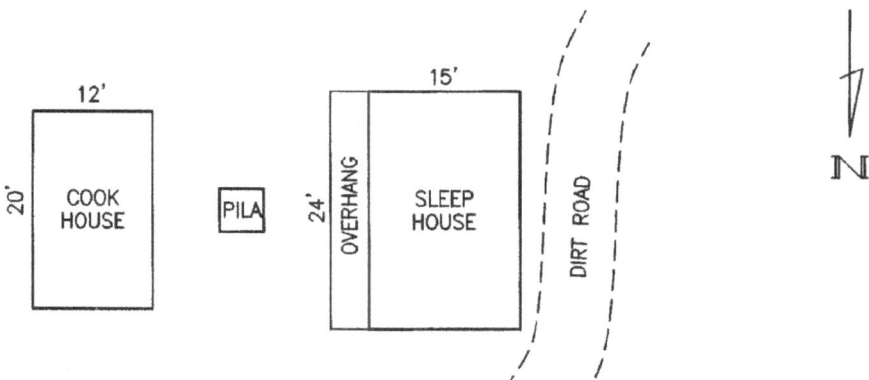

Figure 3.5. Timo's original (and typical) homestead. Drawn by Craig Banghart. Used with permission.

The two "houses" faced each other about 20 feet apart across a small courtyard or patio of packed earth. Each house was constructed of adobe blocks with a tile roof and a single door in the middle, facing the central courtyard. This homestead layout is extremely common throughout the Guatemalan highlands. In the patio between the two houses stood a *pila*, a cement structure for washing clothes and holding water. In the early 80s, Timo's home did not have running water. The women would go to a nearby spring and carry water back to the *pila*, filling it with approximately thirty gallons of water. This water was used throughout the day for washing hands, clothes, and dishes and for preparing food.

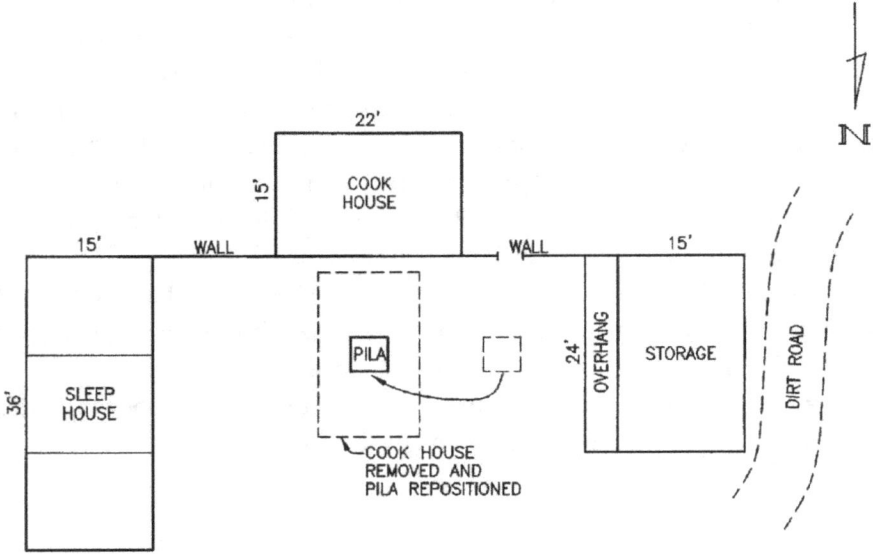

Figure 3.6. Timo's new construction. Drawn by Craig Banghart. Used with permission.

In 1995, Timo's son went to the States to look for work, ending up in an Alabama meatpacking company. He sent money home from time to time, and as is common, this money was put into capital investments, usually the purchase of additional land and construction projects. Timo was able to purchase additional land adjacent to his own, and he decided to expand his homestead site by adding some small buildings. In order to take advantage of the additional acreage, Timo built a block house (approximately 15 feet by 36) behind the adobe kitchen. This building was sectioned into three 12 x 15 foot rooms, each with a door facing the patio area and a small window. These rooms were used for sleeping. Timo then added another building—a new cook house—perpendicular to the block sleep house (figure 3.7).

3.3 From space to place: On the meaning of building

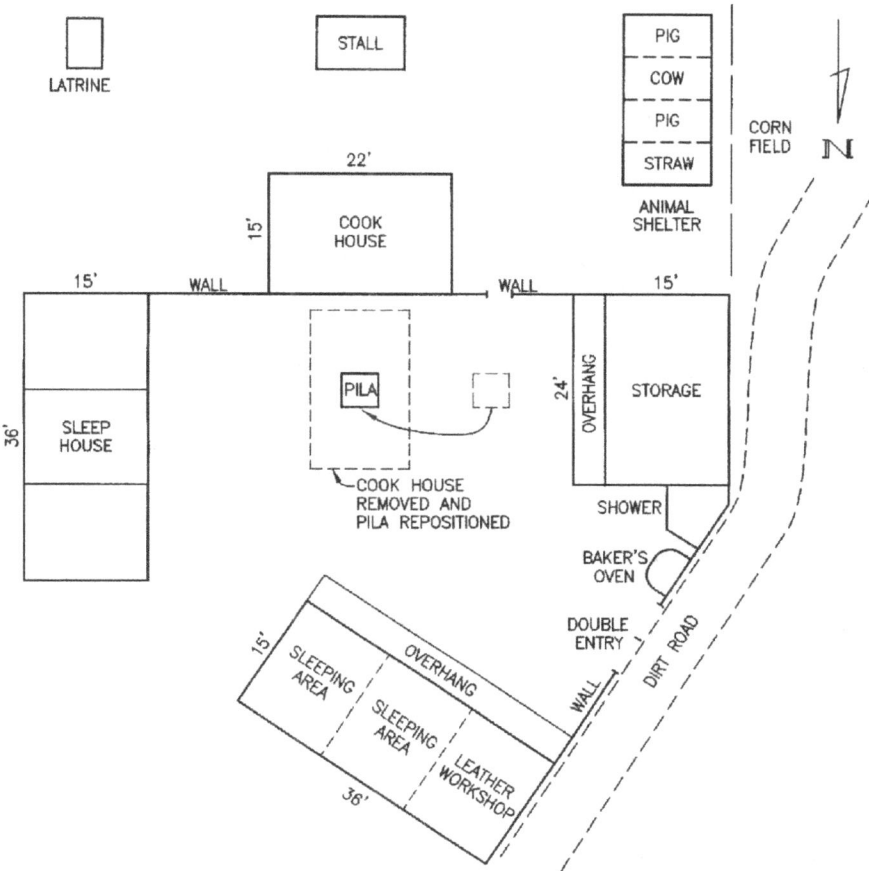

Figure 3.7. Timo's present homestead. Drawn by
Craig Banghart. Used with permission.

When the construction of these two buildings was completed, the old sleep house became a storage area and the old cook house was dismantled. The metal roof was salvaged as were all the beams and boards. The adobe walls were then taken down and the spot was totally vacated, except that the *pila* was moved to take its position in the new center of the courtyard. Later, a third new building was added as a workshop and additional sleeping area. Timo also added separately a shower stall and a large oven for baking bread (figure 3.7).

What I have found interesting about this series of events is that the original cook house and sleep house were built at the same time. They were both in good condition when Timo happened into some extra money from remittances from his son in the States. Nevertheless, with the new construction, while the original sleep house was converted to a storage area, the original cook house was completely eliminated. What seems to be the reason for this is that the original sleep house, being situated on the perimeter of the "new" patio area, still provided a dimension for the central patio, whereas the original cook house was now in the middle of the new basic living area. If the cook house were to remain standing, it would relegate the new sleep house to an area away from the central patio. Its doors would open to the back of the old cook house rather than to the patio, a situation Timo found unacceptable. When I asked Timo why he converted the old sleep house but not the cook house to a storage area, since both buildings were in good shape and salvageable, he said that it was not possible to leave the cook house where it was. Since he had built a new cook house, the old one was unneeded, he reasoned. I suggested that had he left the cook house where it was, he could have taken advantage of the space for a workshop and not spent additional funds on the construction of yet another building.[6]

At this point, Timo gave me one of those looks as he often did when I had asked too many stupid questions. But judging from what Timo actually did, rather than what he said, the original cook house was in the way. There could be no open center area if this area was occupied by an old adobe cook house. Although the old adobe sleep house was fine since it didn't impinge on the new patio area, the cook house now occupied a special space, the center, and it didn't belong there. There was nothing particularly unbalanced about the old cook house being in the center of the new patio area. Rather, it impinged on the new center and therefore had to go.

After knocking down the original cook house, Timo moved the *pila* to the center of the new patio area, the place where it sits today. Today the *pila* is more than just a water storage and washing area. It is connected to running water, a fact which saves Timo's wife and daughters from having to go to the spring in order to keep the *pila* full.

The comparison of what Timo did and what he said is worthy of comment. Geertz would be dissatisfied by a stand-alone, camera-only recording of the events I've mentioned. At the same time, hearing the analysis from Timo's own point of view obscures what may well be behind the action that he took. Neither an etic nor an emic analysis stands alone. Geertz

---

[6] Timo is a carpenter and leather worker. He has always needed space to store his tools and materials and space for a workbench. He also needs what constituted appropriate living space. Practically speaking, the cook house would have been ideal, but it didn't fit Timo's notion of what constituted appropriate living space.

calls, rather, for an interpretation of events, one that takes into account everything—what actually happened, what Timo said, and how the events can be seen against the larger context of culture, something that outsiders tend to be too far away from to understand clearly. At the same time, insiders are far too close to be able to explicate it helpfully. From Timo's point of view, when he told me that it was not possible to maintain the old cook house in its present location, his view was that that should have been enough for me. As Geertz teaches, culture is "out there" and public, interpretable by people's daily practice in lived space. Timo assumed that he had already answered my question. But because Timo lives a life committed to seeking centeredness, centeredness itself is a grounds upon which different figures—construction, health, and faith—are focused. For him, it is the figures, not the grounds, that are salient and meaningful. That I would concentrate instead, and inexplicably, on the grounds was for him the basis for nothing but silly questions. As outsiders, however, it is only through observation of what's going on (the etic point of view) and a meaningful interpretation of the emic point of view that we can come to understand the world in which Timo lives.

The life that Timo lives is not just about what he can experience in regard to health and the constructed world around him; it's also about the world within. As Sheldon Annis says, "If you want to get an Indian's attention, talk to him about God" (1987:3).

3.4 Religion as a search for centeredness

Munro Edmonson (1993) says that the religion of pre-Columbian Maya and present-day traditional religionists is based on reciprocity, the counterbalancing of what is asked of the gods with the value of what is offered in return. Traditional Maya consider their spiritual destiny to be the metaphysical "heart of heaven," the center of paradise, oft-mentioned in the *Popol Vuh*, where everything is in perfect balance and order, a goal which, while strived for, is elusive during life here in the world.

Edmonson approaches Mayan religion in terms of traditional anthropological practice, studying the hieroglyphic record and pre-Columbian texts, particularly the *Popol Vuh*, as well as present religious ritual, and he looks for continuities between ancient texts and present practice. He concludes that for the Maya, religion mimics the early Maya word for religion, *ok olal* 'entering inwardness', or, more idiomatically, 'seeking centeredness', where being 'inside' denotes a safe haven, which is *txolin* 'ordered', *nik'u'n* 'balanced/peaceful', *tz'aqsin* 'adjusted, arranged', *jikytzin* 'straight', *kuj* 'unwavering', and *toj tumil* 'right'.

Edmonson explains that Mayan religion is mystical; it is the province of specialists who understand the esoteric counting of days, the patterning of the tossed beans or corn kernels for predicting the future, the complex sacrificial system, and the requirements of the gods. He says, "The power of the ritual is demonstrated by its ability to placate the demanding gods and actually produce health, fertility, rain, sunrise, predicated planetary movements, and eclipses" (1993:73). The Maya don't pray with empty hands. The priests require a gift commensurate to the importance and value of the item requested of them. In the *Popol Vuh*, not only do men and women depend on the gods, the gods also depend on men and women in a delicate balance of providence for hire. The gods were to be honored and fed the food of sacrifice. In the case of particularly momentous requests, the only "gift to god significant enough...is a human life" (ibid.:83).

Martha Nájera concurs. She says that human sacrifice demonstrated that:

> In order for life to be renewed, it was necessary to produce ritual death, and for this reason, it was required that the community produce such a death, so that the community itself could continue to exist; this idea is in strict relation with *the idea of reciprocity* that should and must exist between mankind and the gods: each needs the other to survive. Human beings, the divine creation, were formed so that they could, with their blood, sustain the gods, and in turn humans need divine power to help them deal with daily problems. The gods are not all powerful beings; they need the human offerings in order to live and it is human beings who are responsible for these offerings. Man considers himself the axis of the Universe, because without his action, everything would be destroyed. (1987:14, emphasis and translation from Spanish, WMC)

Nájera also suggests that it was the heart that was the most important aspect of human sacrifice, since it served as the victim's essence and center, as well as being the preferred food of the gods. In this, she follows Diego Landa (1566) who writes as an eyewitness:

> The executioner came, with a flint knife in his hand, and with great skill made an incision between the ribs on the left side, below the

3.4 Religion as a search for centeredness

> nipple; then he plunged in his hand and like a ravenous tiger tore out the living heart, which he laid on a plate and gave to the priest; he then quickly went and anointed the faces of the idols with that fresh blood. (Landa 1566 [1978]:49)

Nájera's work is largely a history of Maya human sacrifice as depicted in the glyphic record. The title of Nájera's book itself is iconic of our theme: *El don de la sangre en el equilibrio cósmico* 'The gift of blood in cosmic equilibrium' (translation, WMC).

Glyphs occasionally show the *world tree* growing up out of the chest cavity of a sacrificial victim . The tree's branches reach to the heavens; its roots go down into the underworld of death; and its trunk is firmly planted in the literal and ritual center of the religious system, the human heart.

Edmonson (1993:65) goes on to point out that there was no codification of any pre-invasion Mayan belief system. Rather, the city-state political organization of the region militated against a single monolithic religion as each political/priestly/scribal geographical entity tended to portray its successes as stemming from its particular understanding of and relationship to the gods (Johnston 2001). Nevertheless, throughout the Mayan area there was a basic unity of religious concepts: a preoccupation with time and prediction, an obsession with numbers, a strong sense of dualism "profoundly imbedded in Mayan thought and language" (Edmonson 1993:67), a developed notion of reciprocity between humankind and the gods, and a penchant among the masses for wanting to see positive results for their religious and political devotion.

Despite the lack of codification, we still have a reliable witness of pre-invasion religion through the glyphs, art, and architecture of the Classic Maya. Edmonson also says that linguistic reconstruction gives us a good idea of religious categories, as does a reconstruction of the significance of number, particularly as these are compared to the knowledge and practice of modern-day speakers and practitioners of the religion as it has been passed through the generations.

A final source for understanding pre-invasion religion is the writings of the Maya themselves immediately following the arrival of the Spanish. Prime among these sources is the *Popol Vuh*, often called the Mayan bible. The *Popol Vuh* is not so much a treatise about religion, as it is the story of the gods, the creation, the establishment of life on earth, and a history of a number of regional and supernatural conflicts. Much of the content of the *Popol Vuh* deals with interactions among the gods before the successful creation of the first men and women. It assumes an understanding of Mayan religion and therefore doesn't offer much instruction to adherents as to religious practice and belief.

The *Popol Vuh* was written in K'iche' by native K'iche' speakers who wrote their own language using Spanish characters. This was a major challenge since Mayan languages have fifteen or so phonemes that don't exist in Spanish. Nonetheless, modern translators have a good enough understanding of the language and the literacy skills of those who wrote down the *Popol Vuh* that we can be confident of its actual content.[7]

3.4.1 Centeredness and the *Popol Vuh*

In this section I highlight some of the content of the *Popol Vuh* that informs our notion of centeredness. The *Popol Vuh* itself is the story of the present creation. By Mayan accounts, there have been other creations in the past, and there will be more in the future. The present creation began in watery darkness, silent and calm. The creator couple, in conference with other gods, decided to create humans so that these new beings would invoke the name of the gods, fellowship with them, and sacrifice to them. The first attempt to create humans resulted in the creation of animals instead, which were unable to call upon the name of their creators, so the creator couple tried again. The gods used mud to make their flesh, but these were unable to move or reproduce, so they brought down these creatures. Third, they made humans from sticks so that they would not fall apart when they got wet like those made of mud. But these, too, did not recognize their makers; they didn't feed and sustain them, and were therefore destroyed in a terrible sticky, fiery rain.

Before the final (and successful) creation of humans, there is a long interlude about the travails of the twin gods who are lured to the underworld and killed. The sentient talking head of one of the gods is hung on a tree and impregnates with its saliva the daughter of one of the lords of the underworld. She is banished to the surface where she gives birth to another set of twins. When these two become young adults they return to the place of the dead, trick and kill the lords of the underworld, and

---

[7] Like Homer, the writer(s) of the *Popol Vuh* didn't invent the stories they wrote. Rather, they organized and edited them, and wrote them down. It is clear from the glyphic record, carved as much as a thousand years before the invasion, that the stories had been passed down for many generations.

3.4 Religion as a search for centeredness

resuscitate their dead forebears, who would eventually become the sun and the moon.

At this point the creation story is again picked up. The creator couple, also called the *heart of heaven, heart of earth*, created four men from corn. Miraculously, their four wives appeared as well. These are the first Maya-K'iche' and the forebears of the important K'iche' lineages. The sun had not yet appeared, and these people and others wandered the earth in darkness. In their peregrination, they came to where they would receive their gods. The lineages received three gods, but the main god, Tojil—Preuss (1988) says the name means "he who causes rain," and is also translated "Rainstorm" or "Cloudburst"—eventually became the chief god of all the lineages. He also provided fire for these first K'iche', who shared it with other groups. When humans' fires were put out in a hailstorm, Tojil allowed the K'iche' to provide it again to other groups, but only in return for sacrifices. At first, Tojil was content with animal sacrifices of deer and birds, but soon, the priests and sacrificers offered their own blood drawn from their arms and ears. Before long, however, Tojil requested human sacrifices culled from enemy tribal groups, a practice which became more and more bloodthirsty (in addition to human sacrifice, the glyphs show priests bloodletting from their own tongues and penises). In modern K'iche', *tojil* means 'payment'. In Mam, it would mean 'the possession of its inwardness'. This is similar to Edmonson's claim (1993:85), that the Maya term for religion is *ok olal* 'entering inwardness', which I discussed previously.

In some of the ensuing chapters of the *Popol Vuh*, other groups attempted but were unable to overcome the gods of the K'iche' despite numerous attempts and wars.[8] This may well be an attempt by the K'iche' writers to establish their own preeminence among the Maya, which was a scribal tradition. In glyphic depictions of the victory of Mayan warriors, the history of the losers is vanquished and the fingers of their scribes are broken and disfigured (Johnston 2001).

In the *Popol Vuh*, the creator is called both father and mother, two times father, two times mother, grandfather, grandmother, two times grandfather, two times grandmother. This sense of one out of two is common in Mayan ritual rhetoric (Townsend 1980; Neuenswander 1986). In the first

---

[8] For a fascinating summary of the content of the *Popol Vuh*, as well as its allegorical, astronomic meaning, see Tedlock 1996.

attempt at creating humans, the gods requested of the animals that they call on them:

> Praise our name.
> Praise and say that we are
> your Fathers and Mothers,
> we who are Huracán Chipi-Culhá and Raxa-Cuculjá,
> the Heart of heaven and of earth,
> formers and creators,
> Fathers and Mothers of all,
> Speak, invoke our name and greet us. (Ximénez 1722:8)

Here we see the dualistic nature of religious rhetoric. Throughout the *Popol Vuh*, events and persons are often grouped in twos (and fours), and the poetic sections are usually presented in couplets.

Morley observes that "The Maya religion had a strong dualistic tendency" (1956:190). This resonates with comments by Gossen and Martin cited in chapter one about the thematicity of dualism in Mayan culture. Dualism isn't simply the sense of two; it also contains the notion of one out of two, or unity out of diversity.

Neuenswander (1986) discusses how the Maya-Achí ancestors are addressed as 'our long ago mothers, our long ago fathers'; the universe is conceived of as 'the earth and heavens'; the world as 'the mountains and valleys'. Her claim is that the pervasive use of couplets in rhetorical and religious discourse is iconic of the "strong tendency toward dualism" in Maya-Achí culture. I will discuss this further in chapter four.

In the publication of conclusions and recommendations from the *Primer Congreso de Educación Maya en Guatemala* [The first congress of Mayan education in Guatemala] (Curruchiche Otzoy et al. 1994), a number of themes are proposed as basic to an education that respects Mayan worldview. Two of these are duality and the importance of the notion of "fourness." Whereas duality has to do with unity out of diversity, fourness harkens to totality or completeness, like Eugenio's comments about a dog with four legs or a family with four membertypes. Only on four legs is an animal natural, normal, and balanced. Only with a father, mother, daughters, and sons is a family complete. Coe (1999:203) comments on various phenomena regarding the number

3.4 Religion as a search for centeredness

four, and we have seen this ourselves above. The earth is considered four cornered and is "supported by four aged *pawahtuns,* the quadripartite form of the old deity who ruled over the days at the end of the year." The sky also is four cornered, sustained by four bakabs or, by some accounts, four stout trees. The *Popol Vuh* reports four attempts to create humankind, the fourth being successful when the gods made men from corn. Four men were created, followed soon afterwards by their four wives. Four animals were involved in leading the gods to the corn from which the first men's flesh was made. Four owls served as messengers in the underworld, and a road that split in four became the downfall of the first set of twins on their ill-fated visit to the underworld. Dennis Tedlock adds: "the settlement at the center of the K'iche' kingdom embraced a cluster of four citadels" (1996:57). The *Popol Vuh* also mentions a number of other groupings and clusters of four.

It is from present-day Mam that I learned about balanced families having four member-types, that animals need full use of four legs to be considered normal (although this is clearly true in our own culture), and that corn can have four different colors: red and yellow, black and white. Indeed, each of the four basic directions *te twutz tx'otx'* 'on the surface of the earth'—*elnix* 'east', *oknix*[9] 'west', *jawnix* 'up' and *kub'nix* 'down'—has a corresponding color associated with it: red for east, black for west, yellow for downward, and white for upward,[10] with green or blue-green in the balanced center (Mam has one color name for both blue and green). As the colors of the four directions symbolize the importance of corn, which is planted everywhere among the Maya (to the four directions), so the color green in the middle symbolizes tranquility, growth, balance, and health, since the corn plants grow green and tall as the ear is formed. This is symbolized in the quincunx or what is commonly called a god's eye (figure 3.2), its four outlying colors corresponding to the cardinal directions, with green (or blue-green) in the middle.

---

[9] *Oknix* literally means 'toward the entrance'. It means 'west' since that is where the sun enters its house at night. In the same way, *elnix* means 'toward the exit', is east because in the east the sun leaves its house daily to enter the world. Actually, *oknix* and *elnix* are more complicated than this, and the idea of east and west is just part of their story. I won't deal with these details here.

[10] Coe (and others) considers these last two cardinal directions to be south and north, not down and up (1999:203). I agree with England (1978:233) that the four cardinal Mayan directions are east, west, up, and down. A fifth "direction" would be the center in Hanks's and Freidel's terms, for which see section 3.3.

In addition, there are four posts (*tqan* 'legs') that hold up a Mam home of four sides (as per figure 3.1), four sides to a Mayan patio or town plaza, and cornfields historically have four sides, lined up with the sun's trajectory across the sky. Note in figure 3.8 the alignment of the processional route at Dos Pilas with the path of the sun. The center of the central architectural complex aligns with the sun's zenith and its path. As mentioned, the sun's path is important not only to ceremonial centers and the establishing of sacred space, but to the layout of the cornfield and homestead as well. Vogt (1976:72–80) shows that east-west orientation is important to Zinacantecos in healing rituals (the head of the patient is toward the rising sun). In addition, adults are buried with their heads toward the east, while children's heads face the west, albeit both along the path of the moving sun.

There are several direct mentions of the idea of a center in the *Popol Vuh*, albeit few. I take to be the most powerful metaphor of centeredness the idea of *the heart of heaven, the heart of earth*. Martin, following Gossen, mentions the convergence of person and place as a possible cultural theme among the Maya. It denotes at once both the warmth of relationship and the groundedness and situatedness of belonging. The dual designation of the center of both heaven and earth not only is iconic of the dualism mentioned above (and later in chapter four), but it also is inclusive of the two worlds most relevant to the Maya, the here-and-now world of daily practice and the then-and-there world of the afterlife.

The creator couple, conferring among themselves, "in the midst of that darkness, created all creatures and the creation of the trees and all of life was manifest along with everything else that was made by the Heart of heaven" (Ximénez 1722:6, translation from Spanish, WMC). Here we see the creator couple as a basic unity of purpose and power out of the diversity of male and female; we see that it was in the midst of that primal darkness, *en medio* 'from the center' according to Ximénez, that the creation event took place; and it was the exalted person/exalted place of the *heart of heaven* that did the creating. It is the same creator couple, "heart of heaven and of the earth" (Ximénez 1722:99), that eventually created men and women.

Another place where a sense of center is important is in the house of the mother of the deceived gods who met their demise at the hands of the lords of the underworld. Her grandsons (the second set of twins, Hunahpú and Xbalanqué) had left some cornstalks planted in the dry ground of her

3.4 Religion as a search for centeredness 93

patio, when they went to the underworld to avenge their father's death. If the stalks sprouted, it would be a sign to the old woman that they were still alive. After the boys had been gone a long time, Ximénez says, "the old woman was very happy when she saw the stalks sprout, and at that time idolatry began and the burning of incense in the *middle of the house* and *the center or exact point of the middle,* and it was called Cul-nicoh-ha,[11] *stalks of the center* for that's what the *center of the house* has been called…" (1722:92) (translation from Spanish and emphasis, WMC). Tedlock (1996:42) likens this sprouting of the corn stalks to the corn itself, which is dormant and dry as seed, but comes to life after planting.

In this section, we haven't so much seen the details of Maya religious belief, but we've seen a context in which such belief operates. We've had but a glimpse of Mayan religion. It seems that those who wrote down the *Popol Vuh* assumed that their readers would understand the facts of belief. What they offered was the history of the world in which such belief has meaning and place. Although the idea of reciprocity isn't in and of itself a religious notion, among the Maya it does indeed have far-reaching religious implications. The gods created men and women so that men and women could sustain the gods.

I suggest that this relation of reciprocity is an instantiation of our theme of centeredness. In chapter four we will look at the lexicon of centeredness and consider how the Mam themselves talk about such a notion. For now, I suggest that Morley, Edmonson, Gossen, Nájera, Martin, Coe, Neuenswander, and the educators who attended the 1994 First Congress on Mayan Education would agree that Maya life, as instantiated in traditional religion, includes a strong impetus toward seeking the balance of centeredness between the individual and his or her family, between oneself and the gods, between a family and the land, and between an individual and his or her neighbors. Indeed, we will see that agreement and reciprocity are possible only in a philosophical center space of respect, peace, and calm.

3.4.2 Entering inwardness; Mayan Protestantism

In the present world though, it is the lack of centeredness, personal balance, and equilibrium that Scotchmer (1989, 1993) cites as motivation

---

[11] This appears to be cognate with Mam *k'ul niky'jin ja* 'weeds (plants) of the center of the house'. In chapter four we will look at the lexical item *niky'jin* 'center or middle'.

for the unprecedented conversion to Protestantism among the Mam and other Mayan groups. He claims that it is because many Mam see traditional Mayan religion as not delivering on its promise of balance in, for example, social harmony and personal order, and personal peace with God, that they have opted for other religious systems, particularly post-Vatican II Catholicism and, lately, Protestantism. Scotchmer (d. 1995) was a missionary anthropologist whose goal was to provide an ethnohistory of conversion among the Southern Mam.[12] He cites the stories of many Mam men who claim to have beaten their wives and children, and who were addicted to alcohol, who fought with family and neighbors, and who felt ungrounded in the midst of increasing modernization—certainly not the kind of life balance they had envisioned for themselves—and who later found respite from these common yet unhelpful practices.

Scotchmer (1993) suggests that there are three areas in which the Maya seek a broad sense of peace: within the spiritual order, within the created order, and within the human order. This is as much the goal of traditional Maya as for those who convert to Catholicism or Protestantism. I suggest in chapter four that the Mam word for peace, *nuk'b'il*, means not only 'peace' but 'order, where things are as they should be, correctly structured, balanced, safe, calm, and without rancor'. This sense of *nuk'b'il* is the goal of the Maya view of religion, a moral and social center space, where life is in balance in every way. I believe this is why the *heart of heaven,* as both place and person, is such a rich and powerful metaphor to the Maya. It symbolizes all that heaven should be, both personally and geographically intimate and grounded.

Scotchmer shows by citing life stories of the Mam themselves that it is often failure to achieve this kind of balance that triggers the search for something else.

> When ritual performance fails to cure alcoholism, lingering illness, unresolved feuding, repeated misfortune, endemic poverty, social rejection and personal misery, there is an unavoidable crisis of belief. Questions of a very existential nature emerge that challenge not only the way one's ancestors and oneself have lived, but also what one has believed as true, acceptable, and good about reality and one's place in the cosmos. (Scotchmer 1993:509)

---

[12] Southern Mam centers around the town of San Juan Ostuncalco in the department of Quetzaltenango. It is more closely related than Northern Mam (of Huehuetenango) to the Mam of Comitancillo. See Godfrey and Collins (1987) for further linguistic details.

3.4 Religion as a search for centeredness

Scotchmer suggests that because Protestantism deals with many of the same issues of life as traditional religion, it is not seen by adherents as something foreign and necessarily North American. He writes, "Invariably, the believer's conversion story refers to the time when he or she was not a Protestant with strong images of what the old way was like. For the man, the old life usually means alcoholism accompanied by poverty, hunger, illness, violence, jail, indebtedness, loss of valuable land, and finally despair" (1993:508). There is often such a mismatch between how people wish to live and how they actually live that Protestantism becomes an option that is considered by many. Conversion to Christianity deals with these same issues, issues that are very much a part of Mayan life. Because of this touch with the real world in Mayan terms, Protestantism is not necessarily seen as an "outsider religion," but one that deals with the concerns of the Maya and those of humanity in general.

Scotchmer cites one Mam who said:

> *Qajaw Crist* (Our Lord Christ) is the one leader for us, a captain, a general, one who gives wise counsel. He has more authority than that of the people. We essentially are fearful of people with much authority. But *Qajaw Crist* has greater power, and much more authority than do these people. That's because *Tyol Dios* (The Word of God) is a very sacred authority. More than anything it speaks strongly to our hearts. It speaks about our lives and how they need to be opened, about how we may become stronger believers, who are upright and true in our faith like a soldier of *Qman Crist* (our Father Christ, WMC). (1989:301)

In summary, Scotchmer says that the symbols of Mayan Protestantism—*Tyol Dios* 'The Word of God', *Qajaw Crist* 'Our Lord Christ', and *hermano/a* 'brother/sister'—"draw unmistakably on values which are deeply imbedded in the culture and religion of the Maya" (1989:307). So, for Mayan Protestants, they don't see their faith as something from the outside that has been imposed on them, but rather as a response to a very local (grounded) and personal (situated) reality.

Of the many testimonies I've heard about this from Comitecos who are now Protestant believers, the following are indicative.

My friend Flavio told me that before his conversion he would be at the market on pay day and he would determine to go home and take his earnings to his wife and family. But as he passed the *cantina*, his own throat would call out to him for a drink. At this point in our conversation, he paused and gestured, stroking his throat several times. He said that, try as he might, he couldn't get home sober. His life is different now, he says. Now he has the power and motivation to live *tuk'a tumil* 'with direction', as he knows he should.

Victoriano told me that he never had a drinking problem, but that he loved the ladies. He said that he had lived an uncontrolled life, even after his first marriage, but he knew it was wrong. He says that after his conversion, God and the *hermanos* 'Christian brothers and sisters' helped him walk *tuk'a tumil* 'with direction'. The phrase *tuk'a tumil* implies life lived centered on a path leading in the right direction, and not *txalche* 'veering off course, to one side or the other'.

Miguel told me that he and his first wife fought and yelled at each other all the time and finally divorced. His brother had come to believe and pursue the gospel message and he shared it with Miguel who decided to follow it as well. Now, he says, he is remarried (to another woman) and lives in harmony with his wife.

Each of these three men told me that they had converted to Christianity from their old way of life. The term they use for 'convert' or 'repent' is *tu'n tajtz ti'j wanmi'n* 'to come home in regard to my heart', to return to center. Many see their new faith as a return to this sense of centeredness, balance, and harmony. The goal here is not balance—swinging from bad to good—but centeredness and spiritual rest.

In 1984 I attended a meeting of Mam school teachers. The theme of the event was cultural and linguistic revitalization. One speaker said that a Mayan Evangelical is a *coco* 'a coconut', brown on the outside, but white on the inside. This generated a lot of discussion. One teacher said, "Our ancestors didn't wear prescription glasses or drive cars. Are you saying that if we do anything that they didn't do that we're *cocos*?" It continues to be an important topic of discussion among the Maya, but the position that is increasingly held by Protestants is that they are not *cocos*, but rather, they are Maya *actualizados* 'up to date'. They reject the notion that to be Christian is to be less than fully Mayan.

While some (both Maya and non-Maya) consider Christian conversion to be a delinking of the modern Maya with their past, I suggest, based on Scotchmer's work and further interviews with the Mam of Comitancillo, that conversion can be seen as the pursuit of the cultural value of centeredness which, far from being a delinking of the Mam with their past, can be understood as an affirmation of Mayanness. Indeed, 'to return home to one's heart', is to *come home* to centeredness, the basic goal of Mayan life. It is more than mere balance. That the Mam would use such terminology in light of Nájera's emphasis on the heart in Mayan sacrifices is strong support for conversion as cultural continuity and not as cultural delinking. It also affirms the cultural salience of centeredness.

Not only is the basic concept of repentance understood in terms of a return to centeredness, but recall that according to Edmonson (1993:85), the Maya term for religion is *ok olal* 'entering inwardness', which is tantamount to seeking centeredness.

3.5 Conclusion

In this chapter we've considered three areas of Mam life that are part of the daily practice of being Maya: their conception of health and illness, the constructed world that they inhabit, and the spiritual world that gives meaning and understanding to their lives.

What we've seen is that as different as these aspects of life seem to be, they can be understood as instantiations of an underlying cultural goal, that of seeking centeredness. I began with a discussion of disease etiology and how to stay healthy in a world of extremes, both physical and metaphysical. We saw that scholars from the earliest contact with the Maya and, indeed, modern Maya themselves talk about health in terms of a center space of balance and equilibrium with their surroundings. They come to this understanding both as handed down from their parents and grandparents, and from the observation of the cold hard facts of how the world works.

Not only does the idea of centeredness "work" in terms of the maintenance of health and treatment of disease, but it also seems to be the model by which the constructed world is arranged. Mam homes are built around a central four-sided patio. We saw that when this center space is violated by additional construction, the space must be reconstituted and revitalized. Even the earliest and simplest homes, built over a thousand years ago on the outskirts of Tikal, seem to recognize and accommodate the need for a center space around which homesteads were constructed. This is as true today in the town of Comitancillo and its *aldeas* as it was a thousand years ago. I suggested that this sense of center is so much a part of Mam life that it is sometimes disregarded or taken for granted by the Mam themselves, a mere grounds by which to interpret a variety of figures in their lives. But when the sense of center is somehow violated, by new construction, or by an adolescent who is not walking *tuk'a tumil*, the grounds rise to front and center, and buildings and lives need to be rearranged so that the center is respected anew.

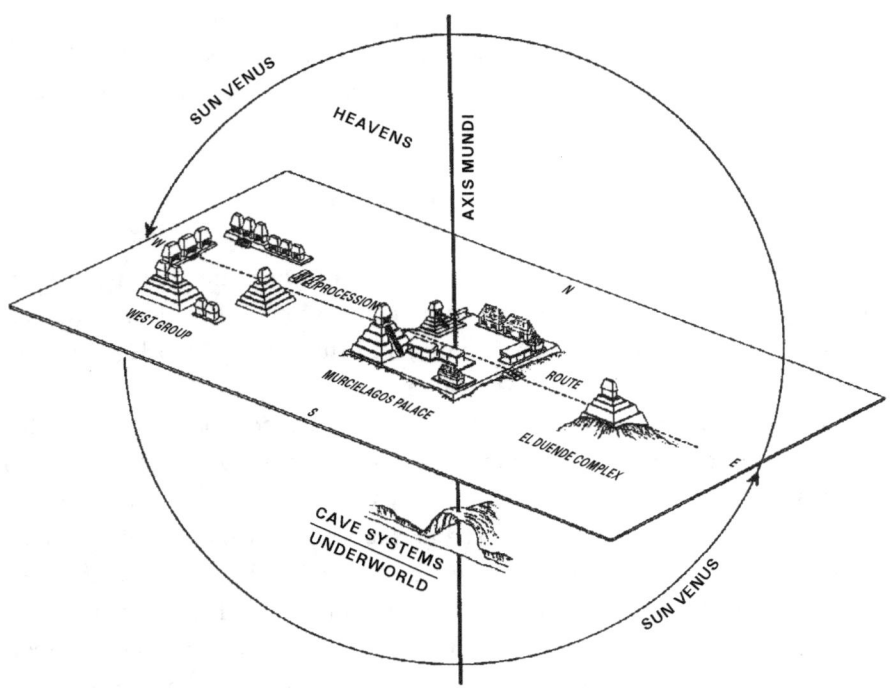

Figure 3.8 Schematic representation of Dos Pilas site, from Demarest et al. (2003). Used by courtesy of A. Demerest, Drawing by L. F. Luin.

Finally, we looked at Mayan religion, both traditional and Protestant. This is an extremely delicate area, especially since I, as a North American Protestant, carry my own ideology and my own understanding of Mam life and belief. What I've tried to do here is let people speak for themselves. The Maya are people of faith, as Annis alluded to in his quote at the end of section 3.3.2, the way to get their attention is to speak of God. The testimonies of Flavio, Victoriano, and Miguel weren't coerced or enhanced. In fact, it is a challenge to get the Maya to talk about things other than religion, since faith is such a basic part of their

3.5 Conclusion

lives. My extractions from the *Popol Vuh* are taken from the translations themselves, particularly Ximénez (1722) and Tedlock (1996). What I've tried to do is show pattern, especially in the continuity of cultural values from the past to the present. I (and thousands of Mam believers) see Evangelical Christianity not as a foreign imposition and disconnect with who they are as Maya, but rather as a response to the values that they hold most deeply and meaningfully, and that they hold on to most tenaciously. As Hendrickson (1995:197) says, "persistence and change are integrally related."

In the next chapter, we will refer to these three cultural matters—health, architectonics, and religion; but we will see them not from a historical perspective, but from the perspective of life lived from day to day and in the words used to explicate a life committed to centeredness.

4

Centeredness as Cultural Practice

4.1 Why ethnography?

Since the most powerful and persuasive evidence for claims about a group should come from an analysis of the daily life and interactions of members of the group rather than from an occasional ceremony (while not ignoring the ceremonies), an appropriate research tool should focus on the mundane aspects of life. This is what ethnography is, a privileging of the emic point of view concerning how locals understand their own lives, or, as Malinowski put it back when the anthropological world was young (and as I cited at the beginning of this study), trying "to grasp the native's point of view, his relation to life, to realize *his* vision of *his* world" (1922:25, emphasis in the original). In summary of the ethnographic method, Zaharlick says:

> Ethnographers establish social relationships with others in order to learn from them their ways of life. Through firsthand, long-term, participant observation, using themselves as research instruments and using an eclectic approach to data collection and analysis, ethnographers view human events in the larger contexts in which they naturally occur…. The knowledge and understandings gained through the ethnographic process are then presented

> in the form of an ethnographic report that describes in rich detail what it is like to be a member of that culture..... A good ethnography systematically describes the flow of behavior in a way that allows others to comprehend at an emotional level the events set before them and to understand the context motivating these events. (1992:121)

This emotional connection with the reader is a hallmark of good ethnography. And the fact that the connection is by means of the participation (whether competently or even incompetently) of the ethnographer in a new culture, helps to make these unknown people and their life ways come to make sense to us, even though our own cultural background is so different from theirs.

The idea that the ethnographer is a participant-observer sets up several professional dilemmas, two of which I mention here. First is the observer's paradox, the idea that the very presence of the observer skews the observed. As I mentioned earlier, this is sometimes called the thermometer effect, in that to measure the temperature of a liquid, one uses a thermometer, but the act of putting the thermometer into the liquid to measure it affects its temperature. Second, since the observer has her own agenda, point of view, history, ideology, and culture, what she "sees" is itself filtered through her own experience and is not objective. So, not only is reality affected by the ethnographer's presence, but the result of the research—the written ethnography of the reality observed—is skewed as per the ethnographer's agenda and ideology.[1]

The ethnographer's solution to these dilemmas is to embrace them. She participates as appropriate in the daily life of the community, while not denying nor ignoring that she is a member of a different culture and a native speaker of a different language, a person with her own personality and history. This gives rise to what Duranti calls "a certain playful element" (1997), where the ethnographer goes back and forth between her world—the one largely known to the reader—and the world new to

---

[1] Another dilemma is the ethnographer's acknowledgement of the idea of culture itself. Some modern writers (Said 1989, is a prime example) consider "culture" to be such an elitist, essentialist, stereotyping, and colonialist notion, that it is pointless to define it, to pursue it, or to trust any generalizations that might be made concerning it. These are important criticisms, but I assume, nonetheless, with Duranti (1997) and Wierzbicka (1997), that culture is a most helpful notion and that understanding human diversity is a wonderful, humanizing pursuit, as per ethnographic study as I've outlined it above. We have more to lose by ignoring culture than we do by studying and understanding it, even if incompletely. Beyond this, I won't defend the basic notion of culture here.

4.1 Why ethnography?

her. She performs this balancing act by attempting to make the strange familiar and the familiar strange, showing how customs that seem unusual are in fact manifestations of our common humanity (for example, the seemingly comic stacking of cans in a tiny basket, which is described later in this chapter), while at the same time, showing how something as routine as walking down the street can have layers of meaning far beyond what we would consider necessary to understand what is going on. The ethnographer includes herself—not just her scholarly opinions—and even acknowledges her own history to the reader in an attempt to "come clean" with her own background and viewpoints as they impinge upon the ethnographic task. In other words, there are multiple voices in good ethnography, not just those of the researched, nor of the researcher's "professional side," but of the researcher's personal side as well, thus, researcher as "subject." The reader of ethnography also speaks, as the ethnographer anticipates the questions and reactions of her readers and responds appropriately. This makes ethnography one of the most readable and accessible of all types of scholarly writing, since it builds on both the reader's understanding of his own culture as well as his motivation to learn about another.

This meshing of voices and this embracing of both the observer's paradox and the observer's filter is what Duranti points to when he says that "An ethnography is an interpretive act and as such should be turned on itself to increase the richness of descriptions, including an understanding of the conditions (personal or otherwise, WMC) under which the description itself becomes possible" (1997).

This is why good ethnography not only privileges multiple voices, but it also maintains several running dialogues at the same time. Along with the voice(s) "telling the story" is a meta-dialogue (an ethnography of the ethnography, or what Duranti calls the ethnography "turned on itself") where the researcher discusses the *process* of ethnography during the telling of the on-the-ground story of the actual ethnography. The attempt to juggle all this is to be enjoyed and affirmed, not dismissed. Good ethnography is a genre of its own, at once scholarly pursuit, linguistic treatise, cultural exposition, travelogue, true confession (within reason!), and readable non-fiction. The interplay and the cross discussion of voices is not tangential; it is the essence of good ethnographic writing.

4.2 Introduction to thick description

The following data are taken from three different occasions as detailed in my field notes. The purchase of boards and ensuing discussion took place over the weekend of September 23, 1989. The marriage proposal by Max's son-in-law occurred in December 1988, and the text by Pablo about marriage customs of long ago was recorded in March 1983. In chapter five I will analyze a short narrative text in order to pursue our topic of grammatical theme, but for now, information from Pablo's text will help us understand some of the precedent and situated meaning of present-day cultural practice related to gift giving and agreement protocol, both of which I claim are instantiations of the pursuit of centeredness. My three main sources—buying boards, an engagement ritual, and a text about decades-old (and perhaps centuries-old) marriage customs—may seem unrelated and far distant time-wise from each other, but there is a thread that runs through them all—one which I will make clear as we understand the events that unfold in the pages that follow and the meaning behind those events.

My goal in this section is to emulate the work of Geertz, particularly his delightful article on Balinese cockfights (1973). He begins with a cockfight, adds linguistic, cultural, and personal data (including puns, sarcasm, irony, and rich detail), continually expands his analysis, and ends up giving us an overview of Balinese culture that is meaning based (thick) and highly contextualized.[2] He claims that the Balinese cockfight is not really about gambling or the life and death of roosters, although these aspects are ever-present. Rather it is about prestige, what Geertz claims is the "central driving force in the society" (1973). In fact, he says that the influence of money and blood cause "the migration of the Balinese status hierarchy into the body of the cockfight" (ibid.). The cockfight is Balinese culture writ small, "a simulation of the social matrix, the involved system of cross-cutting, overlapping, highly corporate groups—villages, kin groups, irrigation societies, temple congregations, all are "castes"—in which its devotees live" (ibid.). The fight also serves as a release for people whose cultural norms require social restraint and coolheadedness on all occasions—except as passions flare both in and around the ring.

---

[2] Geertz borrows (and extends) the notions of thick and thin description from philosopher Gilbert Kyle 1971.

A similar study, although from a different perspective, is by A. L. Becker (1996 [1984]), where he begins with a brief linguistic analysis of a Burmese proverb, and subsequently layers his analysis with rich cultural context until, like Geertz, he gives us an overview of Burmese language-within-culture that rings true. Although Becker enters Burmese culture via a three-line proverb, what he learns about how the Burmese categorize the world, how they perceive all things in their relation to and distance from Buddhahood, and how they enjoy the aesthetic "feel" of their language all fall out from his translation of the proverb: *There are three kinds of mistakes: those resulting from lack of memory, from lack of planning ahead, or from misguided beliefs.*

The two men have different starting points—Geertz with culture, Becker with language—but their goal is the same: richly layered, "thick" description, that is, multiple layers of detailed observation that answers the question, What is it like to be a fully functioning member of this culture? In the writing of these two linguistic anthropologists, Duranti's idea of "a certain playful element" runs throughout, as both authors clearly enjoy the telling of their stories, and they discuss a number of tangential issues as they come up in order to remind us that their ethnographies are from a perspective which is at once personal, yet professional, and playful, yet profound. In fact, their enjoyment in the telling of their respective stories is part of the message that they are trying to get across—that the Balinese and Burmese are people like us, people who have feelings and ideas, friends and enemies, times of ceremony as well as daily grind, times of work and play, joy and fear. The fact that both men bring in so much personal (and what some might call irrelevant) material has a two-fold purpose. First, they want to lay to rest the idea that they would claim to be seen by their readers as disinterested bystanders. Rather, they are full participants, fully invested and fully interested. Second, by talking of their own responses and thoughts, they bring what seem to be strange customs into our own minds and living rooms, helping us to see some of the commonalities we share with people so seemingly different from us.

In their cultural participation, these ethnographers also serve as "instruments" through which they achieve cultural insight. It was Geertz's physical presence and his bodily participation in the events of the police break-up of the cockfight that not only endeared him to the locals and opened up their world to him, but that provided an opportunity for people to include him.

People mimicked and repeated in hilarious detail Geertz's flailing arms and terrified expression as he burst headlong from the illegal ring when the police arrived to close down the grisly business and arrest participants. It was his own clumsiness that provided the grounds or backdrop against which he saw the beauty of Balinese restraint and self-possession in the midst of chaos.

Similarly, it was Becker's speaking the language—even minimally—that opened up a cultural "space" for him to work and relate to locals. But when he began to write the language down and insist that how he did so was really not important, as long as it served him to recall vocabulary and pronounce things correctly, he met with strong opposition. He was surprised that his language tutor told him that Becker's writing system was "hurting the language," forcing it to operate in Becker's foreign style and not in its own natural way, not from left to right, nor right to left, but from the center of the word out, in like fashion to the careful peeling of an artichoke from periphery to its valuable core. Like it or not, the successful ethnographer participates in the local scene, body and soul. And one can never be quite sure when reality, like the tutor's opposition or the police raid on the cockfight, will strike, and embroil the researcher in things he had never considered before.

One of the motivating joys of cultural anthropology is portraying how distinct customs and unusual happenings that occur in other cultures are analogous to thoughts and actions that we experience every day in our own culture, albeit with different trappings. The phenomena that I describe below—a social faux pas, true forgiveness, power issues, a father-daughter relationship, and agreement rituals, among others—are issues that any individual can understand and empathize with, and with which virtually everyone has had to deal from time to time. That these issues are so human and so near to us, while at the same time their cross-cultural analogues are seemingly so foreign and opaque, is at once to recognize the fascination of both the universal nature as well as the particular instantiation of cultural themes. The fact is, however, that it isn't the behavior itself that is so transparent and shared across cultures; it is rather the interpretation of the behavior that is the expression of our common humanity. As Geertz so clearly points out (1973), the difference between a purposeful wink and a meaningless blink or twitch is not in performance, but in the interpretation of performance. The physical act (of winking or twitching) can be significant, but only within a meaningful context. Geertz decries those anthropologists who concentrate on "thin description," the radical behaviorists who, in our winking-twitching example, would not venture to interpret the act, but only to describe it, lest the act be misrepresented. Geertz claims that such uninterpreted events are simply the view that a camera would give us—flat, potentially interesting as art, yet contextless, and therefore meaningless (1973), and for that reason, not within the purview of interpretive anthropology.

4.3 Attaining *b'a'n*

When we lived in Comitancillo, I tried to maintain a fairly strict schedule, doing language-related work during the week, and saving home maintenance and personal projects for the weekend, if at all possible. I had wanted for some time to build a playhouse for our three children, and in late September 1989, the time was right. I cleared a spot in the back yard, and I headed off to look for some lumber. The last thirty years have been marked by a building spree in Comitancillo, much of it facilitated by dollars sent back to the village from people working in the States, as described in chapter two, so boards were not always easy to find, and one had to purchase what was available, without too much complaining about quality. Kiln-dried, planed, squared lumber of uniform thickness and width was (and continues to be) unheard of. Plus, with increased concern over soil erosion in the hinterlands, the Guatemalan government had instituted a system that requires special permission (and fees) to cut and transport boards. So the local need for lumber and its local availability don't normally coincide. With that in mind, when I heard that my friend Rafael had lumber for sale, I went to the market to talk to him. Although the main market days in Comitancillo are Sunday and Wednesday, Rafael maintains a large market stall seven days a week, selling eggs, vegetables, dried fish, chili peppers, and miscellaneous items.

He told me that he did indeed have boards (1 x 12s, more or less), approximately six feet long. I agreed to a price *(Ma tz'ok kymujb'in qyol* 'We paired up our words), and I paid for a dozen recently cut boards. Rafael informed me that the boards were drying in the patio of his home, but I could go there, inform his wife that I had paid him for the boards, and haul them away. My son, Isaac, who was five years old at the time, was with me as my *wuk'i'y* 'my companion'. We walked to Rafael's place, went through the open double gate of the site, and entered an open patio area around which the home compound was built—a sleep house or "family room" in one adobe construction, with a kitchen directly opposite it, about fifteen feet away across a courtyard of hard-packed earth. I whistled for Rafael's wife.[3] She came to the door suckling her youngest child whom she had slung on her back in a shawl, but who was twisted around her side and forward in order to nurse. Two other children, a boy and a girl, grabbed at the pleats of her floor-length skirt or "corte." The entrance to the family room was via "Dutch doors." The bottom half of the door remained shut, while she opened the top half and greeted me, lightly touching my fingertips with her own. Both of us bowed slightly, as I respectfully removed my hat.

Chin q'olb'i'n 'I greet you', I said. *B'a'n* 'It is good', she replied. I told her of my deal with her husband, and that I had come to pick up the boards. As soon as I saw her, I noticed that her left eye was red, swollen, and filled with pus. I very lightly touched her cheek, slightly pulling at the lower lid, and asked her what was wrong. *Jun yab'il ma tz'ok lemtzaj wi'ja* 'an illness has entered against me', she said. I reminded her that my wife, Nancy, had seen and successfully treated many people with pink eye, and that she should come by the clinic. (Recall that Nancy is a registered nurse and ran a small clinic from the patio of our home.) She thanked me and showed me where the boards were—around the side of the house, leaning against a whitewashed adobe wall to dry. I told her that I could only carry a few of the boards at a time, since they were wet and heavy, but I would take some home and come right back for another load.

---

[3] Early in our time in Comitancillo, I was told that whistling is the greeting of choice when approaching a house (particularly a rural house), since people can normally identify a visitor by his or her whistle. Thieves commonly go to the door and make noise and/or knock in order to listen for movement inside the house. That way they can stay anonymous and simply move along if anyone happens to be home.

4.3 Attaining b'a'n

Figure 4.1. Man carrying a load by means of a tumpline.
Drawn by Don Hubacher. Used with permission.

Isaac and I stacked four boards on a table and I drew a tumpline around them and I backed up to the table like a semi-trailer to a loading dock. I balanced the boards on the small of my back, while leaning forward and adjusting the tumpline around my forehead (figure 4.1). The boards were heavy; their rough-cut edges dug into my back. I thought back to a trip I had made almost twenty years earlier to rural Haiti, where a tour guide at a cotton mill told us that specially trained men backed up to docks where they were loaded down with cotton bales weighing 550 pounds each. The bales were then moved around the factory on the backs of these strong men—as if by forklift—for processing. Although my load certainly weighed less than one sixth of those professional haulers' loads, I envied their soft cotton cargo and their special training. I mused to Isaac that much of the harvest of the world is not carried by trucks and forklifts and dollies from place to place, but on the backs and heads of rural men and women as they move thousands of tons of merchandise, firewood, and water a little at a time, from place to place. Lost in my thoughts, albeit philosophically enriched, I made it home with a somewhat battered back and with neck muscles straining from the act of balancing the boards via the taut line extending from the load on my back to my unaccustomed forehead. I nursed a few raw spots on my back, and returned with Isaac twenty minutes later with some extra padding for the next load.

I was surprised to find that the homestead was closed up, with a lock on the outside of the door. Clearly no one was home. I was worried that someone might have seen me hauling the boards and, surmising the source, might have outbid me for the remaining boards, but I knew Rafael, and I was confident that he'd honor our agreement. After all, we "paired up" our words (*Ma tz'ok kymujb'in qyol*), which is one of the ways the Mam say that they have come to common accord regarding a transaction. They also say, *Ma tz'ok qmujb'in qib ti'j jun ti'* 'we have paired ourselves in regard to something'. The idea is one of compromise, chipping away at disagreement until the two "words" or points of view pair up and people meet in the middle. The Mam often gesture this concept laying their index fingers together lengthwise about a foot from their chests, right in the centerline of their bodies.

This "pairing of words" or "pairing of selves" notion is iconic to Mayan dualism, the idea that reality is conceived not just as an underlying unity, but as a balance of oppositions, just as an agreement among the Mam is not conceived as the imposition of one party's will on the other, but a consensus notion of two sides coming together into a common middle ground. They will *kymujb'in kyajb'il* 'pair up their wills' or *kymujb'in kynab'l* 'pair up their minds'.

As I mentioned in the last chapter, Neuenswander (1986) analyzes the use of couplets in Maya-Achí religious discourse as a linguistic reflection of conceptual couplets, that certain aspects of life "consist obligatorily not as one, but as two irreducible elements" (1986, translation from Spanish, WMC). As we've seen, she discusses how the ancestors are addressed as 'our long ago mothers, our long ago fathers'; the universe is conceived of as 'the earth and heavens'; the world as 'the mountains and valleys'. This follows a number of dualistic notions and formal addresses mentioned throughout the *Popol Vuh,* which we looked at in chapter three, section 3.4.1. Morley as well says that "the Maya religion had a strong dualistic tendency" (1956). This resonates with comments by Gossen and Martin in chapters one and three about the thematicity of dualism in Mayan culture.

Several publications by my SIL colleagues in Guatemala have been especially helpful to me in looking at the linguistic corollaries of the cultural theme of

4.3 Attaining b'a'n

centeredness and balance. Neuenswander (1986) discusses dualism in Maya-Achí discourse as further evidence of the importance of balance in Mayan life. She claims that the use of couplets is pervasive in Achí discourse related to religion and prayer as well as in the discourse of other ceremonies and rites. For example, the following discourse was offered as a religious/didactic explanation as to why it is important to offer sacrifices to *dios mundo* 'the world god'. She says the text is "a reminder that one's offerings provide sustenance for the world, thus fulfilling the contract that, in return, charges the world to keep vigil in like manner over those who have made the sacrifice" (1986, translation from Spanish, WMC). This is, of course, reminiscent of Edmonson's and Nájera's claim discussed in chapter three that Mayan religion is based on reciprocity, a cosmic agreement and meeting in the middle of give and take.

> Thus they speak,
> Our grandmothers,
> Our grandfathers:
> Due to the World alone we have our money.
> Due to the World alone we have our coins.
> Due to the World alone we have our food.
> Due to the World alone we have our drink, it is said.
> Because the World feeds us;
> It gives us what we eat, it is said.
> It feeds our cows.
> It feeds our horses.
> It feeds our chickens.
> It feeds our pigs, it is said.
> In this way, the World feeds us,
> It gives us what we eat.
> Here we are in the world, here where we are born,
> Here where we blossom,
> Here where we die,
> Here where we disappear.
> It is thus, that since we are of the World, the World feeds us.
> We also feed the world.
> Thus they say our long-ago mothers of all,
> The long-ago fathers of all, it is said.
>   (from Neuenswander 1986:3, translation from Spanish, WMC)

Neuenswander's point in discussing couplets is both linguistic and cultural. She says that since language "is an aspect of culture, it should reveal certain premises upon which cultural behavior rests" (translation from Spanish, WMC). So we see that Neuenswander affirms the notion espoused by our list of linguistic-anthropological heavy hitters from section 1.2.1. Her claim is that the pervasive use of couplets in rhetorical and religious discourse is iconic to the "strong tendency toward dualism" in Maya-Achí culture. She says that the two parts of the couplet are utilized to instantiate and emphasize a single concept, be it our ancestors, our prosperity, our animals, our lives, or our passing from this world—a unity of meaning out of a dualistic diversity.

It may be more difficult to coerce the notion of centeredness out of Mayan couplets than it has been to see it in the cultural instantiations I've mentioned in the Mam lexicon, and in the formal deictic notions of Mam grammar. Nevertheless, Gossen's notion of dualism as a Mesoamerican theme (1986) includes a sense of balance, wholeness, harmony, and equilibrium, all of which I claim are attributes of centeredness, and which I develop in some detail in chapter three and here in chapter four.

In this light, I consider dualism to be a single notion manifest in two, an abstract sense of balance and the center around which balance is situated. The men and women who in Gossen's account represent the push ahead/pull back of culture change and cultural continuity among the Maya also represent an underlying single culture expressed in a common language and a unified worldview.

Townsend (1980) also discusses the linguistic aspects of couplets while making no claims about their cultural significance. He does, however, support the notion that the focus of couplets is on a single issue and meaning. For example, he cites the words of a Maya-Ixil (Ixil is a Mamean language) *iq'on b'e* 'carrier of the road (a petitioning shaman)' who represents the prospective groom and his family's interests in a ceremony meant to secure a bride. In the portion below, taken from a much longer text, the 'lord' is the girl's father. The shaman comes at dusk to talk to him about the availability of his daughter, 'the quetzal bird, the flower'; terms used here to emphasize the bride's unspoiled beauty and desirability. The girl's mother answers the shaman's call at the homestead entryway, and he says to her:

4.3 Attaining b'a'n

> I have come to waken him a bit
> I have come to rouse him a bit
> Lord of the land
> Lord of the dust.
> You, cradle of life,
>> we have come to wake you;
>> we have come to rouse you;
>>> that about the quetzal bird,
>>> about the flower.
> Not just about anything we have come here to awaken you;
> Not just about anything we have come here to rouse you.
>> (Townsend 1980)

Townsend (1980) says that Maya-Ixil ethnopoetics and ritual rhetoric "depends heavily on a correspondence of semantically similar units (what he calls a rhyming of meaning, WMC)," which is "most evident in parallelisms such as couplets (idem)." He claims that every adult Ixil can employ this discourse style to a greater or lesser degree as the situation arises. In private communication, Townsend agrees that the Ixil consider couplets to be a way to "tell the whole story." In other words, the first line of a couplet seeks a sense of completion in the second. I suggest that Townsend's additional data coincide with Neuenswander's and that the parallel nature of Mayan rhetorical couplets is indeed iconic to the notion of dualism as a cultural principle, one which has been well established (as per Gossen and also Martin in chapter three above) in the Mayanist linguistic-anthropological literature.

This notion of dualism points to the idea of equilibrium: of respect and recognition of two sides of an issue, two points of view in an argument, or two people coming together in agreement. It hearkens to the underlying belief, as Neuenswander suggests, that life can't be reduced to a single concept but is rather a balance of mutually implying ones. The Maya themselves are well aware of the centrality of this notion. Not only do the Mayan masses live it from day to day, but Maya scholars and intellectuals discuss it as well. As I mentioned in the last chapter, in the publication of conclusions and recommendations from the *Primer Congreso de Educación Maya en Guatemala* (Curruchiche Otzoy et al. 1994), the following themes are proposed (among others) as basic to an education that respects Maya world view: unity out of diversity; complementarity (that ideas are not simple in nature, but complex, as per Neuenswander's discussion of couplets); cooperation; duality and the importance of the notion of "fourness"; and the philosophical search for centrality and equilibrium (1994, parenthetical comment and translation from Spanish, WMC). I believe that all of these notions can be derived from a basic understanding of centeredness.

So, in my dealings with Rafael, our "pairing of words" not only fit the social need of the moment—an agreement—but the idea fit a cultural template as well, the concept of an agreement as a symmetry of interests, in this case, a seller's and a buyer's, as well as a compromise, a meeting in the middle—the common ground—on price.

As I pondered my situation, Isaac and I made our way back home, passing Rafael's brother's house. His children were playing in the street and when they saw me, they chanted in Mam, "Wes has got mud on his shoes; Wes has got mud on his shoes." I looked at my shoes and they were no dirtier than usual, certainly not muddy. I had no idea what the kids were talking about.

For the rest of that evening, I continued to think about the hastily locked door and the children's chants, and I concluded that I had most likely offended Rafael's wife, probably by my uninvited touch of her cheek. The fact that the kids were joking about my mud-stained shoes probably meant that Rafael's wife was passing the news of my apparent indiscretion around town. If her nephews and nieces knew of my escapade just minutes after it happened, who else knew, I wondered. I felt that I was clearly innocent of wrongdoing. After all, my wife ran a village clinic; she had seen and palpated body parts far more intimate than a woman's cheek—and my innocent touch was through a Dutch door, no less. Did none of Nancy's license extend to me, her beloved husband? Besides, in careful Mayan fashion, Isaac was along as my companion, and the offended woman was surrounded by her own children, as is culturally appropriate for her moral protection. How could I be realistically accused of anything untoward?

The next day, Sunday, was market day. I discussed my various issues with Julian, an area pastor. He concluded that the alleged mud on my shoes could well have been either what he called "physical" or "spiritual." He suggested that I go to Rafael and simply tell him what happened.

As I thought about talking to an offended husband, I considered the many times Mam men had come to me to request a favor, to seek an opinion, to ask a question, or to pose a deal of some kind, one often involving my

4.3 Attaining b'a'n

money or vehicle. Invariably, these men would bring some kind of gift—a live chicken, turkey, or duck, a dozen peaches or apples, a squash, or at the very least, a can of juice or a Coke from a nearby *tienda* 'store'. Gift giving in relation to an agreement of some kind seemed to be very much a cultural practice. I used to think of these gifts as attempted bribes, that people were trying to buy a favor, but with time, I began to see them more as gifts, a way of somehow leveling the playing field—"you do something for me, and I reciprocate in kind," a common Mayan, if not universally human sentiment. A bribe reeks of indiscretion; a gift is the recognition of something mutual and shared, a friendship that has some history.

There are a number of ways that the Mam talk about an agreement. Commonly, they will say *ma tz'ok kymujb'in qyol* or *ma tz'ok meje qyol* 'our words are paired up, or *ma tz'ok qmub'in qib'* 'we have paired ourselves' ('we've entered into an agreement'), as discussed above. They will also say, *ma qo kyij toj b'a'n* or *ma qo kyij toj wen* 'we have situated ourselves in goodness'. The first two phrases, the pairing of words or selves, is more common in terms of agreeing to a commitment of some kind; the second two phrases more likely imply agreement to a plan of action. They also say *junx qnab'l* 'our minds are together', or 'a meeting of the minds'.

I learned of the importance of agreement rituals almost a year earlier. My friend Max told me he couldn't accompany me to San Marcos (a nearby town) the following Monday as we had planned. There was a special event going on at his house, and he needed to be there. In fact, he said that I would probably appreciate it as well, so he invited me to join him and his family. I inquired further and he told me that a young man was coming to ask him for the hand of his oldest daughter, Alba, in marriage. Since this asking for a daughter's hand is a longstanding custom among the Mam, Max thought that I'd be interested in being there, which, of course, I was.

He invited me to join his family for lunch. They expected the young man, Samuel, and his family to arrive around 2:00 p.m.

On Monday, after a leisurely lunch of *caldo*, a thin stew, and tortillas, we chatted and waited for Samuel. Two o'clock came and went, then three o'clock, then 3:30. Max's family looked concerned. They perhaps wondered if there had been a change in plans. Maybe, on further reflection, Samuel or his family had changed their minds. Earlier, Max had explained to me that Alba had had a son from a past affair. He said that she had strayed from the mark (*Ma txalpaj toj tchwinqil* 'she strayed [from the correct, straight, centered path] in her life'). He confessed that it would be hard for her to find a good man to marry because of her indiscretion, even though she had returned to the faith of her parents and was presently living *toj b'a'n* 'in goodness'. It was very important to Max to settle his daughter into a marriage *toj b'a'n*, or *ttxolil* 'lined up in orderly fashion', or *tuk'a tumil* 'with direction or correctness, straight', with a believing husband.[4]

McArthur (1979:7) says of *b'a'n* (the alternate term *wen* is a borrowing of Spanish *bueno* 'good') that in Awakatek (a Mamean language) it designates "good, good fortune... health, happiness, physical well-being, long life, food, clothing, and any other daily needs." Beach (1994) concurs. In his study of Tektitek (a Mamean language considered by some to be a dialect of Mam) he says that *b'a'n* is a state of goodness, balance, equilibrium, joy, peace—one's main goal in life. Townsend, in a personal communication, agrees. He adds that *b'a'n* is a condition of peaceful relations with everyone, often maintained by disengaging from a person with whom one has strong disagreements in order not to imbalance the relationship.

When asked about someone, the Mam often state that a person is, as Max stated just above, *b'a'n* 'good' or *toj b'a'n* 'in goodness', that is, inhabiting the metaphysical space of goodness, in the center of rightness, harmony, tranquility, and serenity. It is to be in that state of harmony, equilibrium, and correctness that Max so wanted for his daughter, since it would affect not only her, but his own peace of mind and his sense of rightness and satisfaction as a responsible father as well. But at this point, well over an hour and a half late, it looked like the potential husband or the potential husband's family might have changed their minds. After all, Alba had some baggage.

Max's family was anxious; Alba's siblings began to whisper furtively and apprehensively, and I began to feel fidgety, as if I were witness to a well conceived plan of action that had somehow gone sadly awry. Alba's own moral shortcomings—albeit unspoken— were rising to the surface. Why else would the family not show up? And to make matters worse, I was there as well, invited, yet now unwanted, as one whose presence was intensifying and drawing attention to a family's disappointment in this melancholy turn of events. Why did I have to be there with a clipboard taking notes? Why should a family's pain be documented in such a cold academic manner? Maybe the day that started with such promise, would end in a place other

---

[4] Max and other Evangelical Christians consider the term *nimil* 'believer', to apply only to Protestant Christians.

4.3 Attaining b'a'n

than *toj b'a'n*. And the gringo whose presence was meant to add prestige to the occasion was instead adding to the sad reality of hope unfulfilled in the larger, crueler world.

But as 4:00 approached, and as we all brooded in unease, almost two hours late, Alba's younger sister called out, *Lu lo* 'here he is'.

Max, visibly relieved, welcomed the contingent, which included Samuel, his parents, and paternal grandparents, a cousin, a sister, a brother, and an uncle. Along with Max and Alba were Alba's two brothers, her young son, her younger sister, her mother, her maternal grandfather, and me, an obvious intruder, clipboard in hand. Max told the visitors that I was a family friend, and he assured them that I could be trusted, *tu'n tqe kyk'u'ja ti'j* 'your stomachs can sit regarding him'. In other words, "you needn't be jittery or concerned about him, he's ok."

This was a compliment.

Shortly after lunch, several hours earlier, Max had combed his hair and donned a somewhat threadbare suit jacket. Despite the second-hand clothing, he looked noble, as only the Maya can. I felt conspicuously underdressed in blue jeans and a lightweight windbreaker, which I wore against the highland cold. As we entered the sleep house and arranged ourselves, sitting on beds (there were four in the room, one in each corner of the little sleep house) and chairs brought in especially for the event, the women in their colorful *huipiles* 'hand-woven blouses' stood out in the dim interior. There was a single small window, but it was closed and bolted against the wind and cold. The day was gray and cloudy and the sun was low in the late afternoon sky; the sun sets early in the high mountain ranges. The only light was from the open door. The women all wore ankle length, dark blue skirts and the men wore earth tones either by design or from the stain of dirt and sweat and smoke. Max, wearing his navy blue blazer, brought an air of dignity to the scene.

Max's visage changed from one of concerned nervousness just a minute before his future in-laws' arrival to one of formal command.

After some routine small talk about the corn and the weather, Max said, "You've come."

"Yes, we've come," was their reply. "We've come about the situation."

"What situation is that?" replied Max, as if he hadn't been contemplating this very situation for hours that day and for weeks leading up to that very moment.

Samuel's uncle, not wanting to state the family business too directly (and thereby disproportionately) said, "You know, that situation we discussed several days ago."

He had come by earlier in the week to tell Max of their planned visit and to make sure that Max and his family would be at home when they arrived. It was on the basis of this prior visit that Max had invited me to the event.

Max, on the other hand, wanted the supplicant family to be straightforward with their request. This would give him a position of power, not as the weaker entreating party, but as the one being entreated, the one who could grant their supplication, or deny it. "We discussed a number of issues several days ago," he reminded them. "Which one do you mean?"

After a little hemming and hawing, Samuel's uncle gave in, "The situation about our son marrying your daughter."

"Oh, *that* situation," said Max, as if taken by a supreme sense of surprise.

This sense of indirection is very widespread in Mam dealings. On a number of occasions people have stopped by to talk to me (bringing the requisite bottle of Coca Cola or a chicken or squash), and saying something like, "Tomorrow I will stop by and ask you if I can borrow twenty dollars. I'm not going to ask you now, so don't say anything one way or the other. I'll be back tomorrow." Then the following day, they would duly appear (with another Coke or chicken or squash—perhaps for continuity) and say, "I've come about the situation I discussed with you yesterday." This sense of decorum, of unease over being blatant, is part of the Mam commitment to moderation. It is a politeness strategy (Brown and Levinson 1987), a strategy not to be overt and direct in the face of an interlocutor, of not being overbearing or overly demanding, but respectful and deferential. The Coke also prolongs the transaction as interlocutors tarry over sips and business; it's harder to say 'no' while lingering long over a Coke.

This indirection was Samuel's family's cultural *modus operandi,* but Max wanted them to be forthright. He would brook no miscommunication or waffling of motives, nor any challenge to his leadership in the event at hand. He was, after all, the father of the bride. It was his blessing that the entreating family sought. After clearly stating their intentions, Max launched into a mini-lecture about the difficulties of this day and age, and how much a family needs to stay together, how hard it would be for his own wife if Alba, who was an extremely hard worker, were to leave, what a task it would be to raise Alba's son in her absence, etc. Samuel was willing to

4.3 Attaining b'a'n

marry Alba, but he refused to raise her son in their shared home, since this would potentially jeopardize the inheritance he would pass on to his and Alba's future children, an inheritance that would be diluted by the presence of an additional stepson. Max and his wife, although near fifty years old at the time, agreed to raise the boy so that Alba could get a fresh start. (By the way, the boy, now an adult, is doing well.)

With Max's protestations I was almost convinced that he had changed his mind about the marriage. I was in a Mayan home but I was thinking of Shakespeare's famous one-liner "Methinks thou dost protest too much."

"Come on, Max," I was thinking. "Cork it!"

He concluded with these words, "I had considered not sanctioning this marriage, but then I thought, 'What if this is the will of God?'"

Here, Samuel's uncle was quick to pick up his opportunity. It was important for Max not to be too pushy—all things in moderation—but neither did he want to leave the impression that this potential marriage was a non-starter; nor did he want to appear to be "unloading" Alba to any suitor who would take her. He needed some room to maneuver—to agree to the marriage on the one hand without seeming to give his daughter up with no demands or concerns on the other. Despite her indiscretion, Alba was much loved and cherished by her parents. Her father's performance here would become a precious memory for her.

"Exactly," said Samuel's uncle, not failing to respond to Max's slightest of openings. "If this is the will of God, who are we to stand in the way?"

There ensued a short time of affirmation that no one in either of the two families wanted to do anything outside of what God's will was for the couple.

Samuel's grandmother then joined the discussion, somewhat impatient with the theological opining. "They are the ones who will be living together, what do they have to say?" The gathered women all agreed with the wisdom of the suggestion. "Yes, what do they have to say?"

As we all looked at the two young people (who were sitting in separate corners of the room, avoiding each other's secretive glances), first Samuel and then Alba, each agreed that they wanted to be married.

There seemed to me at this point in the whole transaction to be a collective sense of relief on everyone's face and in everyone's posture, as if the heavy lifting were over with. What remained were several important, yet secondary, issues to be resolved. First was a wedding date. Samuel wanted to marry within a month. Max thought this was unrealistic, as Alba's child had not yet been weaned. Plus, it would take his wife some time to acclimate to a home with a young boy without her daughter to help with him or with the extra work occasioned by his presence. Max suggested eight months. He knew that they wouldn't agree to this, but he stated an outside limit in order to be able to move toward the center and the eventual pairing of words *(tu'n kymujb'in kyyol)*, or the 'togetherness or unity of minds' phrases *(junx kynab'l* or *junx kyajb'il* 'unity of wills'), which indicate a coming together and harmonizing of different motives and desires. After about ten minutes of haggling and posturing, they agreed to a late April wedding, four months from the day of discussion. Another, albeit unconfessed reason to postpone the wedding for as long as he could (from Max's point of view), was that during the engagement period, Samuel would be expected to work for Max, visiting his fiancée daily in her parents' home, all the while cutting firewood, helping with fieldwork and taking part in any needed construction projects or other chores. These daily visits are a type of dowry, where the future son-in-law works hard for his future in-laws, not only gaining a wife, but showing his future family how hard a worker he is, thus helping to convince them to see that they had made a good decision in offering her hand to one such as Samuel. After the marriage, Alba's labor would largely be lost to her own family, since she would go to live with her husband's family until the time that Samuel could afford to build his own house separate from, yet near, his own parents' home.

The second issue to be resolved had to do with the marriage ceremony itself. Samuel's father admitted that they were not wealthy people and, although Alba certainly was worthy of the new clothes befitting a lovely bride, they could not afford the money required to purchase all new clothing for her, much less for themselves. Max said that he understood, and that they as well were not wealthy people. The families would just dress cleanly and neatly, with no special purchases,[5] although Max insisted on both a municipal as well as a church wedding, since he expected things to be done *tuk'a nuk'b'il* 'with order', and *toj tumil* 'with direction, in rightness'. He did not want the couple to simply begin living together, which continues to be how many Mam couples marry.[6]

---

[5] Today (2015), new clothing for a Mam woman can cost upwards of $250, a tidy sum when the average rural worker's wage is around $5 a day. These rural workers aren't the ones providing new and lavish clothing for their brides.

[6] A municipal wedding is binding by law and is more difficult to break than a common-law marriage. Subsequently, a municipal wedding gives rights to the woman in case of divorce

4.3 Attaining b'a'n

I saw this first hand on one occasion. I was invited to give a few words of encouragement to a couple getting married in a hamlet a good distance from the municipal seat where we lived. I was expecting to give a short homily on married life for the gathered celebrants. There were lots of family members present from babies through great-grandparents. What I didn't realize was that the couple was not twenty-something and starry-eyed. Rather, the two getting married were the great-grandparents. After living together by common law for over fifty years, they wanted to be baptized, and the local church wouldn't let them unless they abandoned years of shacking up for a formal marriage.

The word *nuk'b'il* 'order' is an interesting one. The verb form *nik'ul* means 'to put in order or to arrange'. It can also mean 'to explain carefully and fully, to orient someone to all relevant details, to clarify', as a judge or lawyer laying out the details of the law in a legal decision, or a teacher marshalling her facts to prove a point. In fact, the term is commonly used in legal and educational contexts. It is often used not in a physical ordering (*txolil* 'to line up, to put in order' is more common in this sense), but in terms of a moral ordering of things, putting one's life in order. A father will tell his child that she needs *tu'n t-xi tnik'u'n tey tze'n tu'n tb'etiy toj tumil* 'to organize/order yourself so that you walk with direction'. This implies that one must stay on the path of a well-lived life, and not veer from the moral center. In fact, the goal of the father's advice here is that a child can live a balanced and centered life *nik'u'nxix wen* 'very well ordered' and *toj b'a'n*, 'in goodness'. The noun form *(nuk'b'il)* extends to the notion of peace and order where things are as they should be: correctly structured, balanced, in order, safe, calm, and without rancor.

With the two issues of date and attire resolved, the agreement proper was complete. The words and families had been paired; the families' interests had been brought into harmony; people were *toj b'a'n* with the results of the discussion. Things were in order, *toj tumil* or *tuk'a tumil*. *Toj tumil* literally means 'in its direction', but it also carries the force of 'manner or way, counsel, teaching, to be correct'. It is also often used as 'the course of one's life', whether good or bad, although unmodified, it implies something good or positive. To walk *tuk'a tumil* 'with direction'

---

which are more likely to be enforced than if the marriage is just by common-law practice. A legally sanctioned wedding is also required by the Evangelical churches for baptism and for full membership status in the local congregation.

or *toj tumil* is commendable. To teach *tuk'a tumil* means to teach correctly and truthfully. If something is characterized as *nti' tumil* 'without direction', it means that it is incorrect or doesn't make sense, or that his course of action will have a negative and hurtful outcome. A Mam father told me that in instructing his children he encourages them with these words: *Il ti'j tu'n kyb'eta toj tumilxix* 'it is needful that you walk with extreme direction', or, *Il ti'j tu'n kyb'eta jikyinxix* 'you must walk very straight (not veering off center to one side or the other)'. He says that this means that they should seek the center of the path of life and not turn aside in either direction.

The word *t-xilin* 'its essence', also has a sense of centeredness or "core" about it. In most instances it means 'essence', such as in the phrase *Ti'tzin t-xilin tyol?* 'What was the essence of his words?' or 'What did he say in a nutshell?' They use the word also to express the essence of what someone knows, thinks, believes, wants, teaches, or learns. It can also stand for the meaning of a symbol or allegory or of a word (for example, *ajo t-xilin yol nuk'b'il* 'the meaning of the word *nuk'b'il*'). It can also be the basic personality or character of a person. Whereas *tumil* encodes the moral direction of a person's actions, *t-xilin* codes his or her core ideas, his or her depth or personality.

Now that the agreement had been reached, Samuel's uncle lowered a large net bag from his shoulder from which he produced a number of small, six-ounce cans of fruit juice. He beamed broadly as he began to pile them into a small basket on the table in front of him. As he piled the cans high, they began to topple and fall onto the dirt floor of the sleep house. He picked up the cans and smiled grandly while continuing to pile others still higher into the basket. This proved to be a futile exercise, since the cans continued to fall on the floor. He then took the basket around the room once and then twice, offering juice to each one of us in the room. Afterwards, he took out handfuls of small hard candies, again piling them into what I thought was a comically tiny basket. Once again, the candies fell to the floor amidst the smiles and joyful enthusiasm of Samuel's family. When he came to me, he said, "*Tzyunxa*[7] 'grab one'. *Q'inxa kab'a* 'take two'. *At nim* 'there are plenty' Take *three!*"

---

[7] This is the same verb, *tzyul* 'to touch, to grab'. that got me embroiled in an awkward situation in the first place. Although it can mean 'to touch', here it implies 'to appropriate, to enjoy', clearly meanings that I didn't have in mind when I lightly touched *(xi ntzyu'n)* Rafael's wife's cheek.

4.3 Attaining b'a'n

My first thought was to go find some larger containers that could adequately hold the items to be shared. Fortunately, I just watched and took notes, obeying the sage and enduring anthropological axiom to just shut up and pay attention. Later, when I asked others about the juice and candy, their reply was that it was merely a gesture to show that there were ample resources to take care of the new bride; or as Max said simply to me, "There is sufficient," the idea being, "Don't worry about your young daughter, we have all we need at our disposal to be able to care for her and provide for her just as her own family would." The deeply touching part of this gesture is that neither family was particularly wealthy. Recall that the immediately previous discussion was about how neither family could afford to dress "lavishly" for the wedding and buy new clothes. In fact the word for 'rich' that they used, *q'ininx*, specifies that wealth is 'out there, beyond them, far away' (the final *x* suffix is a directional particle meaning 'away from where the speaker is' and is discussed at some length in chapter five). The receiving of the humble gifts from Samuel's family was an important part of this ritual. Not only did it show in metaphor that Max's daughter would be well provided for—something on the mind of any caring parent—but by receiving the gifts, Max's family was accepting the proposal. Mayan marriage isn't simply the union of two individuals, but of two families as well. The gifts given and received showed that an agreement had been reached, that words had been paired, stomachs satisfied (for more on stomach terms, see table 4.1 and discussion immediately following). The reciprocal nature of the event was served. A new harmony was established, cultural equilibrium maintained, centeredness achieved, the pressure of tradition assuaged.

After receiving these gifts, to break the agreement by backing out of the engagement would be considered a serious offense. Normally, a father, concerned for his daughter's honor, won't let a boy even talk to her unless he expresses the intention to marry her. Although sexual relations during engagement are frowned upon, it is not uncommon practice. As one friend said to me, "During engagement, one can, but shouldn't, have sex." Another friend, Justino, once agreed to a marriage, cementing it with the giving of gifts just as Samuel's family had done, but after spending time getting to know his fiancée, he decided that they weren't all that compatible after all. This seems prudent and wise to us in the West where we have such open dating customs. But it seemed anything but reasonable to Justino's fiancée's family. When the engagement was broken (even though they hadn't slept together), he was put on church discipline for two years for defrauding the girl and her family. After all, an agreement had been made. Gifts had been given and received. The families and the couple had been *toj b'a'n*. Things were as they should be: correct, harmonious, right, centered. Tradition was respected. Life was in order—only to be derailed by one who refused to honor his word.

The engagement gifts hearken back to a text offered by Pablo early in our time in Comitancillo. Pablo was sixty-two years old at the time of the recording in March 1983. He has always enjoyed talking about the good old days. A Mam co-worker of mine, Gilberto, was doing research for a booklet he was preparing on Mam traditions, when he asked Pablo to tell him about marriage customs back when Pablo was young.

The recording lasts over 30 minutes as Pablo explains to Gilberto how a boy would go about convincing a girl's family (*tu'n tkub' kyk'u'j* 'to lower their stomachs') that he was worthy of her hand. I learned early on in my time in Comitancillo that terms related to the stomach are pervasive and that they often deal with strong emotions (see table 4.1). Although many of these phrases I elicited based on Scotchmer's (1978) discussion of *-k'u'j* terms in Southern Mam (a variant centered around the town of San Juan Ostuncalco; see Godfrey and Collins 1987 for further discussion of differences between Southern and Central Mam), each of these is part of the daily lexicon of Comitecos. Some terms from Scotchmer's study are not used in Comitancillo, and some that I list here are not attested in Scotchmer's data. There are many other phrases that contain the stem for 'stomach' *-k'u'j*, such as *twi' tk'u'j* 'the head of his stomach—his wages', *tk'u'j chemj* 'the weaving's stomach—weaving sticks', *ch'in tk'u'j* 'to have a small stomach—to be touchy or uncaring'. Suffice it to say, the term for stomach has broad semantic reach, stretching its literal, basic meaning of a body part to encompass such concepts as love and commitment, hate and death. As Scotchmer says, "-*k'u'j* comprises one of the most semantically productive and culturally essential lexemes in the Mam language. Body part it is, and yet is it any wonder that the Mam (and the Maya) chose that which is central to him physically to extend semantically to include a much greater universe than his own belly?" (1978: 30). He goes on to say, "I would suggest that *-k'u'j* 'stomach' really is best translated 'the stomach-heart', or 'the core of the person including his physical and psychological needs'."

4.3 Attaining b'a'n

The term, -*k'u'j*, then, is a clear example of what Wierzbicka (1997) calls a *key word*, a term which is "important and revealing in a given culture." She says that these words are culturally elaborated, that is, they occur in many contexts, and they must be defined in relation to cultural notions, not simply in terms of what they literally mean. They also occur frequently in daily discourse, particularly in certain semantic domains, although our -*k'u'j* terms cut across many such domains. But her main criterion for determining the terms' status as key words is whether or not we "are able to say something significant and revealing about the culture by undertaking an in-depth study of them" (ibid.). Think back to Wierzbicka's comments about Americans' sense of equality and the linguistic gyrations we go through in order to not use the imperative. These grammatical constructions, according to Wierzbicka, say something important about American culture. I suggest, then, as per Scotchmer's definition, that -*k'u'j* terms are indeed iconic of the notion of the cultural relevance of centeredness in daily life. Even a cursory study of verb phrases in which -*k'u'j* terms appear shows the strong sense of emotion and physical groundedness of such phrases, as well as, assumedly, the importance of the metaphor behind such emotions. The stomach for the Mam, like the heart for English speakers, is never far from consciousness, as evidenced in a number of lexical items in English such as *hearty, heartbroken, heartsick, soft-hearted, cold-hearted, warm-hearted, hard-hearted, wholehearted, disheartened, heartache, heartfelt,* and even terrifying terms like *heart-stopping, heart attack,* and *heart failure.* The Mam love, not with all their hearts, but with all their stomachs, which implies what "with all our hearts" does for us: fully, passionately, and all-encompassingly, with all our being and strength. Wierzbicka adds, "By exploring these focal points in depth we may be able to show the general organizing principles which lend structure and coherence to a cultural domain as a whole, and which often have an explanatory power extending across a number of domains" (ibid.).

There are two other terms the Mam use to denote a sense of center. *Niky'jin* means 'half or middle'. They use it to denote the middle of a lake or river, or something that is halfway up the side of a mountain. *Niky'jin q'ij* means 'noon, middle of the day', while *niky'jin aq'b'il* means midnight. It can denote half of one's possessions, half of one's land; and half of a measure, such as half a year, half an hour, half an inch, or half an *ajlab'* 'four kilometers'. (I've been told that an *ajlab'* is the distance a man can walk in an hour with a 100-pound load on his back.) *Niky'jin* can also be used to situate something in the center of an area, like the center of town, the center or heart of heaven, the center of a path. The second related word is *niky'sil* 'to split in half or to divide in two'. It is likely that *niky'jin* and *niky'sil* for the idea of the middle or center or split are related to the Mam verb *niky'il* 'to know, understand, recognize, calculate or estimate, to aim at a target, to zero in (to center in the crosshairs)'. The idea seems to be that the root, *niky'* 'to know something', is 'to get to its center, its essence'. There appears to be a strong morphological connection and a clear semantic relation among these terms.

A final word used for the notion of centeredness is *tanmin* 'one's heart'. Fray Diego de Reynoso's 1644 Mam dictionary doesn't mention this term at all, but rather *k'u'j oloj*, a phrase which Scotchmer doesn't venture to parse any further. He does mention, however, that *k'uj* in K'iche' means 'one's entire being', a definition fully compatible with our discussion of Mam -*k'u'j* terms. Edmonson (1993:85) claims (see section 3.4 above) that *ok olal* 'entering inwardness' is the Maya word for 'religion'. It's unclear what he means here by the term "Mayan"—probably Yucatecan or perhaps an early, even a proto-Mayan, term. In any event, *ok* means 'to enter' in Mam, and *olal* is possibly related to *okslal* in northern Mam, which is the word for 'believer' or 'religious', a term likely built on the same root as *o:kil* 'to enter'. The -*k'u'j* substitution for *ok* 'to enter' in the Reynoso dictionary would literally describe the stomach (center or middle) of inwardness, which seems to be a plausible rendering of the idea of *heart* as we've discussed it so far. As mentioned above, in Reynoso's dictionary, the Mam word for heart is *k'u'j oloj*, which could mean something like 'in the interior', or 'the real interior', as per Edmonson. Interestingly, Reynoso reports the word for stomach as *titzi nak'u'j* (with spelling slightly regularized, WMC), which possibly means 'the younger sibling of the *k'u'j*', or, perhaps, 'the companion of the center', so the illustrative phrase for *stomach* plays off of the meaning of *heart*. I may be wrong on these terms; after all, Reynoso published his dictionary over 350 years ago, and he didn't distinguish many of the "exotic" consonant sounds that the Mam so routinely produce in daily speech, and we can't necessarily count on his word breaks, although he seems to have done pretty well on the vowels.

4.3 Attaining b'a'n

Table 4.1. Verb phrases containing -k'u'j 'stomach' terms

Mam	Literal meaning	Gloss
tu'n tk'u'jlin	'to cause to stomach'	to love
tu'n tk'u'jin	'to stomach'	to defecate
tu'n tul toj tk'u'j	'to arrive at one's stomach'	to lament/to remember
tu'n tk'ulb'in tk'u'j	'one's stomach goes down'	to meet (someone)
tu'n tok tjtz'o'n tk'u'j	'to tighten one's stomach'	to work very hard
tu'n tel naj jun ti' toj tk'u'j	'to lose it from one's stomach'	to forget
tu'n tjaw tk'u'j	'to raise up the stomach'	to hate, to doubt
tu'n tkub' tk'u'j	'to lower one's stomach'	to convince
tu'n t-xi' tk'u'j	'to have one's stomach go'	to be concerned
tu'n tpon tk'u'j	'one's stomach arrives there'	to lust or to divine
tu'n tb'aj tk'u'j	'to finish off one's stomach'	to be frustrated
tu'n tiky' tk'u'j	'to pass by one's stomach'	to defecate
tu'n tkyij tq'o'n tk'u'j	'to leave/give one's stomach'	to defecate
tu'n tkanin ti'j tk'u'j	'to arrive at the stomach'	to sense something
tu'n tjulk'aj tk'u'j	'to awaken one's stomach'	to remember suddenly
tu'n tel tk'u'j	'for one's stomach to leave'	to be dying
tu'n tqe tk'u'j	'for one's stomach to sit'	to have confidence in
tu'n tjaw ti'n tk'u'j	'to carry (up) one's stomach'	to be alarmed
tu'n tel ti'n tk'u'j	'to carry away one's stomach	to put it out of mind
tu'n t'xi t-xo'n tk'u'j ti'j	'to throw one's stomach at it'	to commit oneself
tu'n tajtz ti'j tk'u'j	'to return home in regard to one's stomach'	to repent
tu'n tkab'in tk'u'j	'to do twice his stomach'	to vacillate
tu'n tpatz' tk'u'j	'to flatten one's stomach'	to die
tu'n t-xtz'u'yin tk'u'j	'for one's stomach to cramp'	to have dysentery
tu'n tlakj tk'u'j ti'j	'for one's stomach to rip'	to have pity
tu'n tq'aq'in tk'u'j	'for one's stomach to burn'	to have compassion/to be hungry
tu'n tjulin tk'u'j	'for one's stomach to roar'	to be hungry
tu'n tlipin tk'u'j	'for one's stomach to fly'	to be jittery
tu'n tok tk'u'j	'to enter one's stomach'	to trust
tu'n tk'ant tk'u'j	'for one's stomach to burn'	to eat too many chiles
tu'n tjaw we' tk'u'j	'for one's S to stand up'	to be convinced

tu'n tjaw ti'n tk'u'j	'to carry up one's stomach'	to be on the verge of giving birth
tu'n tnimsin tk'u'j	'to make large one's stomach'	to encourage
nti' tk'u'j	'to have no stomach'	to have no desire

Today, however, *anmin,* a borrowing of Spanish *anima* 'soul' has come to mean 'heart' or 'departed soul' throughout the Mam area (Godfrey and Collins 1987). Assuming that Reynoso is correct with his Mam heart term *k'u'j oloj,* the word *k'u'j* did double duty (at least in part) as a lexeme for both 'heart' and' stomach'.[8] Sustained contact with Spanish speakers has provided ample opportunity for the distinction between heart and stomach to be more fully lexicalized (i.e., become part of the vocabulary over time). The stem *-k'u'j* apparently has maintained the meaning of 'stomach', while 'heart' called for a new term, *tanmin,* which, while coming to mean 'heart', it has lost the morphological make-up of its former parts 'the center of inwardness'. The present term for heart, *tanmin,* is more restricted than present-day *-k'u'j,* that is, it deals basically with the body part or one's inner being or soul, and it doesn't enter into near the number of extended meanings as *-k'u'j* terms do. The only figurative uses for *anmin* that I've heard are listed in table 4.2

Some of the phrases in table 4.2 can also be used with *tk'u'j* 'one's stomach' terms instead of simply *tanmin* 'one's heart'.

Table 4.2 Figurative uses of *tanmin* 'one's heart'

Mam	Literal meaning	Gloss
tanmin nq'ob'a	'the heart of my arm/hand'	skill, ability to do something
tanmin kya'j	'the heart of heaven'	the center of heaven
tu'n tajtz ti'j tanmin	'to return home to the heart'	to repent
tuk'a tkyaqil tanmin	'with all one's heart'	wholeheartedly
che'wx tanmin	'to cool/calm one's heart'	to console/to be humble

---

[8] If *(t)k'u'j oloj* means 'heart', or literally 'the stomach of inwardness'. in light of Edmonson (1993), it would mimic other phrases like *twi' qq'ob'* 'the heads of our hand— our fingers', where a single lexical meaning 'finger' is expressed as a phrase using a relational noun (see chapter five for details). As per our discussion (see Nájera 1987 and comments in section 3.4), it seems plausible that terms for stomach and heart were at one time (partially) conflated. The idea that *-k'u'j* may have meant 'heart' is strengthened by the fact that Mayan priests excised the heart and not the stomach of their ceremonial victims.

4.3 Attaining b'a'n

at tanmin toj tq'ob'	'for one's hand to have heart'	to have feeling in one's hand
chyo'n tanmin	'for one's heart to eat'	to be upset
nka'min tanmin	'to be double hearted'	to doubt or vacillate

As we've seen, the Mam have ample ways to talk about centeredness: -k'u'j terms, *tanmin, niky'jin, nuk'b'il, tumil, t-xilin,* and *tu'n tten toj b'a'n* 'to be in goodness' (among others), but what interests us presently is the giving and receiving of gifts, centeredness as represented by reciprocal exchange.

Pablo says that in order to pair up their words (agree to the marriage proposal) when he was a youngster, the boy's family would bring *chicha,* a very intoxicating (and inexpensive) wheat or corn liquor, or *q'e'n,* 'moonshine', an alcoholic sugar cane derivative. This would be passed around among both families until they all (aside from the marrying couple) would get extremely drunk. Then the boy's family would pass around hand-rolled cigarettes for leisurely smoking. This exchange of gifts sealed the agreement—the pairing of words—all of which took place so that there would be order and harmony in the new relationship, and that tradition and reciprocity would be respected, and the new couple could enter into a life *toj b'a'n,* on the inside of goodness.

Although Max's and Samuel's families, as practicing Evangelicals, would not drink *chicha* or smoke, they found suitable cultural equivalents that, while respecting their religion's ban on vices, nonetheless enabled them to engage in the culturally meaningful giving and receiving of gifts in order to affirm, indeed, to cement, the pairing of words, and to respect the engagement ritual protocol. Interestingly, the *chicha* was substituted by juice, something that is drunk, while the hard candy, which is sucked on, substituted for cigarettes, which are also "sucked on." And the satedness of drinking until one is rip-roaring drunk is substituted by the quantity of juice and candy that is so plentiful that even the baskets provided can't contain it all.

So gift giving is more than social grace for the Mam. It is akin to an American handshake, which we consider binding ("Hey, we shook on it!"). And what is bound in this agreement ritual are the paired words, the words of two families coming together, meeting in the middle, and establishing a new home.

All of this swirled around in my head as I thought of Rafael. If I wanted to put things back on track and come back onto the path of moderation and good conduct, I needed to apologize, and have the apology accepted. I've seen on several occasions, men offering gifts of one kind or another to someone at the town plaza. Sometimes the gifts are warmly received—as I hoped mine would be. But other times, I've seen the would-be receiver put his hands in the air, as if the victim of a hold-up. He wouldn't receive the gift; he refused to pair up his words, to unify his stomach, to enter together into goodness and share "center space" with his interlocutor. In such circumstances, the supplicant has to dig deeper and offer a gift of greater value, somehow commensurate to the weight of the discussion at hand, whether a request for forgiveness, an agreement to buy or sell a horse or a house, or the supplication by a suitor for a bride.

My plight was the epitome of what ethnographers mean when they say that the ethnographer himself or herself is the research instrument (see section 1.3.1 and particularly Zaharlick 1992). In this situation, instead of reporting on the behavior of others as an outsider watching from the sidelines, I was in it up to my neck all by myself. I was a true participant observer, both playing a role in an actual event, as well as analyzing my involvement in the event. Like Geertz, whose flight (together with his wife) from the Balinese authorities opened the door for his acceptance into the community, my connection here was not as a bystander, but rather as a full participant, one invited into the lives of wonderful people of another culture. But, once accepted into a cultural system, I was expected to know and play by the cultural rules that I had unwittingly violated. This is truly applied anthropology in the largest sense.

So I searched for a gift that I thought would be meaningful—one adequate to my blunder. It couldn't be too much—it was an honest mistake; I had just wanted to help a sick woman. But at the same time, I had to step up and realize that my action was indeed an indiscretion, so at the same time that it couldn't be too much, it couldn't be too meager either.

I had a nice ballpoint pen that had a small LCD dial on it with a date and time function—back when such an item was far more of a novelty than it is today. This seemed to me to be sufficient. It was unusual enough to be meaningful and appreciated, but not expensive enough to overstate the weight of my transgression.

With pen in hand, I went to the market to talk to Rafael. Interestingly, by Mam custom, it wasn't Rafael's wife whom I had offended; it was Rafael himself. Had I spent more time with her trying to right the wrong, the situation would have simply deteriorated. It was being with her "alone" (despite the presence of our 'companions'), which had precipitated the problem in the first place. Going back to her to try to resolve my guilt would have only made it worse.

I greeted Rafael and asked to speak to him. He quickly walked to a private section of his market area and we stood close together. I told him that I had inadvertently wronged him by innocently touching his wife. He recounted that she had come immediately after my visit and told him that I had grabbed her.[9] I explained that I had no intentions toward his wife, and Rafael and I had a friendly exchange. Nonetheless, I asked him to *tkub' tnajsin wila* 'forgive my wrongdoing', which he did. I offered the pen to him; he received it graciously. From that moment on, I've never been reminded of my indiscretion by him, by his wife (although I make it a practice to steer clear of her if she's by herself), or by anyone else, nor have the children ever recounted to me the time that I had mud on my shoes.

4.4 Conclusion

What I have tried to do in this chapter is show that centeredness is a salient cultural principle in the daily lives of the Mam. Not only do they allude to it in dozens of distinct *-k'u'j* constructions that lexicalize strong emotions (pity, compassion, trust, courage, love, premonition, among many others) and important notions (health, birth, and death, to name just a few), but additional terms such as *niky'il* 'to understand, take aim', *tanmin* 'one's heart', *niky'jin* 'the middle', *nuk'b'il* 'order', *t-xilin* 'one's essence or core', and *tumil* 'one's direction' and others are all called upon in myriad contexts to set children on the right direction in life, to counsel others not to leave the straight and narrow, or to come back to it, and to otherwise encourage others, including the speakers themselves, to seek centeredness.

We have also seen how the language of agreement protocols involved in seeking either forgiveness or a wife (the unity of minds or wills, the entrance into goodness, the situating of disputants in goodness, and the pairing of words or selves) all share the notion of coming together in mutual understanding around a metaphorical center space of unity, mutual accord, equilibrium, harmony, and balance.

---

[9] The verb *tzyul* in Mam means either 'to touch' or 'to take hold of', an unfortunate lexical extension which implied quite a bit more than I had intended.

Since these notions, both cultural and linguistic, are pervasive in the daily life of the Mam, I chose to present the data in this chapter by means of an ethnographic account that highlights the actions and vocabulary of the Mam as they go about living their lives. Throughout the telling of this story, I have maintained a meta-dialogue with the reader about the notion of ethnography itself, anticipating questions concerning both the methodology as well as the cultural and linguistic facts, while at the same time defending the concept of good ethnography.

I use the phrase "good ethnography" here and throughout the chapter because ethnography has unfortunately become a catch term for all non-quantitative analysis. Robert Cyders, a friend and education professor, reported in a personal communication that in the educational literature, titles like "An ethnographic account of teacher-student interaction" are ubiquitous. He goes on to say that some of these articles are based on observations made during one class period per week over the span of six weeks. There are no interviews with students, little discussion of context, no multiple voices, no microscopic reporting, no emic analysis, and no researcher participation, just fly-on-the-wall observation. There's nothing ethnographic about it—other than the lack of formal statistics.

I started the chapter with a discussion of what one can "prove" with ethnography and why a researcher would chose it as an exploratory and explanatory method. Gold is not valueless simply because we can't eat it. In the same way, the ethnographic process and product are valuable even though the notions described cannot be weighed or measured positivistically. Rather, the social facts must be interpreted and understood in relation to a concept "within which the observations find a natural place" (Chafe 1994). I suggest that centeredness is just such a concept, explanatory to cultural outsiders and pursued by the Mam themselves.

5

Grammatical Aspects of Centeredness

5.1 Introduction

In chapter four, I mentioned that one of the ways I intend to establish a link between language and culture is to seek patterns in both the linguistic and cultural data that we observe. And while the patterns should be independently verified (see section 1.2), we should be able to unite them under the common cultural umbrella of centeredness. Hymes says that a basic practice of anthropological study is "the showing of a pattern, fashion of speaking, or style among a number of traits" (1966). Pattern, while not a conclusive link between language and culture, is certainly indicative of a relationship between the two, especially in the minds of locals, who don't bother making technical distinctions between what they know about the world (culture) and how they talk about what they know (language).

In this chapter, I pursue what Hymes calls this "number of traits" in the formal linguistic structure of Maya-Mam. In chapter four, woven through the ethnographic discussion of our theme, I discussed how centeredness is instantiated in the lexicon, or, for our purposes, the words or semantics of the language. Specifically, we looked at a number of terms: *-k'u'j* 'stomach', and *tanmin* 'heart', *nuk'b'il* 'order, peace, moderation', *tumil* 'one's direction in life', *tniky'jin* 'middle', *niky'il* 'to understand, to zero in on', *niky'sil* 'to split', and *t-xilin* 'one's essence'. I talked about how the concept of centeredness pervades each one. We've also seen how the Mam talk about agreement protocols, using phrases such as *junx kynab'l* 'together their minds', *tu'n kykyij toj wen* 'to stay in goodness', *tu'n kyten toj b'a'n* 'to be situated in goodness', *tu'n kymujb'in kyyol* 'to pair up their words', *tu'n kymujb'in kyib'*, 'to pair themselves up'. Each of these is iconic of the sense of center reached in a compromise, a pairing up of interests, an entering into the grounded center of mutual accord, where people commit viscerally and wholeheartedly to a common cause.

I consider that centeredness is well established in the Mam lexicon as per my discussion in chapter four on different ways in which centeredness is talked about by the Mam and how they use it as an organizing principle in their daily lives. In addition, Wierzbicka's claims about the cultural scope of key words which I discussed in section 1.1.1 above seem very much to hold true of Mam *-k'u'j* terms in particular, along with other Mam terms related to the notion of a physical or moral center. The lexicon straddles the artificial line between language and culture. As Wierzbicka says, "There is a very close link between the life of a society and the lexicon of the language spoken by it" (1997). This agrees with Sapir, as we have seen, who claims "vocabulary is a very sensitive index of the culture of a people" (Sapir 1949). What people code, they can talk about. What they talk about is important to them.

Much of Sapir's contribution to the Sapir-Whorf Hypothesis is related to the lexicon, and how the vocabulary both opens up and narrows down the world that individuals live in. Whorf 1974 [1941]) was more interested in what he called the "habitual thought" of speakers, how the formal structures of different languages shepherd the speakers of those languages toward certain observations and a specific understanding of how the world works. Of these observations and understandings, he says: "They do not depend so much upon *any one system* within the grammar (e.g., tense, or parts of speech, or even the vocabulary [parenthetical comment, WMC]) as upon the ways of analyzing and reporting experience which have become fixed in the language as integrated 'fashions of speaking' and which cut across the typical grammatical classifications, so that such a 'fashion' may

5.1 Introduction

include lexical, morphological, syntactic and otherwise systematically diverse means coordinated in a certain frame of consistency" (1974; emphasis in original).

So Whorf saw habitual thought inhabiting not only the lexicon of a group (as did Sapir), but even more so the formal grammatical categories of the language. He goes on to say, "A category such as number (singular vs. plural—or, in some languages, dual or trial forms [parenthetical comment, WMC]) is an attempted interpretation of a whole large order of experience, virtually of the world or of nature; it attempts to say how experience is to be segmented, what experience is to be called 'one' and what 'several'." But it is a subconscious interpretation. Whereas word choice—the lexicon—is the storehouse from which we choose what it is we want to say; grammatical categories come along for the ride at no extra cost. In Spanish, for example, one can't discuss dogs, or, to be more abstract, the notion of "dogness" without specifying one or many dogs, male or female. We consciously choose the topic of discussion, the dog; then grammatical categories force certain additional nuances of meaning upon us beyond the topic choice by means of the sheer act of speaking our native language. Spanish requires number (singular or plural) and gender—*perro* or *perra*. There's no escaping these additional notions in Spanish.

Our interest in Whorf's view on this is that this "habitual" thought is congruent to the partially hidden grammatical themes which are so powerful in both the formation and formulation of speakers' understanding of the world. They are less salient to speakers than is the lexicon, since they don't show up in speech as "dictionary items," which reflect the clear coding of the perceived world. Rather, grammatical themes—ideas of number, gender, noun classification, tense and aspect, evidential and deictic marking, among others—are less conspicuous, albeit more pervasive, and as such, they are all the more constructive of the basic notions by which speakers understand and live in the world. This is somewhat akin to Lakoff and Johnson's (1980) claims that the under-the-surface nature of metaphor is what is so powerful about it. Although metaphors aren't grammatical structures in the same sense that tense and aspect are, their influence, according to these authors, can be just as hidden, just as formative of our "conscience collective," and just as pervasive. For an in-depth look at such things, see Lakoff's *Women, fire, and dangerous things: What categories reveal about the mind* (1987).

In the remainder of this chapter, I look at how centeredness as a function of spatial deixis is evidenced in the morphology, syntax, and narrative discourse of Mam grammar. I suggest that centeredness is a "fashion of speaking" in Whorf's words, or what Martin (1977) and England (1978) call a grammatical theme. England defines grammatical themes as "the underlying organizational principles of a language linking [grammatical, WMC] structure with semantics" (1978:226). Martin adds that they are "pervasive semantic categories with profound grammatical force" (1977:366). They are what Hale calls "lexico-semantic themes or motifs which function as integral components in a grammar" (1986:234). In light of these three quotes, I suggest that we consider a grammatical theme to be a meaning-based notion that is realized across a number of grammatical categories. That it is meaning based makes a grammatical theme culture specific, since meaning derives from cultural practice and understanding. That it is realized grammatically (irrespective of, or in the present case, in addition to its lexical presence in the language) adds to its distribution throughout the language as a pervasive meaning "motif." In other words, the idea of centeredness shows up all over the place, not only in the culture, as laid out in the first four chapters, but in the grammar as well. Remember what Wierzbicka said back in chapter one about how the American commitment to democracy seems to have affected the expansion of causative constructions in the grammar of the language, while at the same time the grammar of the language is one of the culture's most powerful tools in our education and acculturation. This is the patterning that Hymes talked about and it adds to the fascination of our look into language and cultural diversity.

The study of these fashions of speaking are the purview of a relatively new field in linguistics called "ethnosyntax," a term introduced by our friend Anna Wierzbicka in 1979. Nick Enfield, in his book *Ethnosyntax* (2002:3), defines the field as "the study of connections between the cultural knowledge, attitudes, and practices of speakers, and the morphosyntactic resources they employ in speech." Goddard adds that these morphosyntactic constructions should, more narrowly, "encode a specifiable culture-related semantic content" (2002:53). He also suggests that in the study of ethnosyntax, these linguistic structures "literally encode [a] particular 'ethnophilosophy'" (2002:55). As an example of this ethnosyntactic relation between language and culture, he cites the work of Wierzbicka (1992, 1997). She talks about the Russian concept of *sud'ba* 'fate, destiny, a sense

5.1 Introduction

of impending doom or dreadful justice'. Goddard mentions a number of impersonal, agentless, dative (i.e., third-party) constructions where the powers that be—both physical and metaphysical—are the only real (albeit unspecified) agents, while powerless individuals are subject to the capricious and perhaps whimsical or even heinous determinations of such powers. From Wierzbicka's work and his own, Goddard cites seven such agentless constructions in Russian. In addition, he mentions common constructions in Russian colloquial speech that mean 'it is indispensable', 'one may not', 'it is required', 'it is necessary', 'one ought to', 'one has to', "and the sundry infinitive and reflexive constructions conveying meanings related to helplessness, obligation and necessity" (2002:58). Wierzbicka claims that in all these constructions, language follows culture, mirroring in the formal structure of Russian grammar, the underlying sense of what she claims is a widespread sense of helplessness of the Russian masses in the face of almost certain and ultimate disappointment.

Showing a direct correlation between language and culture may not be possible, but clearly there is a pattern among the agentless constructions mentioned here and Wierzbicka's reports on the reality of Russian life where nameless powers usurp personal initiative and add to cynicism within the general population. We can dispute any causality in this pattern, but Wierzbicka informs us that during communist rule, the language police, in a futile act of language planning, tried to eradicate the use of these agentless passives, calling them archaic, obsolete, unscientific, uneducated, and irresponsible in the sense of speakers' not taking personal responsibility for their situation, but by blaming others—often the bureaucracy (1979:372–373). Despite the view that the use of such constructions was irresponsible and anti-modern, they were (and are) so pervasive that political authorities felt that action must be taken to bring the cultural worldview into line with the political worldview espoused by the communists. Apparently the Soviet government interpreted the relationship between culture and language as a bit too close for comfort.

Wierzbicka and Goddard have set the stage for us. Grammatical themes are pervasive, meaning-based multi-level phenomena that encode notions important to the culture. I suggest that centeredness in Maya-Mam is just such a phenomenon. It shows up in daily life and in daily speech. The idea is absolutely unavoidable if one is to speak or think in Mam at all.

The following discussion, based primarily on the linguistic notion of deixis, is technical in spots. You might consider skimming over some of this unless you are particularly interested in the mechanics of how centeredness shows up in the grammatical function of the language.

5.2 The centeredness of spatial deixis

Linguistically, the idea of a center that serves as an origin point for grammatical notions is called an origo or deictic center.

In chapter one I discussed various general treatments of deixis, namely, those of Lyons (1977) and Fillmore (1997). These studies largely agree on what are included as deictic notions, but I've opted for Lyons' definition: "By deixis is meant the location and identification of persons, objects, events, processes and activities being talked about, or referred to, in relation to the spatiotemporal context created by the act of utterance and the participation in it, typically, of a single speaker and at least one addressee" (Lyons 1977:637).

Routinely, we think of deixis in three categories: person, time, and place, anchored to a deictic center or anchorage point, what Levinson calls the "space-time-social centre" of the entire world (1983). Repeating Fillmore's commentary from section 1.3.2: "I carry around with me, everywhere I go, my own private world. The spatial centre of this world is my location…the temporal centre of this world is the passing moment of my consciousness… the social centre of this world is me" (1998:40–41). The speaker (ego) is the center point from which all deictic notions are determined. By most accounts, deixis is quintessentially egocentric, based on where the speaker is at the moment of utterance. This deictic center serves like a surveyor's monument stake, a binding starting point from which all measurements are calculated.

Because centeredness is primarily a spatial notion, it is spatial deixis, measured from a deictic center or anchor point, that is most relevant to our discussion. Of course, the notion of origo is not specific to Mam. Indeed it seems likely to be a universal grammatical principle. What I suggest in this study is that what is peculiar to Mam culture (and to Maya culture in general) is the way in which the notion of centeredness as both a grammatical and cultural theme reflects speakers' means of organizing their experience of the world. In the same way that -k'u'j terms can be seen as the lexical manifestation of centeredness that both reflects as well as constructs the Mam notion of centeredness, I suggest that the use of grammatical categories that depend on the deictic center is part of the mechanism used to acculturate speakers to this view of the world.

5.3 Mam intransitive verbs of direction

Mam has twelve intransitive verbs of direction that are different in meaning and distribution from other Mam action verbs. Godfrey (1981:88) says that most Mam intransitive verbs of motion like *ajqelil* 'to hurry', *pasyalil* 'to walk without a load', *b'etil* 'to walk', and *rinil* 'to run' specify manner of motion, but not change of location in relation to some reference point. Of course, running, hurrying, and walking (with or without a load) imply a change of location, but exactly how that motion resulting in change of location translates into movement (or lack of it) in relation to a reference point of some sort is left unspecified in terms of the meaning of the verb itself.

The twelve intransitive verbs of direction that are found in Mam, in contrast to other intransitive verbs of action, specify movement in relation to a sense of center or a reference point, an origo, without specifying manner of movement. They are also distinct from other verbs in their ability to combine as reduced auxiliaries in complex verb phrases (see section 5.4).

Table 5.1 Mam intransitive verbs of direction

Intransitive verbs of motion	Gloss
tza:jil	to come toward speaker
xi'yil	to go away from speaker
u:lil	to arrive here where speaker is
po:nil	to arrive there from where speaker is
o:kil	to enter from where 'other' is
e:lil	to leave from where 'other' is
ja:wil	to ascend from where 'other' is
kub'il	to descend from where 'other' is
a:jil	to return to one's habitual place
iky'il	to pass (by)
kyijil	to stay, remain
b'ajil	to complete

Both Godfrey (1981:100–108) and England (1983:167–174) discuss the semantics of these intransitive verbs of direction, but situate them neither specifically in a deictic system nor in terms of a deictic center. Godfrey discusses the meanings of these verbs in terms of a change of distance (increase or decrease) from a reference location and whether the course or path of distance traveled focuses on the start of movement or its completion. This is quite clever, if esoteric. So for the first verb in table 5.1, *tza:jil,* distance decreases during the movement toward the reference point (the speaker), and the pathway focuses on the initiation of movement at some place distant. Movement starts somewhere else and moves toward the speaker, as in (1).

(1) K-chi   tza:jil   n-k'wala   nchi'j.
    POT-they   come   my-child   tomorrow
    'My children will come (to visit) tomorrow.'

(2) I   xi'   ila'   maj.
    they.REM   go   various   time
    'They went various times.'

(3) I   u:l   tzalu'n   ewa.
    they.REM   arrive   here   yesterday
    'They arrived here yesterday.'

(4) Taj   tu'n   tpo:n   Txeljub'   yol-il   tuk'a.
    wants   to   arrive.there Xela   to.speak-INF   with (him)
    'She wants to go to Xela to speak with him.'

For *xi'yil,* movement starts at the speaker and moves away. By Godfrey's account, distance from the speaker increases (as in (2)). For the verb *u:lil,* the same direction of movement as *tza:jil* is encoded (distance from the speaker decreases), but the endpoint of motion (arriving where the speaker is) is in focus for *u:lil* rather than the initiating point of movement as in *tza:jil* (compare (1) and (3)). Likewise, *po:nil* involves the same directional movement as *xi'yil* (distance from the speaker increases) but the pathway focuses on the endpoint (arriving 'there' after having begun where the speaker is) rather than the initiation of movement away from the speaker as in *xi'yil* (compare examples (2) and (4)).

England (1983:167–174) spends a lot more time discussing directional auxiliaries (see section 5.4) than the intransitives from which they derive, but her glosses for the intransitives, while not as detailed as Godfrey's, are congruent with Godfrey's analysis.

5.3 Mam intransitive verbs of direction

We can take Godfrey's idea of reference location and recast it in terms of centeredness without doing damage to his semantic analysis of the directional intransitives. What I suggest is that looking at reference location in terms of centeredness enables us to generalize over the twelve directionals while maintaining Godfrey's (and England's) basic idea of what the terms mean, particularly in Godfrey's double rubric of pathway and change of distance.

The first four verbs listed in table 5.1 are what Fillmore (1997) calls deictic verbs, since they depend on a traditional deictic center for their meaning. Deictic verbs are those like *bring* and *take* which code action in terms of speaker location or origo. The movement described by these verbs depends on the location of the speaker at the time of utterance. This is prototypical deictic usage.[1]

The next four verbs in table 5.1, *o:kil* 'to enter', *e:lil* 'to leave', *ja:wil* 'to ascend', and *kub'il* 'to descend', I've glossed in relation to 'other'. These verbs depend not on the location of the speaker, but of the subject of the sentence, usually someone or something other than the speaker. For example, in (5) below, the verb phrase *i o:k* 'they enter' makes no reference to the location of the speaker of the sentence. Both the speaker and the speaker's location are ignored. But there is reference to the relative location of the subject of the sentence, the people. The verb *o:kil* denotes movement from the position that the people occupied just before the action of the verb takes place into some kind of enclosure, physical or otherwise, which is denoted by the action. It is movement starting outside, and moving inside.

(5) *I   o:k-x   xjal   toj   ja.*
    they.REM enter-going   people   in   house
    'The people entered the house.'

(6) *K-chi   e:li-x   ichin   toj   ja.*
    POT-they   leave-going   man   in   house
    'The men will leave (from within) the house.'

---

[1] Fillmore (1997) shows that it isn't quite so simple. We can say, "Bring it to work tomorrow," even if we don't happen to be at the work location at the time of utterance. Nonetheless, *bring* anticipates that I will indeed be at work when the action of bringing takes place. The prototypical sense of *bring* is action toward origo, whether actual or projected, origo being the quintessential "me, here, and now" locus of deictic measure.

(7) I   ja:-x   tata   twi'   wutz.
     they.REM   ascend-going   man   top   mountain
     'The men ascended the mountain.'

(8) I   ku'-tz   tata   twi'   wutz.
     they.REM   descend-coming   man   top   mountain
     'The men descended the mountain.'

Similarly, in (6) the movement denoted by *e:lil* starts inside some kind of enclosure and ends up outside it. For *o:kil* and *e:lil*, I assume that the reference location is that of the individual(s) in focus (whom/what I've called 'other' in my glosses in table 5.1), in relation to some sort of enclosure.

The same basic idea obtains for the next two verbs, *ja:wil* 'to ascend' and *kub'il* 'to descend'. They encode movement from a starting position before the action of the verb takes place to one either higher (as in the case of *ja:wil* in example (7)) or lower (as in (8)) than the starting point. For now, we will ignore the final -*x* in *e:lix* and *ja:x*, in (6) and (7) and the final -*tz* in (8), although they are important and we will pick them up below in section 5.5.

I've suggested that for the first eight verbs that we've looked at from table 5.1, the reference point, the deictic anchorage, is either the speaker (for the first four verbs) or the subject of the sentence (for the next four) that the speaker is coding. Ascending and descending are measured from the point in which the person or thing was situated when brought into the discourse and not from where the speaker was located. From that point, the subject moves up or down. For example, we can use the verb 'descend' in a sentence like *The man descended on the mountain from the tree line to the highest cornfields*. So even though he is (assumedly) still higher than the speaker when the sentence was coded, this fact is irrelevant to our understanding of the sentence. His descending is not relative to speaker location, but to the location of the subject of the sentence—from where the man was located before the action began, not at the top of the mountain, but at tree line—to where he ended up—not at the bottom, but at the height of the highest corn fields.

With this in mind, I suggest that for the first four verbs, the prototypically deictic verbs, the reference point or deictic center is the speaker herself. For the next four, the reference point is 'other'. In other words, just as 'I' as speaker serve as origo in terms of movements toward and away from me, I recognize that 'others' have this same sense of center, and movement can

5.3 Mam intransitive verbs of direction

be in relation to them and their situatedness in the world, just as it can be in relation to me and my situatedness.

The difference in deictic anchorage between speaker and 'other' is part of that which is specified by the verbs themselves. Linguists say that this anchorage is part of the lexical entry for that verb. In other words, our mental dictionary doesn't just store meanings but elemental vignettes that situate the meaning of these verbs in terms of the participants involved. *Tza:jil, xi'yil, u:lil,* and *po:nil* normally code the speaker as deictic center. *O:kil, e:lil, ja:wil,* and *kub'il* normally code 'other' as the deictic center. This second group of verbs is not speaker-centric as is the first set, but "other-centric."

The final four verbs from table 5.1, *a:jil* 'to return', *iky'il,* 'to pass', *kyijil* 'to stay or remain', and *b'ajil* 'to complete' are different again. I suggest that for these verbs, origo is arbitrary. It isn't coded in relation to the speaker or 'other', but rather to an arbitrary location, sometimes not even a physical location. *A:jil* 'to return' can mean returning from anywhere to almost anywhere (see example (9)). Use of this verb usually implies that the place returned to is "home," but one's actual home isn't a necessary component of meaning. Rather, one can return to any salient location, particularly one which somehow inheres to the person (or thing) in question, like a market stall from which one routinely sells to the public, or one's cornfield, or one's hometown. Remember what we said in chapter three about the notion of repentance being to return "home" regarding the heart. One can return 'here' or 'there'; actual location is arbitrary, and so it must be either implied or explicitly mentioned in the discourse. As we've seen with the first eight verbs mentioned, in contrast to these last four, specific deictic anchorage is part of the lexical meaning of the term. In these last four verbs it is not. These last four verbs code an arbitrary deictic anchorage. There is still a sense of groundedness (either being in a place or in some relation to a place or an action), but neither origo nor movement in relation to it is specified.

(9) Ma   chin   a:ja   n-ja'y.
     REC   I   return my-home
     'I am going home.'

(10) In   iky'a   tzma   jawnix   ewa.
     I.REM   pass   to   upper.area   yesterday
     'I passed by the high area yesterday.'

Just as *a:jil* codes an arbitrary origo, *iky'il* 'to pass (by)' does as well (example (10)). Someone can pass someplace far away or near. They may actually arrive at the place in mention, or they may simply pass near it. Both direction and reference location are arbitrary.

Kyijil 'to remain' also is arbitrary in reference to origo. It denotes lack of movement, no direction at all. It indicates suspended motion, not necessarily completed action. For example, in (11), we can assume that my little brother eventually makes it home, but from the perspective of the sentence, the action of a round trip to town has been suspended.

(11) *Ma Ø kyij w-itz'i'n   toj tnam.*
     REC he stay my-little.brother in   town
     'My little brother stayed in town.'

B'ajil 'to complete', on the other hand, means that the motion or action in question has been completed, as in (12) and (13). I include both of these words *b'ajil* and *kyijil* as members of the set of intransitive verbs of direction even though they don't specify actual movement in the same way as the rest of the set. Lack of motion is a movement notion just as we can consider zero to be a measure of quantity. Plus, *b'ajil* and *kyijil* (actually, their directional counterparts) combine to form complex verb phrases just like the rest of the set of intransitive verbs of direction, so they seem clearly to belong to this special set of intransitive verbs.

For both *kyijil* and *b'ajil* origo is again arbitrary. The (in)action of the verb inheres to the situation of use. Reference location is irrelevant because there is no focus on movement from one place to another. Whatever location is salient, that's where the movement stays; whatever action had occurred, it is over and done with.

(12) *Ma   b'aj   jun   ti'   wi'ja.*
     REC completed.action   one   thing to me
     'Something happened to me.'

(13) *Ma   b'aj   te   xjal.*
     REC completed.action DEM   person
     'That person died.'

As discussed above, the differentiation in deictic anchorage is part of the lexical meaning of each of these twelve intransitive directional verbs. Whether the

5.3 *Mam intransitive verbs of direction*

anchorage is speaker centered, other centered, or arbitrary, it is coded in the word choices that people make every day. Not only does the anchorage contrast in Mam depend upon the different verbs employed in speech, it can also shift in complex ways. For example, I can tell my friend at breakfast, "Last night my wife told me, 'If I catch you bringing that mess in here you can just camp outside from now on'." In quoted speech, the "here" and "now" is projected onto a different context and frame, triggered by the use of the quoted speech structure. "You" in our sentence above is actually the speaker—me—the one who is telling my friend what my wife told me. "I" is not me, but my wife; and "here" is not the space that I presently occupy, but rather the space that my wife ascribed to herself when she was speaking. In the same way, "now" doesn't mean 'now' in the traditional sense, but 'then'—last night. So the deictic center can flit around. This is sometimes called projection or transposition, where origo is projected or transposed elsewhere. So, as with everything, it isn't as clear as it first seems, but the basic notion still holds.

The use of any of these verbs calls upon a sense of origo, since the verbs denote action that is either speaker centered, other centered, or arbitrary in terms of origo. Mayanist John Haviland says that "the very use of directional verbs always indexes some deictic origo" (1996:276). In other words, word choice (not grammatical structures like quoted speech) necessarily triggers a specific frame for deictic anchorage. We will also see that the calculation of origo is more complex than simply being part of the lexical entry for these twelve intransitive verbs of direction. The use of directional auxiliaries, which we will see directly, shifts the conception of deictic anchorage from the semantic component of the lexical entry to a pragmatic calculation of direction, often metaphorical, based on origo not as a physical center space, but as a norm of some kind.[2]

---

[2] I suggest in this study that the intransitive verbs of direction have a sense of direction tied to an origo as part of their lexical meaning. For the directionals, this meaning must be computed, as I will discuss below. But to illustrate, consider the directional *jaw,* which can be used in a verb phrase to give each of the following meanings, the details of which must be calculated pragmatically (i.e., based on the individual context of use): to choose, to stand, to resurrect, to take, to be astounded, to see, to speak out, to fall, to make fun of, to insult, to be astonished, to be born, to grow, to scream, to pray, to shiver, to open, to be confused, to pull, to move, to sit, to doubt, to obey, to be sad, to pull, to jump, to be in an uproar, to be jealous, to get drunk, to hurry, to argue, to believe, to hang, to speak against, to vacillate, to awaken, to be happy, to die, to strangle, to read, to change, among dozens of others. The pragmatic sense of "up" must be determined by the context for each of these cases. I discuss this further in section 5.4.1. The border between semantics and pragmatics is recognized as an area for further study, one which I will not pursue here. We do similar things in English with *look up, think up, dry up, build up, tear up, wash up, write up,* etc.

5.4 Directional auxiliaries

England defines Mam directionals as "auxiliary elements in the verb phrase which indicate direction of movement and are derived from intransitive verbs of direction" (1983:167). Table 5.2 repeats the intransitive verbs of direction with their corresponding directional auxiliaries.

Table 5.2 Mam intransitive verbs of direction and corresponding directionals

Intransitive verbs of direction	Directionals	Gloss
tza:jil	tzaj	to come toward speaker
xi'yil	xi	to go away from speaker
u:lil	ul	to arrive here
po:nil	pon	to arrive there
o:kil	ok	to enter from where 'other' is
e:lil	el	to leave from where 'other' is
ja:wil	jaw	to ascend
kub'il	kub'	to descend
a:jil	aj	to return
iky'il	iky'	to pass (by)
kyijil	kyij	to stay, remain
b'ajil	b'aj	to complete

Other than the presence of the infinitive suffix *(-il)* of the intransitives, the difference that we notice with the directionals is that any complex vowels from the first column of intransitive verbs of direction (either long vowel or vowel plus glottal, as in *xi'yil*) are shortened or streamlined in the directionals. (In the case of *kub'il, iky'il, kyijil,* and *b'ajil,* the vowels are already short so no simplification takes place). Both the intransitive verbs of direction and the directional auxiliaries (from now on, simply *directionals*) occur very frequently in normal speech. England says that directionals are "almost obligatory with two-topic verbs" (1978:227). She adds, "almost all transitive verbs are always accompanied by directionals" (1983:170), although they occur occasionally with non-transitive verbs as well. Typical examples of the directional verbs follow:

5.4 Directional auxiliaries

(14) *Ma   tzaj   t-q'o'n   Pegr   jun   u'j.*
     REC   DIR.come   he-give   Peter   one   book
     'Peter gave me a book.'

(15) *Ø   Xi   n-q'ma'n   jun   n-yol-a   kye.*
     REM   DIR.go   I-tell   one   my-word-EX   them
     'I told them something.'

(16) *I   ul   kanin   n-xjalil-a   pasyalil.*
     they.REM   DIR.arrive.here   arrive   my-people-EX   to visit
     'My relatives came to visit.'

(17) *B'e'x   i   pon   kanin   jni'   xjal.*
     immediately.PAS   they.REM   DIR.arrive.there   arrive   all   people
     'All the people arrived there.'

In these four sentences we can see how the directional affects or adds to the meaning of the main verb. The directional *tzaj* in (14) indicates movement toward the speaker (compare with (1) above), which is what happens when Peter gives me a book. It moves from him to me. In (15) my words go from me to the receiver, *kye* 'them'. So the basic notion of *xi'yil* 'to go' is retained, which is movement from the speaker to somewhere else. In this sentence, it is my words that go from me to them. Even though the main verb in the sentence is *nq'ma'n* 'I told', the directional still adds the meaning of direction away from the speaker to the act of my telling.

In (16) and (17) *ul* and *pon* both team up with *kanin* 'arrive', the difference in the directional indicating the relation to speaker-as-origo, where the arrival takes place, either starting elsewhere and arriving at origo or starting at origo and arriving elsewhere.

(18) *Ma   chi   ok   t-b'yo'n   k'wal   tx'yan   tuk'a   tze.*
     REC   them   DIR.enter   s/he-hit   child   dog   with   stick
     'The child hit the dogs with a stick.'

(19) *El   naj   jun   ti'   toj   t-k'u'j-a.*
     DIR. leave   lose   one   something in   your.stomach-EX
     'You forgot something.'

(20) *Ma   jaw   tz'aq   q'a   toj   b'e.*
     REC   DIR.ascend   fall   boy   in   trail
     'The boy fell in the trail.'

(21) O-taq   kub'   q-b'isi-'n   qa   mi   tu'n q-xi'y.
     PER-PAS   DIR.descend   we-think-EX   that NEG that we-go.EX
     'We had thought that we wouldn't go.'

In (18) the action of hitting by the child is perceived as entering into the dogs. The pain of being hit "penetrates," as one man said to me. It enters the bodies of those being hit. In (19) the directional *el* indicates that whatever it was that was lost has left—gone out from—my stomach, the place where things are stored and remembered. In both (18) and (19) the basic meaning of the directional is the same as for the corresponding intransitive verb.

The same holds for (20) and (21). I've noted two explanations for the directional in (20). It would seem that falling wouldn't find a place for the directional *jaw* 'up'. One claim is that in falling, the *jaw* directional codes the upward flailing of the boy's arms as he fell, while another view codes the position of the boy after he has fallen—*bocarriba*—in Spanish 'face up'. In both cases, origo is clearly the boy, not the speaker. And the "upwardness" of the directional is very much a live topic to the Mam such that they attempt to describe how the meaning of "up" obtains in the basic meaning of the verb phrase which is 'to fall down'. Either his arms are flailing up from his body as he falls or, after the fall, his mouth is "up" in relation to the rest of his body.

Contrast this with the idea of being *fed up* in English. We use this as an idiom or figure of speech while ignoring both the "up" part of the construction as well as the "fed" part. In this English phrase, *fed up* is not a live notion at all, just a two-word way to express exasperation, discontent, being sick of something or someone, etc. It is what is called a dead or frozen form, not one whose meaning is recoverable from the words themselves—like a round table discussion which is neither round nor a table. This is not true of the Mam use of *up* in (20). With them it is a "live" notion.

In (21) *kub'* indicates the stereotypical downward gaze of someone deep in thought, like Rodin's famous statue. Again, *down* signals movement from the norm, which is the person's neutral gaze straight ahead; it doesn't indicate 'down' from the deictic anchorage of the speaker, but rather from the subject of the sentence. Again, the Mam whom I queried on this directional have claimed that it is a physical movement of the head downward in relation to the act of thinking or praying. Like *jaw* above, the downwardness of *kub'* is a live topic, one that has not been sufficiently grammaticalized that people separate it from its basic, lexical meaning.

5.4 Directional auxiliaries

The arbitrariness of origo for the final four verbs in table 5.1 we can again see in (22) and (23).

(22) I   aj   t-meltz'in   tata   chej
     them.REM DIR.return he-give.back man horse
     'The man returned the horses.'

(23) Ø   Iky'   t-i'n   nana   t-ikitz
     it.REM DIR.pass.by she-carry woman her-load
     'The woman passed carrying her load.'

In (22) the horses are returned to where they belong, but where that is, we haven't a clue—the home of their owner, one presumes. In (23) the woman passes someplace, the whereabouts of which are ignored, except to imply that the place is a recognizable location.

(24) Ma   kyij   naj   n-xjab'-a   toj plas
     REC   DIR.stay   lose   my-sandals-EX in   plaza
     'I lost my sandals at the market.'

(25) Ma   b'aj   n-b'inchi-'n.
     REC   DIR.complete I-do-EX
     'I just now did it.'

The use of *kyij* in (24) indicates that the lost sandals are assumedly still in the plaza. They 'stayed' in lostness. In (25) *b'aj* signifies that my doing is done with.

In each of these constructions, (14)–(25), the directional adds to the action described by the main verb in the sentence. The main verb carries the basic meaning; the directional fine tunes it. Some directionals are very common with certain verbs and are virtually coterminous with them. For example, *kub' tb'yo'n* 'he down killed', *el tniky'* 'he out understood', *kub' meje* 'he down kneeled', *el tmatz'in* 'he out kissed', *jaw xhch'in* 'he up screamed', *jaw anq'in* 'he up resurrected'. Some of these meanings may seem harder to grasp than others, but the Mam explain the use of directionals in these and all constructions in terms of physical motion in space (in reference to the relevant deictic anchorage encoded in the different verbs) and the basic meaning of the directionals themselves. For example 'to kiss' is understood as drawing something out of the one kissed (even if one kisses a newborn baby on the forehead). Each of these directionals, even in relation to a main verb, still maintains its lexical denotation of its respective center as discussed above.

5.4.1 Directionals and deictic centeredness

Although the directionals in the sentences cited so far seem to participate in the same deictic nature as their intransitive counterparts, this is not always the case. Whereas the intransitives maintain a deictic profile as I've outlined above, the directional auxiliaries often have a more extended or perhaps even metaphorical meaning. Compare (26), where the intransitive verb does not have a metaphorical sense and (27), where it does:

(26) I   e:tz   kye   nana   ky-ja   qlixjexix wen   ewe.
     they   leave   they   woman their-house   early   very yesterday
     'The women left their houses early yesterday morning.'

(27) El   naj   xjal   toj   t-umil
     leave   lose   person in   her/his-way
     'The person lost her/his way (lost her/his moral compass).'

In (26), the intransitive verb *e:lil* 'to leave' is modified slightly with the *-tz* suffix to denote that the leaving is from the house and toward the speaker of the sentence. The notion of 'leaving' is the prototypical meaning of the transitive verb *e:lil* as we saw in (6) above (albeit with a different suffix).

In (27), however, the directional auxiliary *el* no longer deals with the deictic center of the subject of the sentence as it does in (26). Rather, it treats the 'leaving' in a metaphorical way—not from a physical place, but from a metaphysical place from which this person has strayed, the place of *b'a'n* or of a correct direction in his or her life.

(28) Xi   t-q'ma'n   junjun   t-yol-a   kye.
     DIR.go   you-tell   various   your-word-EX   them
     'You told them something.'

(29) Xi   t-yek'in   Pegr   jun   chej   te   Juan.
     DIR.go   he-showed   Peter   one   horse   to   John
     'Peter showed John a horse.'

(30) Xi   ky-k'ayin   xjal   tx'otx'.
     DIR.go   they-sell   people   land
     'The people sold the land.'

Examples (28)–(30) show clearly that the directional does not code movement in relation to the speaker, but rather in terms of the subject of the

5.4 Directional auxiliaries

sentence. In each case, there is movement away from the subject: *you, Peter* and *the people,* respectively. The movement is of the telling itself or the words in (28); the demonstrating (the verb also means 'to indicate, to show', or 'to point out'), where Peter directs John's gaze and attention toward the horse and away from himself; and the selling of land, where what is distanced is not the land itself but ownership of the land. This last sentence exemplifies the most extended meaning of all in the sense that both (28) and (29) involve the notion of movement—either words or gaze—from the subject of the sentence to a place somewhat distant. In (30) however, there is no movement at all, just a sense of distance from the intimacy of ownership to the new relationship to the land as non-owner.

The deictic anchorage of the actual speaker in these sentences is not coded in (28)–(30) in any way. Compare (28) with (15) above. In (15) the subject of the sentence also happens to be the speaker, so we can't tell for sure whether it is the subject or the speaker that determines the deictic anchorage for the verb. In (14), (16), and (17), however, the speaker is not the subject of the sentence and yet he or she still constitutes the deictic center. I take these occurrences to be the prototypical meaning of the directionals, that is, the same as their corresponding full intransitive forms, with movement conceived in terms of an origo. Nevertheless, a "demoted" sense of center is clear with the directionals, as in (27) as well as (28)–(30), where the deictic anchorage is not the speaker, but is determined from the context.

Similarly, in (31) auxiliary *tzaj* no longer acts as if the deictic center is the speaker as it does in its intransitive form in example (1) or in the prototypical (14). Rather, the father—not the speaker—is the center, and the movement is not towards him in a physical way, but in a metaphorical or extended way; it's the love that he feels for his daughter that moves toward him and grips him.

(31) B'e'x   tzaj   q'aq'in tej   mamb'aj tk'u'j   ti'j.
     PUNCT.PAS DIR.come   burn   that   father   his.stomach   toward.her
     'The father felt compassion for her.'

What we've seen is that the special set of intransitive verbs—the verbs of direction in relation to a speaker—are based on the notion of the deictic center. The directional auxiliaries are derived from these intransitives; they lose phonological size with the simplification of their complex vowels, and their centeredness can be more local or metaphorical than their intransitive counterparts. The deictic anchorage of the intransitive verbs of direction is part of the lexical entry (the basic meaning) for each verb. These are determined by the semantic content of each one. The meaning of the directionals, however, is determined pragmatically (i.e., in relation to the context of their use). They maintain their basic meaning of movement away from center (for *xi* and *pon*) or toward center (for (*tzaj* and *ul*), but their meaning in context must be calculated, as is basic to all pragmatic contributions to meaning in a specific context.

Nevertheless, deictic anchorage is still in view, whether lexically or pragmatically. Mam speakers must situate action in terms of where it begins and where it goes—all in relation to a deictic anchor or center.

To summarize, centeredness is not only a cultural theme, one which continually arises in the thoughts and daily lives of the Mam, it is also an integral part of the language as well. Godfrey says "just about half of the approximately 5700 clauses in the text corpus contain some kind of directional verb" (1981:93). England reminds us that directionals are "almost obligatory with two-topic [subject and object, WMC] verbs" (1978:227). This means that the Mam are continually dealing with the concept of centeredness as a grammatical theme, since, repeating Haviland, the use of directional verbs "always indexes some deictic origo" (1996:276), either their own as speaker, or another's, or an arbitrary center of reference.

We have already seen the importance of the lexicon in coding centeredness; in this chapter, we've seen that centeredness is what Hale (1986:234) calls a lexico-semantic theme, a grammatical category that is expressed in different morphosyntactic constructions and on different levels of the grammar. This is what Slobin means when he says that certain obligatory grammatical expressions *must* be expressed. They are "required by the grammatical organization of the language" (1996:71). He calls this "thinking for speaking," the idea that certain grammatical categories must be tended to in order to say anything at all. And once said, they affirm the importance of the center as a grammatical theme, here showing up in the lexical meanings of a special set of intransitive verbs or as verbal auxiliaries within the verb phrase.

In sections 5.5 and 5.6 we will see how directionals and their concomitant deictic anchorage play a further role in Mam morphology.

5.5 Complex directionals

Both the directionals and the intransitive verbs can be more fully specified by adding a directional suffix to the root.[3] As seen in table 5.3, we will limit ourselves to just two of said suffixes. Despite their reduced phonological forms, the *-tz* an *-x* suffixes (except as discussed below) maintain their full lexical meaning.

Table 5.3. Reduced suffixal forms of two direction-related verbs

Intransitive verb/directional	Reduced suffixal form
tza:jil/tzaj	*-tz*
xi'yil/xi	*-x*

(32)
    a. *ja:w* 'go up' + *-x* → *ja:x* 'go up away from speaker'
    b. *ja:w* 'go up' + *-tz* → *ja:tz* 'come up toward from speaker'
    c. *e:l* 'leave' + *-x* → *e:x* 'leave moving away from speaker'
    d. *e:l* 'leave' + *-tz* → *e:tz* 'leave moving toward speaker'

The long vowels in (32) identify these verbs as intransitives (as opposed to directionals which have only short vowels). The suffixes can also be added to directionals as in (33).

(33)
    a. *Ma jax tkanin xjal.* 'the person arrived up there away from speaker'
    b. *Ma jatz tkanin tzalu'n.* 'the person arrived up here where speaker is'
    c. *Ex rinin.* 'he left running away from speaker'
    d. *Etz rinin.* 'he left running toward speaker'

The *-tz* and *-x* suffixes are common throughout Mam discourse, particularly narrative discourse.

---

[3] There are other directional suffixes mentioned by both Godfrey (1981: especially page 99) and England (1983:168). These directional suffixes constitute an issue that needs further study.

In table 5.4, I show the *-tz* and *-x* suffixes with a number of directionals. While the 'come' and 'go' meanings of the *-tz* and *-x* suffixes are clear, both forms have taken on additional meaning beyond their simple directional meanings exemplified in (32) and (33) above.

Table 5.4 Directional combined forms with *-x* and *-tz*

Base form				Reduced form		Fused form	Gloss
el	'leave'	+	-x	→		*ex*	leave away from speaker
el	'leave'	+	-tz	→		*etz*	leave toward speaker
ok	'enter'	+	-x	→		*okx*	enter away from speaker
ok	'enter'	+	-tz	→		*oktz*	enter toward speaker
jaw	'ascend'	+	-x	→		*jax*	ascend away from speaker
jaw	'ascend'	+	-tz	→		*jatz*	ascend toward speaker
kub'	'descend'	+	-x	→		*kux*	descend away from speaker
kub'	'descend'	+	-tz	→		*kutz*	descend toward speaker
iky'	'pass by'	+	-x	→		*iky'x*	pass by on far side
iky'	'pass by'	+	-tz	→		*iky'tz*	pass by on near side
aj	'return'	+	-x	→		*ajx*	return away from here
aj	'return'	+	-tz	→		*ajtz*	return here

What the addition of *-x* and *-tz* does to the meanings of these verbs (either the intransitive or the directional auxiliary) is to recenter origo from 'other' or 'arbitrary' to 'speaker'. *El*, for example, means 'leave', but it gives no indication as to whether the motion of leaving is toward the speaker (thus 'leave coming out') or away from the speaker ('leave going out'). The affix provides this additional information.[4]

The use of directional affixes begins early in life. I stopped to visit a friend one morning and his toddler daughter (barely three years old) was in the yard. I greeted her, holding my hand low to touch hers. *Chin q'olb'i'n* 'I greet you', I said. She took my hand and gently touched it to her bowed

---

[4] Phonological reduction, as in the forms of *-x* and *-tz*, from *xi* and *tzaj*, respectively, is common in the discussion of grammaticalization. However, the fact that the reduced forms maintain their full semantic denotation is not.

forehead and kissed it. Mam children are taught this greeting ritual even before they can speak. I asked if her father was home and she said that he was in the house. *Ku to:kxa* 'go in', she said. *Ku* is the imperative marker; the prefix *t-* and suffix *-a* constitute second person singular, leaving us with just *o:kx* 'enter + movement away from the speaker'. Had she been inside the house and invited me to enter, she could have said *ku to:ktza*, using the *-tz* allomorph meaning 'come toward me' rather than *-x* 'go away from me', or she might simply have said *ku to:ka* 'enter'. This *(ku to:ka)* is the common way to invite someone into the house and it is what I learned to say if someone comes to the door and I am inside. This sentence leaves the idea of motion in relation to the speaker as unstated, since, as we've seen above (table 5.1 and subsequent discussion), the origo for the verb *o:kil* 'to enter', is 'other'. In the present case, the 'other' is me, the one being addressed, who is 'other' from the little girl's perspective. In *ku to:ka,* I'm being told to enter irrespective of the location of the speaker.

But my juvenile interlocutor had learned something beyond the greeting ritual. Since the verb *o:kil* denotes an origo of 'other', if she wanted to include herself in the picture, she needed a shift in spatial frame. She accomplished this shift by employing the *-x*. Indeed, the use of *o:kil* (or *e:lil, ja:wil* and *kub'il*) without affixation when referring to oneself is less common, since there is a mismatch between the denoted 'other' origo of the verb and the speaker-centric origo of the act of speaking. It is far more common to recast the frame by adding an *-x* or *-tz* in such situations as spelled out in tables 5.3 and 5.4 and in the discussion following.

With this in mind, my young friend was perhaps just learning to use directional affixes in a way that situated herself as a deictic center.

5.6 Extended use of *-x* and *-tz*

From the above discussion of intransitive directional verbs and directional auxiliaries we see that the principle of deictic anchorage is part of the denotation of these terms which is reflected not only in the lexicon (i.e., the semantics), but also in the morphology (for example, by the use of *-tz* and *-x* in the formation of words) and the syntax (in the use of directional auxiliaries as part of complex verb phrases).

Above, I commented on the phonological reduction of *xi* and *tzaj* to *-x* and *-tz* respectively, while they maintain the full semantic force of the full forms (either the directionals or the intransitive verbs of direction). I mentioned that this kind of phonological reduction is common as words take on more grammatical function (see Hopper and Traugott (1993) for extensive discussion). But I also mentioned that grammaticalized forms tend to be semantically bleached as well, as they take on a more grammatical function. Although we saw that this is not the case in the examples already cited, in the following discussion we will see that the directional suffixes -*tz* and perhaps -*x* have indeed been affected in this way.

5.6.1 A narrative context for directional suffixes

The narrative text cited in these pages and included as an appendix, was spoken and then transcribed later that same day by Oscar, a personal friend of mine and a local schoolteacher. Oscar was 26 years old when the recording was made in 1994. Early that same morning, he had accompanied me and another friend to *El Triunfo*, an important market town a two-hours' drive away from Comitancillo, Oscar's hometown. He came along to help sell books and to visit an area he had heard about for many years, but which he had never actually visited. When we got back to Comitancillo that same evening, Oscar recorded the day's experiences at my request. I asked him to tell the story of the day's events as if speaking to a Mam friend—although only I was in the room running the tape recorder when he told the story. After taping, Oscar produced a written version of the text and made some minor corrections to his version as he listened to it again. It was then edited once again by native Mam-speaking co-workers. I've glossed the text in some detail for those interested, but mostly just to the extent necessary for the purposes of this study.

In Oscar's text, he talks about the trip to *El Triunfo*, and he starts out with a few remarks about the roads and the beauty of the area (lines 1–10). The bulk of his talk (lines 11–35) is about the selling itself—how we went about setting up and reading from the books that we were offering for sale. Finally, in line 36, he talks about packing up our table, boxing up the books, and heading back home.

What particularly interests me in the text are the words for 'come' and 'go' and the directionals and suffixes derived from them. My specific interest is in the discourse function of the suffixal form of *tzaj*, although we will look at *xi* also (i.e., -*tz* and -*x*) as charted in tables 5.3

5.6 Extended use of -x and -tz

and 5.4. We will cite occurrences of these suffixal forms throughout the text and consider several related meanings for their different occurrences. The careful reader senses me hemming and hawing a bit on the *xi* forms. Well observed. We have less relevant data for these forms, and there are homonyms to the *-x* forms that will keep me mitigating the claims concerning *-x* and *xi*. However, I think the claims about *tzaj* and *-tz* are strong and will carry the point, which is that the directionals find their way into the discourse structure of Mam texts, to go along with their presence in other levels of the grammar (the lexicon, the morphology and the syntax).

5.6.2 -x in context

The suffix *-x* occurs 13 times in Oscar's text. Its most transparent use is as a directional suffix appended to an intransitive verb. For example, in line 27 of the text (repeated here as (34)), the word *e:x* is the same as that illustrated in (32c) above. It signifies that the people who attended the market went (in a direction away from Oscar at the moment he was telling the story) in order to sell their goods at *El Triunfo*.

(34) Ma   nintz-x   xjal   e:-x   k'ay-il   toj-jo   k'ayb'il   a'.
     very many-AUG people leave-go to.sell-INF in-SPEC market   that
     'A large number of people went to sell at that market.'

This same *-x* directional suffix also occurs in lines 25 and 34 of our text, repeated below as (35) and (36) respectively. In these cases *-x* is suffixed to the directional verb *el* 'leave'. In (34), *e:x* does not function as a directional auxiliary. First, the long vowel precludes such a function, and second, the word is followed by an infinitive. This structure is similar to the English gloss included for (34) of this sentence where the second verb (*k'ayil* 'to sell') serves as an infinitival complement to its immediately preceding intransitive verb (*e:x* 'went' as in 'went to sell').

In (34), *e:x* is what is predicated about the people who have gone out (away from where Oscar is when he is telling his story) in order to sell at the market. In contrast, in (35) and (36), *ex* has a short vowel and it is followed by a tensed verb. This is the archetype occurrence of a complex verb phrase that includes a directional auxiliary. So we see that that there is syntactic participation on the part of our *-x* directional.

(35) *At-taq   n-e-x   t-laq'on-te   tu'j   Marks*
     exist-PAS   PROG-leave-away s/he-bought-it   book   Mark
     'There were some who went to buy the book of St. Mark.'

In (36) and (37), *ex tlaq'o'n* implies that people out-away-bought books, that is they bought books, taking them away from the place where they were sold.

(36) *At-taq-te   n-e-x   laq'o'n-taq   tu'j.*
     exist-PAST-he   PROG-leave-go   s/he-bought-PAS   his.books
     'There were those who bought books.'

In line 10 of the text, repeated here as (37), *-x* is affixed to the preposition *tzma* 'toward'. giving us *tzmax Twi' Chlub'* 'toward *Tuichilupe* (a town), but away from where Oscar was at the moment of speaking'.

(37) *A-tzin   t-xilin-jo   b'e   iky-jo   tzen-ku'*
     that-well   its-essence-SPEC   camino   similar-SPEC   like-down

   b'e   n-tzaj   xkye   tzma-x   Twi' Chlub'.
   road   PROG-DIR.come   begin   at-go   Tuichilupe.
   'The way we went was similar to the road that comes toward us from the town of Tuichilupe.'

Aside from its use as a directional suffix, *-x* can also be used as an augmentative suffix. The following words are taken from the text, lines 4 and 6. The entire words (including the affixes) are listed as (38), (39) and (40).

(38) *t-b'an-il-x-ch'in*
     s/he.POS-good-INAL-AUG-little
     'pretty good' (literally 'very good, a little')

(39) *nintz-x*
     many-AUG
     'very many'

(40) *quq-x-tz*
     dust-AUG-then
     'a lot of dust, then'

These augmentative uses are related to the directional meaning discussed above in examples (35) and (36), and they have similar force. Something big (augmented) goes beyond the norm in terms of size or

5.6 Extended use of -x and -tz

quantity (as in 'very good', 'very many', and 'a lot of dust' in (38), (39), and (40), respectively), so the augmentative sense is that of moving away from a standard of some sort. It's not uncommon to hear the Mam say in Spanish *más allá* 'further away', to signal a contrast with a person who is smarter than another or more widely traveled or richer, as in English 'he's *far and away* smarter than his brother', where there is semantic overlap between distance away from the speaker and the sense of augmentation. So the metaphorical use of *-x* is conceived of as being beyond some sense of standard—if not in terms of actual motion away from a deictic center, at least a metaphorical movement beyond a norm. For example, if a lucky woman were to win the lottery, the Mam would say something like, *Ma q'ininx te nana* 'the woman became rich'. Note the *-x* suffix on the verb *q'inin* 'to get rich'. If someone gets rich, she figuratively moves away from the rest of the group which is considered to be not rich.

There are two occurrences of *-x* in Oscar's text that seem to fit neither the directional, nor the augmentative function. I'll discuss these interesting examples below in sections 5.7 and 5.7.2.

5.6.3 *-tz* in context

There are twelve occurrences of the suffix *-tz* in Oscar's text. As seen in (14) and (31) above, *-tz* has directional force. We can see this in line 39 of Oscar's text, repeated here as (41).

(41)   *Ex*   *b'e'x-sin*   *o*   *a:j-tz-tz-a.*
        and   PUNCT.PAS-well   we.REM   return.home-come-then-EX
        'And we returned home.'

In (41), the intransitive verb *a:j* (see example (9)) is affixed with two *-tz* suffixes. The first carries directional force. We returned home, here, the place where Oscar was narrating his story. The second *-tz* has discourse specifier function and will be discussed below in sections 5.7 and 5.7.1.

Another interesting use of the *-tz* suffix is in line 22 of the text, repeated here as (42).

(42) Ex   nchi   b'in-xjal   ti'j   u'j   n-ja-tz
     and   PROG.they listen-people regarding book PROG-DAR.up-then

u'jin-taq.
read-past
'And the people listened to the book that was being read.'

Here, the word *njatz* is a directional that pairs with and precedes the (tensed) main verb *u'jin* 'read'. The directional here is denoting that the words that the man is reading are coming up (the *ja* part of the directional) out of his mouth (or possibly from the book itself) and toward (the *-tz* part of the directional) the hearers. This is exactly the same directional form *jatz* as demonstrated in example (33b), although its meaning must be calculated based on context. Here the *-tz* doesn't signal Oscar as the speaker, but rather those hearing the reading. So, just as Oscar's text exemplified both conventional (speaker-centered) and extended meanings for *-x* (compare examples (35)–(37) with (38)–(40)), so the text also contrasts the conventional uses of speaker-centered *-tz* in (41) with an extended 'other center' in (42).

5.7 The discourse function of *-tz* and *-x*

Neuenswander and, more recently, Zaharlick, both in personal communications, have discussed the metaphor of body position vis-à-vis the cultural conception of time. We in extended European cultures normally think of ourselves looking toward the future, with our back to the past, as we march boldly forward into the unknown.

Many non-European cultures are not nearly so bold about the unknown. Both Neuenswander and Zaharlick talk about Amerindian groups metaphorically facing the past, with their backs toward the future. They conceive of their situation not so much as marching wisely and briskly into the future but as having the future overtake them. The future becomes the present as they experience it and then, as they recall it, it is part of the past. There certainly is an emic logic to this idea of body position vis-à-vis time, since we have experienced the past (and can therefore "see" it), while we don't know the future, despite an English future tense that claims "I will do such and such." Indeed, Mam has at least five past tense grammatical aspects, and only one future, which carries along with it the sense of the

5.7 The discourse function of -tz and -x

dubitative or unknowable. The language is far more specific about the past, which has been experienced, than the future, which they consider unknowable. For example, when my family and I left Guatemala in 1998, we were feted at a special party where many of our friends wept and carried on. I told them to ease up, because we would be back within six months to visit, to which they replied, "Who are you to claim to know the future? You don't know for sure that you'll be back. Maybe you will return, and we can rejoice, but today we assume that we will never see you again. Let us be sad."

Metaphorically, with this in mind, it's more realistic to consider the Maya as facing, and more intimate with, the past—that which they know and have experienced—while the future—that which they don't know and haven't yet experienced—is behind them, creeping up on them unbeknownst.

To extend this cultural metaphor in linguistic terms, the *-tz* suffix denotes movement, either actual or metaphorical, toward the deictic center, whereas the *-x* suffix moves away from the deictic center. The sense of 'to come', then, is more intimate, near, and known than 'to go', which represents apartness and distance. I suggest that our suffixes *-tz* and *-x* mimic this idea of the known and the unknown, and reflect a coherence strategy in Mam discourse, a linguistic strategy for helping a text "hold together."

Eve Danziger discusses spatial deictics in Mopan Maya, a Yucatecan language of northern Guatemala. She discusses a four-way contrast of locatives: *waye'* 'here (near speaker)', *ta'kan* 'there (near addressee)' *tilo'* 'there (near a visible third person)', and *te'* '(invisible, away from everyone)'. She goes on to point out that these deictics are used in discourse as well, to refer to information that the speaker is presenting as new or old. She concludes by saying, "No reference to deictic location can in fact be made in Mopan without invoking semantic contrasts relevant both to the social situation in which reference is made, and to the medium of reference and state of shared knowledge of the discourse participants" (1994:904). In other words, deictic referents do double duty in Mopan as discourse markers, helping to manage the presentation and interpretation of narrative text, thus forging strong discourse cohesion.

According to Halliday and Hasan (1976), languages have ways of showing that a natural text is qualitatively different from a mere concatenation of disjointed sentences. The difference is that a text displays discourse *texture*—a cohesive unity based on linguistic strategies which link later text with what has come before. Mam, of course, is no different. Mam speakers employ discourse strategies to articulate well-formed texts. One of these strategies seems to be the use of extended notions of *-tz* and *-x* in order to specify or highlight discourse-old and discourse-new information. I suggest that the Mam suffix *-tz*, by representing nearness and intimacy, extends to text that is discourse old and known, while *-x*, which represents apartness or distance, extends to text that is new to the discourse and unknown.

5.7.1 A discourse function for *-tz*

As mentioned in 5.6.3, there are twelve occurrences of *-tz* in Oscar's text. Three of these have directional force, as shown in example (41), and one in (42) is used with an extended, non-speaker center meaning, as discussed previously. I suggest that the rest have discourse function signifying that the stem that they attach to is discourse old, that is, previously mentioned in the text. In line 3 of our text, repeated here as (43), *-tz* is affixed to *ayi'n*, meaning 'me', a participant that was mentioned as part of the 'we' in sentences 1 and 2 by entailment, since 'we' includes 'me', which is immediately accessible from the previous text. So the *-tz* affixed to 'me' identifies 'me' as evoked by or previously mentioned in the text.

(43) *A-tzi'n   q-b'aj-a,   a   Julián   ex-sin   ayin-tz-a.*
     that-well   our-number-EX   that   Julián   and-well   me-then-EX
     'So our number included Julián and me.'

Here *-tz* affixes to a pronoun. And although it doesn't here seem to have the meaning of 'come', either as speaker center or 'other' center, it nonetheless suggests something known and recently mentioned or something 'close by', something intimately or recently experienced.

In sentences 5 and 6 of Oscar's text, here as (44) and (45), all *-tz* occurrences point back to the trip, mentioned in 1, 2, 4, and 5.

(44) *Noq-tzin   tu'n-tz-jo   te'   q-xi'-ch'il-tz-a*
     only-well   regarding-then-SPEC   when   we-went-a.bit-then-EX

   tu'n   q-kanin   Triunfo,   nya-xix   wen   b'e
   in.order.to   we-arrived   Triunfo   not-very   good   road
   'Regarding this (trip) when we went (from Twimuj) to Triunfo, the road was not very good.'

5.7 The discourse function of -tz and -x

(45) *Ma   nintz-x   jul,   ex-sin   manyor   quq-x-tz.*
quite big-AUG holes and-well much   dust-AUG-then
'There were big holes and a lot of dust.'

In 21, here as (46), *-tz* is attached to *Josué* (by which I'm known by many of my Mam friends), who was first mentioned in 2, but who was kept close to the story since it was *Josué* who actually made the tape of Oscar's story and was present as it was being recorded. In addition, he was part of every mention of "exclusive we" in our text, lines 1–5, 9, 11, and 14–17.

(46) *Ok   ten-pe-tzin   te   Josué-tz   yol-il   kyi'jjo jni' u'j*
DIR.enter begin-?-well he Josué-then to.speak-INF about all   in

toj   q-yol
book our-language
'Then Josué began to talk about all the books in our language.'

In 36, included here as (47), *-tz* reappears after a fairly long hiatus, referring to book sales, still the main topic of the discourse, and clearly discourse old.

(47) *B'aj   k'ayin-tz-a   ja'lin,*
DIR.complete sell-then-EX   now
'Then (we) finished selling,'

In 39 and 40 of our text (48), Oscar completes his narrative. The mention of home reflects the full circle traveled that day and the place where the day had begun and where the discourse was originally spoken.

(48) *ex   b'e'x-sin   o   a:j-tz-tz-a,*
and PUNCT.PAS-well we.REM return.home-come-then-EX

tu'n   q-u:l-a   kyxol   aj   Txolja.
in.order.to we-arrive-EX among resident Comitancillo
'and we returned home in order to come again to our own pueblo.'

So, it appears that *-tz* when used in its discourse function, points to preceding context, that which is accessible within Oscar's discourse (or implied by it), not forward in the text or to new information. Because of this, I consider this marker or discourse particle, *-tz*, to have discourse status as a true deictic or specifier. I don't consider it to be a discourse marker in the technical sense, since it doesn't "manage" text portions, it only selects or refers to them. This is different from other discourse markers (DMs), which actually manage portions of text. For example, the DM, *nevertheless,* points both ways in a text, taking what occurs before it and considering it as grounds that have been somehow overcome by what comes after it in its containing sentence. Fraser (1999) says that DMs "impose a relationship between some aspect of the discourse segment they are a part of, call it S2 (for Sentence 2), and some aspect of the prior discourse segment, call it S1." Our particle *-tz* seems not to impose such a relationship, since it doesn't impose any analysis on S2; it merely points to or highlights something in S1 or in the broader preceding context. Nevertheless, even though it isn't a DM in Fraser's sense, it supports text cohesion and "texture" as per Halliday and Hasan, by reaching back into previous text in order to keep it discourse current.

The suffixes *-tz* and perhaps *-x* are what Levinson (1983) calls discourse deictics. To exemplify, he suggests a sentence like *That was the funniest joke I ever heard,* where the deictic *that* points not to a specific object in the physical context, but to a linguistic object (perhaps a sentence or series of sentences or an entire discourse).

5.7.2 A possible discourse function for *-x*

Although *-x* occurs frequently in Oscar's text, it doesn't occur as often as a discourse specifier as *-tz* does. There are only two possible occurrences in the limited text that we will discuss here. In line 13, Oscar mentions that Julian had gone to sell his wares. Then in line 14, repeated here as (49), he says that we also went to sell. This is the first mention of the merchandise that we had brought to sell.

(49) Ex   iky-x-jo   qe',   o   xi'   qe'   k'ay-il
     and   similar-AUG-SPEC   us.EX   we.REM   go   us.EX to.sell-INF

   ti'j-jo   q-k'axhjil-a,   a   iqin-taq.
   regarding-SPEC   our-merchandise-EX   which   carry-PAS
   'And we also went to sell the goods that had been brought.'

He then goes on to talk about setting up a small table and laying out books for sale—all first mentions.

In line 18, repeated here as (50), the first word in the sentence is *noq-x* 'only'.

5.7 The discourse function of -tz and -x

(50) *Noq-x   te'   t-lon-te   tnejil   xjal,   b'aj   tzaj*
     only-then when   he-saw-it   first   person   DIR.complete   DIR.come

   qi'yj   txqan-l   xjal.
   gather   all-remaining   people.
   'When the first person saw our goods, everyone else gathered as well.'

Both the first person and everyone else are first occurrences. There had been no mention in the text of buyers up to this point (although we might certainly consider them as inherent to the buying-selling process). So both *ikyxjo* and *noqx* seem to look forward into the text to what is coming. This contrasts with the discourse use of *-tz*, which looks back in the text to what has already been mentioned.

There is another difference in distribution between the two suffixes which may prove to be important. The *-x* suffix, when used as a discourse specifier, occurs early in its containing sentence. In our three examples, it occurs affixed either to the first or second word in the sentence and it seems to take scope over the entire sentence. In contrast, *-tz* tends to occur at the end of its containing clause, and it seems to take scope only over the word that it is attached to, particularly if its host is a noun or verb. Of the eight occurrences as a discourse specifier, only once is it attached to a word other than a noun or verb. This is in line 5 where a noun (the trip) is implied, although the suffix is attached to *tu'n* 'regarding'. Also, this is the only instance where *-tz* is suffixed to a word early in the sentence.

Despite these distributional differences, it seems possible to consider that the affixes *-tz* and *-x* and work as a cohesion team in Mam discourse, specifying text as known (old) or unknown (new) in the unfolding of the story being told.

In this chapter, I've traced the meaning and function of Mam directional forms from the intransitive verbs of direction to their corresponding directional auxiliaries to several affixal forms. In each instantiation of these terms we've seen a subtle effect on meaning. The full intransitives code deictic anchorage as part of their formal semantic character, a basic relationship between the form and the world. But we saw that with the directionals, although the same basic meaning holds true, deictic anchorage must be recalculated dependent upon the local context of speech. With the affixal forms, we saw a fairly stable sense of deictic anchorage and movement in relation to it, where the allomorphs *-tz* and *-x* serve to fine-tune the directions coded in the fuller forms. But we also saw that these suffixes can be extended to meanings that seem not very directional in nature. For example, -*x* can be used as an augmentative, intensifier, or as an affix meaning 'all', as in *tkyaqilx* 'all, every one', or as an affix meaning 'one and the same', as in *Ax tata* 'that very man'. Finally, I suggested that the affixes -*tz* and -*x* are used to identify information in Mam discourse as discourse old or new.

5.8 Relational nouns as an instantiation of centeredness

A final place where we will consider the projection of origo is as it relates to the use of Mam relational nouns, which are based in part on the physical body in space. As Hanks says, "Body space has a schematic structure...and it is related to other spatial schemata by processes of analogy, homology and transformation" (1990:81). The Mam use the vocabulary for certain body parts to recenter an origo from speaker center to some other projected center of reference and locate noun phrases in relation to a projected origo of the body in space. These relational nouns have "live" denotative meaning, such that a spatial relation is evoked in many grammatical relationships that are handled in other ways in other languages like English or Spanish. For example, the Mam will say that something is *twutz ja* 'in front of the house'. *Twutz* literally means 'its face (at the house's face)'. Likewise something can be *twi' ja* 'on top of the house (at the house's head)', *ttzi ja* 'at the entrance to the house (at the house's mouth)', *ttxa'n ja* 'at the edge of the house (at the house's nose)', *ttxlaj ja* 'beside the house (at the house's side)' or *t-xe ja* 'under the house (at the house's root)', where *twi', ttzi, ttxa'n, ttxlaj,* and *t-xe* mean 'its head, its mouth, its nose, its side and its root, respectively.[5]

England describes the extensive use of relational nouns in Mam. "All sentence constituents except the verb, the direct agent, patient, or subject, and adverbs are indicated by relational noun phrases. This means that all non-direct cases and most locations occur in relational noun phrases" (1983:153). This suggests that in order to speak at all, the Mam must take into account not only the deictic spatial relations of verbal semantics as discussed above, but also spatial relationships between noun phrases as expressed in body terminology that ground these relationships in space via analogy with the

---

[5] Some relational nouns are *not* possessed body parts (although all are possessed), and some relational noun phrases indicate not noun phrase locative (or positional relations), but case relations.

5.8 Relational nouns as an instantiation of centeredness 167

physical body. As Duranti says, "We often forget that the human body is the first instrument we experience" (1997:322), mediating between our thoughts and the world. Many relational nouns have a sense of center, particularly in positional relations like 'in front of the house', 'around the house', 'above the house', 'on the house', 'under the house', 'behind the house', etc. where the house is seen as projected center stage, and the noun phrases located in relation to it are situated in association to the "body" of the house itself.

Table 5.5. Mam relational nouns

Relational noun	**Usage**	**Literal meaning**
A.		
twutz	'before'	'its/his face'
ttzi	'at the entrance to'	'its/his mouth'
twi'	'on top of'	'its/his head'
ttxlaj	'beside'	'its/his side'
(tzkyel) ti'j	'behind'	'its/his back'
ttxa'n	'at the edge'	'its/his nose'
B.		
tuk'a	'with'	'its/his companion'
t-xe	'at the base'	'its root'
tu'n	'by, by means of'	
te	'to, of, for'	
txol	'between, among'	
ti'jila	'around'	
tib'aj	'over'	
tjaq'	'under'	
toj	'in'	
tzma (tsma?)	'at'	
tumil	'in the direction of'	

For example, table 5.5 shows how relations coded by several English prepositions are coded in Mam. The nouns in set A of table 5.5 reference body parts, while those in set B do not.

Examples (51)–(56) exemplify the relational nouns in set A of table 5.5, those which are based on body parts.

(51)	*A xjal at twutz tja.*	'The person is in front of (at the face of) his/her house.'
(52)	*A nana at ttzi jul*	'The woman is at the entrance to (at the mouth of) the cave.'
(53)	*Jun pich' at twi' ja*	'A bird is on (at the head of) the house.'
(54)	*Lu at ttxlaj ja.*	'Here it is beside (at the side of) the house.'
(55)	*At jun tze ti'jxi ja.*	'There is a tree behind (at the rear of) the house.'
(56)	*Jun pich' at ttxa'n ja.*	'A bird is at the drip edge (at the nose) of the house.'

By stating that the Mam consider these relational nouns to have "live" denotative meaning, I mean that the Mam consider these terms in light of an actual body in space, even if the body in question belongs to a house or a car or a chair. There is wide agreement, for example, that the "nose" of a chair is the front edge of the seat. Plus, if something is in front of me, I wouldn't say, **Lu jun xjal twutz nwutza* 'Here is a person at the face of my face', but rather, *Lu jun xjal nwutza* 'Here is a person at my face', where my own body is the basis of the relational use of the noun. In other words, the relational nouns have not been so grammaticalized that they have lost the "live" denotational meaning of the body in space and its accompanying sense of center.

What these relational nouns do is force an origo of 'other' into the context of speech. This holds for all of the relational nouns, not just those in set A of table 5.5. In every case the deictic anchorage shifts from the speaker to that of the "body" of the noun phrase that follows the relational noun. For example, in (51) the person is situated in front of the house. This implies that the house has become the new anchor point of the sentence, and the person is situated not in terms of her location in regard to the speaker, but rather, in terms of the new anchor point, the house. In this case, the person is somewhere near the wall of the house in which the front door is located.

5.9 Conclusion

In this chapter I have built on the notion that centeredness is a cultural theme and showed that it is a recurrent notion in the grammar as well. In chapter four we looked in detail at the way a number of lexical items are

5.9 Conclusion

built around a sense of centeredness. In the present chapter I suggested that in similar fashion, the intransitive verbs of direction contain in their lexical meanings a reference location or deictic center. Four of these verbs *(tza:jil, xi'yil, u:lil,* and *po:nil)* code the speaker as their deictic anchor or origo; four code 'other' as origo *(o:kil, e:lil, ja:wil,* and *kub'il)*; and four code an arbitrary origo *(a:jil, iky'il, kyijil,* and *b'ajil)*.

A corresponding set of directional auxiliaries is derived from these intransitive verbs of direction. They are phonologically reduced and their meaning, while consistent with that of their corresponding intransitive, is affected as well. Whereas the intransitives have deictic anchorage coded into their basic meaning, origo for the directionals is calculated pragmatically, that is, based on context. The directionals can be further reduced phonologically to single-phoneme suffixes, two of which, *-tz* and *-x,* we've looked at in this chapter. Although further phonologically reduced, we saw that these suffixes can still have full directional meaning just as their intransitive and directional counterparts do. Just as the directionals code meaning beyond that of the intransitives from which they derive, so the affixes have meaning and functions beyond those of the directionals. Nevertheless, we've seen that the Mam consider these meanings to be largely equivalent, and that deictic anchorage must be tended to for each of the full intransitives, the directional auxiliaries, and the directional suffixes.

I showed why I think that what seem to be grammaticalized forms of these directional affixes have come to have discourse function, based on the extended meanings of the forms for 'to come' and 'to go'. In this chapter, we've seen how the notion of centeredness is a theme that runs through a number of grammatical categories, specifically the morphology (in terms of directional suffixes and relational nouns, both of which require deictic anchorage), the syntax (in the pervasive use of directional auxiliaries in transitive sentences and the high percentage of intransitive verbs of direction in Mam speech), and the discourse. At the level of discourse, we've looked at directional suffixes which highlight or specify text as discourse old or new. We've also considered the use of couplets in Mayan ritual rhetoric (see chapter three) as iconic to the notion of dualism which I claim is another instantiation of centeredness. The mention of couplets here is relevant to our topic since such couplets are a mainstay of certain discourse genre.

That deictic anchorage is basic to each of these grammatical categories makes the calculation of centeredness as important grammatically as we've seen it to be culturally. This, of course, is the basic premise of this study, that centeredness functions as an organizing principle throughout Mam language and culture.

At a meeting with Mam Evangelical village leaders in March 2005, we were discussing instantiations of centeredness as a cultural theme. The gathered men affirmed that centeredness is indeed a formative principle in their lives, and Mesac said, only partly in jest, "This explains why our people are so hard to work with. Each of us thinks he is the center of everything." In saying this Mesac realized not only that the seeking of centeredness is a Mam cultural value, a motivating and organizing principle, something external and "out there" to be pursued, but the fact that each individual constitutes a center from which the pervasive Mam notion of movement and spatial relations is lexicalized by the language and grammaticalized in the language makes it a principle that is internalized and all the more pervasive as well.

I consider Mesac's off-hand remark an affirmation of my premise that centeredness is both a cultural and grammatical theme, and his statement is just the kind of comment we would expect since centeredness sort of "busts out" all over. The seeking of centeredness and the construction of it in terms of architectonics, religious choice, the conception of health and illness, and even the lexicalization of centeredness in -k'u'j and other terms discussed in chapters three and four, situate centeredness as a cultural theme. But the idea of reflecting on *oneself* as center is a notion deriving from the habitual thought or fashion of speaking required by the grammar itself.

6

Conclusion

6.1 What we've seen

In this book, we've seen that centeredness is a cultural theme for the Maya-Mam, a recurrent thread of cultural understanding and practice that points toward shared underlying values and worldview. England says that such themes "override community differences; they are defined for cultural groups as a whole" (1978:226). Martin adds that they "are part of the history and behavior of whole cultural groups" (1977:366). A cultural theme is what Hale calls World View 1, "the central propositions or postulates in a people's theory of how things are in the world" (1986:233).

We have considered four wide-ranging instantiations of centeredness which point to its existence as a cultural theme: the constructed world, health practice and illness etiology, religious choice, and the practice of daily life.

I suggested with Low (2000) and Bourdieu (2003 [1971]) that both the ruins of the Mayan central plaza and the present-day Mayan homestead itself are each microcosms of how the Mam, and, more generally, the Maya, think about the world. Gossen (1974) points out that the Chamula Tzotzil consider their town to be the navel of the earth. In the same way that the town of Chamula is considered the epicenter of all that matters in the world, so Mayan homes are built around a patio that defines a center space in and around which all home activity takes place. When this center area is violated, something has to happen to restore the center. For example, when Timo wanted to add on to his homestead, renovation was required to reestablish an appropriate center space that "felt right."

In addition, Low (2000, 1993) suggests that the Latin American plaza is iconic of the sense of center "with buildings arranged so as to symbolically equate the architectural center of civic power with the center of the universe," what she calls a "sacred geography" (2000). She goes on to suggest that the appropriation of such sacred space—the imagery of centeredness—may well have added a sense of gravitas to the invading Spaniards' eventual success in exerting hegemony over the Maya. This was affirmed in an interview I had with Agustín where he talked about the plaza as a place of comfort, knowledge, peace, harmony, and unity amidst diversity. The plaza is a grounded and physical center space where one senses that he or she truly belongs.

In terms of illness etiology, Redfield says that good health involves "maintenance of that median condition which the native expresses in terms of heat and cold" (1941). Recall that diseases considered hot by the Maya are considered to be caused by overexposure to things or situations considered hot, while cold diseases are caused by overexposure to cold. Recall as well that we discussed the notions of hot and cold in terms of intrinsic qualities and not necessarily physical temperature. As discussed in section 3.2, diseases are treated with herbs, infusions, medicines, foods, and ceremonies that are meant to counteract the overabundance of hot or cold built up in the ailing body. Cool medicines and special cool foods are brought to bear on hot illnesses, while warmer medicines and foods are used to treat cold illnesses.

This idea is more than simply the notion of balance. Balance, rather, is a strategy for attaining centeredness, what Redfield (1941:128) called "that median condition" between hot and cold. Treating illness utilizes a balance paradigm in order to restore equilibium to the body, a sense of *b'a'n,* well-being and centeredness. It is centeredness—"that median condition"—not the balance or reciprocity used to attain it, that is the goal of the Maya. Balance is a mechanism, the means to an end.

Perhaps the most powerful picture of the notion of centeredness is the Mayan religious concept of *the heart of heaven* conceived as both a

6.1 What we've seen

personality and a position. As Martin (1977) suggests, there is a Mayan notion of the convergence of person and place. Mountain deities are identified with the high places they inhabit. People identify not so much with the larger language group, but with the *municipio* where they were born. There is no straightforward Mam word for the notion of "family"; rather, they speak of "those in the same house," where location is given priority over kinship in expressing this important relationship of an individual to his or her biological family. They occupy the same space.

In chapter three we looked at Mayan religion in light of reciprocity—offering to the gods a gift commensurate with what a supplicant has requested of them. The *Popol Vuh* lays out a give-and-take relationship between humanity and the gods that is mutually beneficial and mutually dependent. I suggested that the idea of agreement or bargaining in this area of life is a metaphorical center space that promises a life of harmony and proper relationships between people and the gods, people and the land, and people and each other. Recall that Edmonson claimed that the Mayan word for religion is *ok olal* 'entering inwardness', which is tantamount, in our view, to seeking centeredness.

Historically, this balance was achieved, at least on major occasions, by human sacrifice, offering the red blood of a victim to the gods so that they would send the red dawn of a new day. Nájera discusses the heart as the center and essence of humanity, and it is this that is offered to the gods in exchange for the equilibrium essential to life here in the world.

It is also noteworthy that to the extent that people are unable to achieve the kind of personal centeredness they seek from their faith, the door is opened to faith alternatives. Citing Scotchmer and my own interviews, it was the lack of personal balance that drove many Mam to consider new ways to conceive of their relationship to the supernatural. The unprecedented conversion to Evangelical Christianity among the Mam is not necessarily a rejection of "Mayanness," but rather a confirmation of the importance of the cultural value of centeredness and the Mam's willingness to pursue it. Indeed, the Mam phrase for repentance and turning to faith in Christ is *tu'n tajtz ti'j tanmin* 'to return home in regard to one's heart'. The use of *heart* in this phrase and in light of the heart as conceived as the essence of humanity and the food of the gods presents powerful support to the salience of centeredness to the Mam. And as mentioned above, reciprocity is not a goal in and of itself. Rather, it is a strategy for attaining that median condition—centeredness.

In discussing how the Mam talk about centeredness, we looked at terms such as *niky'jin* 'half, middle', *niky'il* 'to understand, to aim, to center', *niky'sil* 'to split' (lit. 'to cause to be halved'), *tanmin* 'one's heart', *-k'u'j* 'stomach', *t-xilin* 'one's essence', *nuk'b'il* 'peace', *txolb'in* 'order', *tumil* 'one's direction', and *jikyin* 'straight', all of which point to a sense of being grounded in some kind of moral or actual center space. We also looked at Mam agreement protocol and how they talk about making a deal or coming to agreement. These phrases—*tu'n qkyij toj b'a'n* 'that we remain in goodness', *tu'n qten toj wen* 'that we occupy goodness', *tu'n kymujb'in qyol* 'to pair up our words', or *tu'n kymujb'in qib'* 'to pair up ourselves'—commit both sides to an agreed-upon compromise, a social center space where both can be happy with the agreement that has been hammered out.

In addition to seeing that centeredness is a cultural theme, we saw that it is a grammatical theme as well. England defines grammatical themes as "the underlying organizational principles of a language linking structure with semantics" (1978:226). Martin adds that they are "pervasive semantic categories with profound grammatical force" (1977:366). They are what Hale calls "lexico-semantic themes or motifs which function as integral components in a grammar" (1986:234).

The formal notion of a deictic center could be considered the formal, grammatical corollary to the cultural theme of centeredness. The closed set of twelve intransitive verbs of motion must be analyzed in terms of motion in reference to a deictic center, either speaker as center, other as center, or an arbitrary center. From this set of intransitive verbs is derived a corresponding set of directional auxiliary verbs that maintain the basic meaning of their intransitive counterparts, but extend it beyond the simple notion of movement in relation to a deictic center. Movement about such a center is part of the meaning of the intransitive verbs of motion, while the directional auxiliaries' precise meaning must be calculated pragmatically, that is, based on the context. From several of these directionals is derived a set of single-phoneme suffixes that denote direction from a deictic center, or other meanings related to movement toward or from a norm of some kind. Finally, we see that grammaticalized versions of two of these suffixes (*-tz* and likely *-x*) function in Mam discourse to tag information as discourse old or discourse new.

The Mam relational nouns also contribute to the grounded notion of centeredness, These, as we have seen, are a closed set of preposition-like words

6.1 What we've seen

that establish relations between noun phrases in Mam. About half of these relational nouns are possessed body parts that express relations such as in front of, on top of, at the side of, behind, etc. These forms as well depend on the notion of the live metaphor of a body or center from which these relations are calculated.

The pervasiveness of the Mam intransitive verbs of motion, the directionals, and the directional affixes, plus the relational nouns guarantee that virtually every utterance requires some degree of attention to the grammatical concept of an origo or deictic center. As I said earlier, such attention is inescapable, not only as the Mam conceive of the world, but also in how they formulate their minute-by-minute utterances in relation to their place in the world.

Finally, we saw that the use of couplets in Mayan ritual discourse is iconic of the principle of centeredness where the balancing of notions, as in the following invocation from the *Popol Vuh* petitioning the gods to create human beings, is a strategy for attaining centeredness:

Midwife, matchmaker,
our grandmother, our grandfather,
Xpiyacoc, Xmucane,
let there be planting, let there be dawning
of our invocation, our sustenance, our recognition
by the human work, the human design,
the human figure, the human form.
So be it, fulfill your names:
Hunahpu Possum, Hunahpu Coyote,
bearer twice over, begetter twice over,
Great Peccary, Great Coati,
lapidary, jeweler,
sawyer, carpenter,
plate shaper, bowl shaper,
incense maker, master craftsman,
Grandmother of Day, Grandmother of Light.
(Tedlock 1996)

I suggested, following Neuenswander, that the use of couplets is an instantiation of the Mayan value of dualism mentioned by many, including

Morley (1956), Gossen (1986), and Coe (1999), as thematic among the Maya. Neuenswander and Souder say, "The aspect of the Achí language selected as the focus of [their] study is the stylistic characteristic of rhetorical parallelism or, specifically in Achí, the formation of couplets in poetic discourse" (1977:1). She says that in dualism, a single entity is in view, or two aspects of a single entity. This sense of "unity out of diversity" is a paradigm of balance that, while highlighting the two sides of the dualistic frame, at the same time points to the fulcrum upon which the balance hinges, the center.

Attention to center pervades the lexicon, morphology, syntax, and discourse structure of Mam.

6.2 Where do we go from here?

A book often gives rise to more questions than it actually answers—particularly for the writer. Among recommendations for further study, I'd like to suggest several:

First is the idea of homonymy between the ergative markers and the possessive markers. They are identical, and they may not be homonyms at all, but similar senses of the same terms. Since relational nouns are possessed, there is a sense of center involving a body in space. If we could consider the ergative marking on verbs to be possessed action as opposed to simply person marking, there might be some interesting discoveries.

Second, I ignored many of the allomorphs of the directionals as well as other directionally-related affixes (see footnote 3, chapter five). Here my goal was to present a principled few. An exhaustive study—probably by a native speaker—would be a wonderful addition to what little we as outsiders know about Mam. Another discourse particle *-tzin,* or its allomorph *-sin* may also have a role in the marking of information as new or old. Let's look at this as well.

Third, would be other areas of life where centeredness might be an organizing principle. For example, Hendrickson says that the Maya themselves "explicitly argue for the worth of indigenous dress as a symbol for all things Maya" (1995:196). She suggests that "our mother tongue" and "our costume" are the closest and most emotional of connections that we have with any cultural object. Figure 6.1 shows a *huipil,* a woman's traditional blouse with the head opening in the center, circled by a motif of the sun and other symmetrical figures, also concentrically arranged. Why do they do this?

The rich ornamentation and symbolism of Mayan weaving would be an important place to seek analogues of centeredness (see De Jongh Osborne 1965:ch. 8), especially among women.

I also think it would be helpful to pursue the idea that direction and origo are part of the "lexical entry" for intransitive verbs of motion, whereas these are calculated pragmatically for directionals. Such a study would impinge on issues of mutual interest to practitioners of both semantics and pragmatics, and it would help us understand some of the inner computations the Mam employ in order to calculate and assign pragmatic meaning.

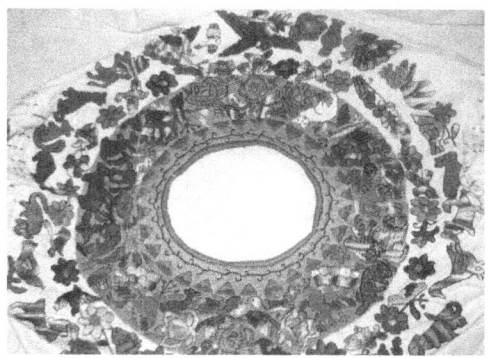

Figure 6.1. *Huipil* (blouse) with center sun motif and embroidered concentric circles, from San Andrés Xecul, a Maya K'iche' town. Photo and *huipil* from the collection of Judith Oltrogge. Used with permission.

6.3 So why the commotion?

We have established the importance of a sense of center in the cultural and linguistic practice of the Mam—that centeredness is indeed both a cultural and grammatical theme. The age-old question remains: Is there a causal relationship between the two? We would certainly think that the things that are important would be coded so that that they would be easy to talk about. This was Sapir's view, and it was wrapped up mostly in the lexicon. Following Boas, he said: "Vocabulary is a very sensitive index of the culture of a people" (Mandelbaum 1949:27). The words and lexical meanings of a people group make explicit those issues and features that are salient to speakers. Languages are different because cultures are different. It is not the case that we simply have different words across cultures for the same concepts. Rather, the semantic pie is cut in different ways by different people groups. Each culture has its categories, its fashion of speaking, "its genius," according to Sapir (1921:32, 120). Our goal as linguists is to plumb the depths of that genius to see and describe how it works as an integrated conceptual system. As anthropologists, we try to understand how such a system works "on the ground," that is, how people talk about the things that matter to them and how they live in the specific context that their language has helped create.

Hymes (1966) recognized this. He said that just as language affects culture, so culture affects language and privileges certain fashions of speaking, certain ways of cutting the pie.

That said, I believe with Everett (2005:37), Wierzbicka (1997:5), and Hoijer (1954:100) that culture basically drives language. There seems to be nothing about any universal properties of language that coerces any particular cultural analogues. Rather, it appears that culture, as its members interact with the real world (and each other), selects among the potential ways to slice up the semantic pie that privileges a certain linguistic code. What is important to people of a culture, they name, and what they name they can talk about. It is the grammar of this "talking about" that interested Whorf, those fashions of speaking or grammatical themes that forced themselves upon the minds of speakers by their obligatory nature. As Boroditsky et al. (2003) point out, if our native language codes gender, then gender becomes a salient and inescapable theme by which we categorize the world. That gender is also reflected in the reality of how the world works only serves to solidify the theme as a legitimate understanding of the world. This is why cultures are so resistant to change. Like Abel's mother in chapter three, she has seen her perception of how the world works confirmed time after time after time.

So at the same time that I claim that culture basically drives language, it is language that carries culture and instills it in those who learn the language in the very act of watching it be affirmed in the real world. This is behind what Enfield says about language and culture. They are not only connected, but "interconstitutive, through overlap and interplay between people's cultural practices and preoccupations and the grammatical structures they habitually employ" (2002:3–4).

This sense that language and culture are interconstitutive reflects Bourdieu's notion of a structured and structuring *habitus* (1990:52) where

6.3 So why the commotion?

language and culture are mutually implying, that is, language realizes the culture of those who speak it, while at the same time it is through language practice that culture emerges and is built up over time, or, as Duranti claims, language "both presupposes and brings about ways of being in the world" (1997:1).

Yet to claim that language and culture mutually imply is not to show that they do. In chapter one I laid out a rubric that I would follow in this study to show the nature of the overlap between cultural and grammatical theme, and to try to "prove" some kind of relationship. I suggested that we adopt a different kind of proof regimen that dealt not with positivism, the idea of measureable, mathematical entities, but hermeneutics—the interpretation of events not by measuring them, "but through understanding meanings, intentions, values, norms, or rules, and [reflecting] upon what has been understood" (Itkonen 1978:20). To review the "proof" rubric that I suggested in chapter one:

1. Itkonen reminds us that meaning exists only in social context (1978:63–64.) So, instead of trying to extract ourselves from social context, we embraced it in this study. This participant observation technique was our main strategy for understanding the emic categories and point of view of the Mam.

2. We sought historical continuities. If cultural and grammatical themes are indeed an appropriate window on Mam culture, they should not only be pervasive within the culture, but they should be instantiated historically among the greater Maya diaspora. By citing scholars from throughout Mesoamerica and by looking at the historical record (the *Popol Vuh*, cross-group comparison, and early writings), we've seen that this theme is both geographically widespread and persistent through time.

3. We sought patterns in the data that we observed, both linguistic and cultural; the more disparate and atomistic the data, the more helpful an encompassing theory "within which the observations find a natural place" (Chafe 1994:21). And while the patterns were independently verified (see chapter three), we were able to unite them under the common cultural umbrella of centeredness. Hymes says that a basic practice of anthropological study is "the showing of a pattern, fashion of speaking, or style among a number of traits" (1966:117). This was the goal of my study—to explain how such diverse observations as religious choice, the constructed world, the perception of health and illness, daily language use, and aspects of the formal grammar of Mam are all instantiations of a single theme.

4. Itkonen says that the people themselves—the Mam—must be able to understand and accept the description arrived at in our research (1978:64). This is what Zaharlick, in a personal communication, called the "Aha! factor." When Mesac said that the idea of centeredness "explains why our people are so hard to work with. Each of us thinks he is the center of everything," he was affirming the overlap of cultural and grammatical theme. He realized not only that the seeking of centeredness is a Mam cultural value, a motivating and organizing principle, something external and "out there" to be pursued, but the fact that each individual constitutes a center from which the pervasive Mam notion of movement and spatial relations is lexicalized by the language and grammaticized in the language makes it a principle that is internalized and all the more pervasive. The other men gathered at this meeting experienced just such an "aha moment," affirming that deictic anchorage and a cultural center space are cut from the same cloth.

5. When someone acts outside of the cultural norm, that is, if centeredness is ignored or flouted, we can expect and seek perturbations in behavior. A cultural value becomes salient via its absence. I discussed this in terms of Timo's patio. When centeredness was considered compromised, a renovation had to take place to reestablish the central patio. I had some repair work of my own to tend to in the case of the offended husband, where the center space of communal peace and tranquility was upended by my careless indiscretion.

Similarly, when parents want to give advice to their children who have wandered from the norm, they talk in such a way as to bring the prodigal back to the center, the road of life that should be traversed down the middle without deviating to the right or left.

6. Finally, we expected our theme to be manifested in many ways in the daily life of the Mam. In chapters three and four, I showed how centeredness is pervasive as an organizing principle among the Mam and how the vocabulary of centeredness is coded lexically in a number of terms and in the details of agreement protocol.

These six observations perhaps don't prove that language and culture are interconstitutive in a measurable, empirical way, but I believe that I have satisfied the hermeneutic approach to the problem, interpreting data in a patterned way, consistent with how the Mam themselves view the world, how they see their place in it, their description of it, and their practice within it.

Appendix A: Text

1. *Jun   qlixje,   o   xi'-y   toj jun q-b'e-'y   k'ay-il.*
   one   morning   we   went-EX   in one our-trip-EX   to.sell-INF
   'One morning we went on a trip to sell (at a market).'

2. *Oxa   q-b'aj-a;   o   xi'-y   tuk'a   t-karr   Josué.*
   three our-number-EX   we   went-EX   with   his-car   Josué
   'There were three of us that went in Josué's car.'

3. *A-tzi'n   q-b'aj-a,   a   Julián   ex-sin   ayin-tz-a.*
   that-well our-number-EX   that   Julián   and-then   me-well-EX
   'So our number included (Josué), Julián and me.'

4. *A-tzi'n   te   q-xi'-y,   t-b'an-il-x-ch'in   q-b'e-'y*
   that-well   when   we-went-EX   its-good-INAL-AUG-little   our-road-EX

   tej   q-kani-'n   Twi'muj.
   when   we-arrived-EX   Twimuj
   'Now when we went, the road that took us as far as Twimuj was pretty nice.'

181

5. *Noq-tzin tu'n-tz-jo, te' q-xi'-ch'il-tz-a*
only-well regarding-then-SPEC when we-went-a.bit-then-EX

   tu'n q-kani-'n Triunfo, nya'-xix wen b'e.
   in.order.to we-arrived-EX Triunfo not-very good road
   'Regarding this (trip) when we went (from Twimuj) to Triunfo, the road was not very good.'

6. *Ma nintz-x jul, ex-sin manyor quq-x-tz.*
quite big-AUG holes and-well much dust-AUG-then
'There were big potholes and a lot of dust.'

7. *Te' q-xi'-y Txolja o-taq tz'o:k wajxaq tajlal te*
when we-went-EX Txolja PERF-PAS entered eight its.count of

   qlixje.
   morning
   'When we left Txolja (Comitancillo), it was eight in the morning.'

8. *Ex tej q-kani-'n o-taq tz'o:k lajaj te qlixje.*
and when we-arrived-EX PERF-PAS entered ten of morning
'And we arrived (at Triunfo) at ten in the morning.'

9. *Ponix-jo tal najb'il, ja' o kanin-i'y.*
nice-SPEC DIM place where we arrived-EX
'The place where we went was very nice.'

10. *A-tzin t-xilin b'e iky-jo tzen-ku'*
that-well its-essence road similar-SPEC like-down

    b'e n-tzaj xkye tzma-x Twi' Chlub'.
    road PROG-DIR.come begin toward-at.away Tuichilupe.
    'The way we went was similar to the road that comes toward us from the town of Tuichilupe.'

11. *A-tzi'n te' q-kanin-tz-a, ma nintz-x xjal*
that-well when we-arrived-then-EX very big-AUG people

    n-k'ayin-taq Triunfo.
    PROG-sell-PAS Triunfo
    'When we arrived, a lot of people were selling there in Triunfo.'

12. *N-we'*　　　　*karr*　*ja'lin,*
    PROG-stop　　car　　now
    'Now the car stops'

13. *ex*　　*b'e'x*　　　　　　*xi'*　　*te*　　*Julián*　*k'ay-il.*
    and　　PUNCT.PAS　　went　he　　Julián　　to.sell-INF
    'and Julián went off to sell.'

14. *Ex*　　*iky-x-jo*　　　　　　　*qe',*　　　*o*　　　　　*xi'*　　*qe'*
    and　　similar-then-SPEC　　us.EX　　we.REM　　went　us.EX

    k'ay-il　　　*ti'j-jo*　　　　　　　　*q-k'axhjil-a,*　　　　　　*a*
    to. sell-INF　regarding-SPEC　our-merchandise-EX　that.which

    iqin-taq.
    carry-PAS
    'And we as well went to sell the goods that had been brought.'

15. *Ex*　　*tib'aj*　*jun*　*tal*　　*netz'*　　*mexh*　　*o*　　　　　*k'ayini'-y*
    and　　on　　　a　　　DIM　　little　　table　　　we.REM　　sold-EX

    toj　*plas.*
    in　　plaza
    'We sold (our things) on a little table at the plaza.'

16. *Ex*　　*a-tzi'n*　　　*q-k'axhjil-a*　　　　　　*iqin-taq:*　　*tajlal*　　*ab'q'e,*
    and　　that-well　　our-merchandise-EX　carry-PAS　counter　year

    jun　*t-u'j*　　　　*San Juan,*　*ex*　　*ma*　　*nintz-x-taq*
    one　　his-book　　San Juan　　and　　very　　big-AUG-PAS

    txqan-l　　　　　　　　*u'j.*
    other-remaining　　book
    'And the goods we brought to sell (were) calendars, Gospels of San Juan, and a lot of other books.'

17. *Kub'*　　　*yek'-it-tzin-tz-jo*　　　　　　　　　*tal*　　*q-k'axhjil-a.*
    DIR.down　show-PASS-well-then-SPEC　　DIM　　our-merchandise-EX
    'We laid out our little bit of merchandise.'

18. *Noq-x te' t-lon-te tnejil xjal, b'aj*
    only-then when he-saw-it first person DIR.complete

    tzaj qi'yj txqan-l xjal.
    DIR.come gather other-remaining people
    'When the first person saw our goods, everyone else gathered as well.'

19. *Tzen-lila e:l-ila toj ky-wutz*
    how-uncertain leave-uncertain in their-minds

    xjal-la.
    people-uncertain
    'What could the people have been thinking?'

20. *Noq b'aj jaw ka'ylaj.*
    only DIR.complete DIR.up amazed
    'They were amazed.'

21. *Ok ten-pe-tzin te Josué-tz yol-il kyi'jjo*
    DIR.enter begin-?-well he Josué-then to.speak-INF about

    jni' u'j toj q-yol.
    all book in our-language
    'Then Josué began to talk about all the books in our language.'

22. *Ex n-chi b'in-xjal ti'j-jo u'j*
    and PROG-they listen-people regarding-SPEC book

    n-ja-tz u'jin-taq.
    PROG-DIR.up-then read-PAS
    'And the people listened to the book that was being read.'

23. *Ex iky-x-taq we-ji'-y noq-taq n-xi b'i'n*
    and also-AUG-PAS I-EMPH-EX only-PAS PROG-DIR.go listen

    we'.
    me
    'And even I myself was listening,'

24. *tu'n tnejil maj in xi' we' k'ay-il tuk'a Josué.*
    since first time I.REM go I.EMPH to.sell-INF with Josué
    'since it was the first time I had ever gone to sell with Josué.'

Appendix A: Text 185

25. *At-taq   n-e-x   laq'on-te   tu'j   Marks*
    exist-PAS PROG-DIR.leave-go bought-it book   Mark
    'There were some who bought the book of St. Mark'

26. *mo   ti'j-jo   txqan-l   u'j-taq*
    or   regarding-SPEC other-remaining book-PAS
    'or some of the other books.'

27. *Ma   nintz-x   xjal   e:-x   k'ay-il   toj-jo   k'ayb'il   a';*
    very many-AUG people leave-go to.sell-INF in-SPEC market   that
    'A large number of people went to sell at that market.'

28. *noq   ja'-chaq-ku   n-chi   b'aj   tza:j-e.*
    only where-disperse-down PROG-they DIR.complete come-HAB
    '(God only knows) where all these people come from.'

29. *Ex   xi   ky-laq'o'n   ky-u'j.*
    and DIR.go they-bought their-books
    'And they bought books.'

30. *Tu'n-pe-tzi'n,   o   k'ayin   qe'   wen.*
    for-?-well   we   sold   us.EX   well
    'For this reason, the books sold well.'

31. *Ex   nya   jotx   b'aj   loq'in.*
    and not   everyone DIR.complete bought
    'And not (even) everyone bought.'

32. *At   te-tz   noq   n-kanin   ka'y-il,*
    exist s/he-then   only   PROG-arrive   to.see-INF
    'There are those who are coming only to watch,'

33. *ex   mina   n-loq'in   ni   jun   u'j.*
    and   no   PROG-buy   nary   one   book
    'and they didn't buy a single book.'

34. *At-taq-te   n-e-x   t-laq'o'in-taq   t-u'j,*
    exist-PAS-him/her PROG-DIR.leave-go s/he-buy-PAS   his/her-book
    'There were those who went to buy a book'

35. | *tu'n* | *n-ok* | *t-ka'yin-taq* | *tu'n* | *b'a'n-taq* | *te*
since | PROG-DIR.enter | s/he-see-PAS | that | able-PAS | he

mos *yolin* *toj* *q-yol*
non.Mam speak in our-language.
'simply because they heard a foreigner speaking our language.'

36. *B'aj* *k'ayin-tz-a* *ja'lin,*
DIR.complete sold-then-EX now
'Then (we) finished selling,'

37. *ex* *o-taq* *tz'o:k* *kab'lajaj* *te* *q'ij,*
and PERF-PAS enter twelve of day
'and it had passed 12 o'clock noon'

38. *ja* *q-nik'u'n-tz-a* *q-k'axhjil-a.*
where we-arranged-then-EX our-merchandise-EX
'at which time we packed up our merchandise.'

39. *Ex* *b'e'x-sin* *o* *a:j-tz-tz-a,*
and PUNCT.PAS-well we.REM return.home-come-then-EX
'And we returned home'

40. *tu'n* *q-u:l-a* *kyxol* *aj* *Txolja.*
in.order.to we-arrive-EX among resident Comitancillo
'in order to come again to our own pueblo.'

Appendix B: List of Abbreviations

AUG	augmentative
DEM	demonstrative
DIM	diminuitive
DIR	directional
EMPH	emphatic
ERG	ergative
EX	exclusive
HAB	habitual
INAL	inalienable (or intimate) possession
INF	infinitive
PAS	past
PASS	passive
PERF	perfect aspect
PL	plural
POS	possessive
POT	potential (future)
PROG	progressive aspect
PUNCT	punctual (at a certain point in past time)
REC	recent completed aspect (near past)
REM	remote completed aspect (far past)

SG	singular
SPEC	specifier

Appendix C: Notes on Orthography

The examples throughout this book are in the Central Mam practical orthography with the exception of <xh> which is explained below. Assume Spanish pronunciation for all vowels with the following proviso: Although the Mam do not write vowel length, I have written it here with a colon (:) to distinguish the directionals (which contain short vowels) from their corresponding intransitives (which may contain long vowels). The following consonants are pronounced as in Spanish: ch, k, l, m, n, p, r, s, t, w, and y.

The consonants <j> and <q> are uvular fricative and uvular stop respectively, formed far back in the throat; <xh> is an alveopalatal fricative (the same as English <sh>), while <x> without the accompanying <h> is the retroflexed version of the same sound. You can try making this sound by forming your tongue for an English <sh> and then, before starting your pronunciation, pull your tongue tip back sort of like a fish hook and then try to pronounce the <sh>. What comes out should be identifiable as a retroflexed version of the English <sh>. Notice the more "hollow" resonance of the retroflexed sound. The <tx> is a retroflexed alveopalatal affricate (a <ch>, but with the same "retroflex gymnastics" involving the tongue tip as with the <x>); <ky> is a palatal stop similar to the <k> in *keen* (which is much more fronted in the mouth than say the <k> sound in *call;* <tz> is an alveolar affricate, and it sounds just like the *ts* in *cats*.

The consonant <b'>, commonly called the "Mayan b," is an implosive bilabial stop. Implosive means that it is formed with inrushing air, rather than outgoing. Interestingly, for those with a phonological bent, the "Mayan b" is the only voiced obstruent in Mam. All other obstruents are voiceless, and there is clear indication that the "Mayan b" is moving toward [p'] with speakers of the present generation. On the other hand, all non-obstruents in Mam (vowels, semi-vowels (y and w), flaps (r), laterals (l), and nasals (m and n)) are voiced. This is universalist phonology at its best.

Consonants plus apostrophes (') are glottalized consonants (ch', k', ky', q' t', tx', tz'). These, plus the retroflexed sounds, give Mam a beautiful explosive and exotic voice. A vowel plus glottal stop is considered to be a complex vowel and is written a', e', i', o', and u'.

You might enjoy the challenge of following along with native speakers as they read a chapter from the Gospel of Matthew. Go to:

http://www.bible.is/MVCNVS/Matt/2

You may be able to follow along and see how the different sounds that I wrote about actually sound tripping effortlessly from the mind and mouth of a native speaker.

Good luck!

References

Aissen, Judith L. 1992. Topic and focus in Mayan. *Language* 68:43–80.
Altman, Patricia B. and Caroline D. West. 1992. *Threads of identity: Maya costume of the 1960s in Highland Guatemala.* Los Angeles: Fowler Museum of Cultural History.
Annis, Sheldon. 1987. *God and production in a Guatemalan town.* Austin: University of Texas Press.
Beach, Edgar. 1994. B'a'n as a life goal among the Tektitko. Ms.
Becker. A. L. 1996 [1984]. Biography of a sentence: a Burmese proverb. In Donald Brennais and Ronald K. S. Macaulay (eds.), *The matrix of language: Contemporary linguistic anthropology,* 142–59. Boulder, Col.: Westview Press.
Boas, Franz. 1911. *Handbook of American Indian languages,* Vol. 1. Bureau of American Ethnology, Bulletin 40. Washington: Government Print Office (Smithsonian Institution, Bureau of American Ethnology).
Boroditsky, Lera, Lauren A. Schmidt, and Webb Phillips. 2003. Sex, syntax, and semantics. In Deidre Gentner and Susan Goldin-Meadow (eds.), *Mind: Advances in the study of language and cognition,* 61–80. Cambridge, Mass.: M.I.T. Press.
Bourdieu, Pierre. 1990. *The logic of practice.* Richard Nice trans. Palo Alto: Stanford University Press.
Bourdieu, Pierre. 2003 [1971]. The Berber house. In Setha M. Low and Denise Lawrence-Zúñiga (eds.), The *anthropology of space and place: Locating culture,* 131–141. Oxford: Blackwell Publishing.

Brewster, Thomas, and Elizabeth S. Brewster. 1976. *Language acquisition made practical.* Colorado Springs: Lingua House.

Brown, Penelope, and Stephen Levinson. 1987. *Politeness: Some universals in language usage.* Cambridge: Cambridge University Press.

Carroll, John B. 1956. *Language thought and reality: Selected writings of Benjamin Lee Whorf.* Cambridge, Mass.: M.I.T. Press.

Chafe, Wallace. 1994. *Discourse, consciousness, and time: The flow and displacement of concious experience in speaking and writing.* Chicago: University of Chicago Press.

Coe, Michael D. 1999. *The Maya,* sixth edition. New York: Thames and Hudson.

Collins, Wesley, M. 2010. The center as cultural and grammatical theme in Mam (Maya). *Space and culture* 13(1):17–31.

Collins, Wesley, M. 2005. Codeswitching avoidance as a strategy for Maya-Mam linguistic revitalization. *International Journal of American Linguistics* 71(3):239–276.

Cruz, Emiliana. 2004. *Oradores de la palabra del alma: Desplazamineto lingüístico y pérdida cultural en comunidades chatinas.* Paper presented at the Symposium for language and cultural maintenance in Mesoamerica. University of Texas at Austin, April 1–3, 2004.

Curruchiche Otzoy, German, Ernestina Reyes de Ramos, and Margarita López Raquec. 1994. *Conclusiones, recomendaciones, y resoluciones del primer congreso de educación Maya en Guatemala.* Guatemala City: Ministerio de Educación.

Danziger, Eve. 1994. Out of sight, out of mind: Person, perception, and function in Mopan Maya spatial deixis. *Linguistics* 32:885–907.

Demarest, Arthur, Kim Morgan, Claudia Wolley, and Héctor Escobedo. 2003. The political acquisition of sacred geography: the murciélagos complex at Dos Pilas. In Jessica Joyce Christie (ed.), *Maya palaces and elite residences: An interdisciplinary approach,* 120–183. Austin: University of Texas Press.

Dodsworth, Robin. 2005. Linguistic variation and sociological consciousness. Ph.D. dissertation. The Ohio State University.

DuBois, John. 1985. Competing motivations. In John Haiman (ed.), *Iconicity in Syntax,* 343–365. Amsterdam: Benjamins.

Duranti, Alessandro. 1997. *Linguistic anthropology.* Cambridge: Cambridge University Press.

Duranti, Alessandro. 1992. Language and bodies in space: Samoan ceremonial greetings. *American Anthropologist* 94:657–691.

Durkheim, Émile. 1988 [1938]. Rules for the explanation of social facts. In Paul Bohannan and Mark Glazer (eds.), *High points in anthropology,* Second edition, 234–251. New York: Alfred A. Knopf.

Edmonson, Munro S. 1993. The Mayan faith. In Gary H. Gossen (ed.) in collaboration with Miguel León-Portilla, *South and Meso-American native spirituality: From the cult of the feathered serpent to the theology of liberation.* New York: Crossroad Publishing Company.

Enfield, Nick J. 2004. *Ethnosyntax: Explorations in grammar and culture.* Oxford: Oxford University Press.
England, Nora C. 1998. Mayan efforts toward language preservation. In Lenore A. Grenoble and Lindsay J. Whaley (eds.), *Endangered languages,* 99–116. Cambridge: Cambridge University Press.
England, Nora C. 1996. The role of language standardization in revitalization. In Edward F. Fischer and R. McKenna Brown (eds.), *Maya cultural activism in Guatemala,* 178–194. Austin: University of Texas Press.
England, Nora C. 1990. El Mam: semejanzas y diferencias regionales. In Nora C. England and Stephen R Elliott (eds.), *Lecturas sobre le lingüística maya,* 221–252. CIRMA: Guatemala.
England, Nora C. 1983. *A grammar of Mam, a Mayan language.* Austin: University of Texas Press.
England, Nora C. 1978. Space as a Mam grammatical theme. In Nora C. England (ed.), *Papers in Mayan linguistics,* 225–238. Columbia: University of Missouri Press.
Everett, Daniel L. 2005. Cultural constraints on grammar and cognition in Piraha: Another look at the design features of human language. *Current Anthropology* 46(4):621–646.
Fillmore, Charles J. 1998. Deixia and context. In Kirsten Malmkjaer and John Williams (eds.), *Context in language learning and language understanding,* 27–42.
Fillmore, Charles J. 1997. *Lectures on deixis.* Stanford: CSLI Publications.
Freidel, David, Linda Schele, and Joy Parker. 1993. *Maya cosmos: Three thousand years on the shaman's path.* New York: William Morrow and Company, Inc.
Garzon, Susan, R. McKenna Brown, Julia Becker Richards, and Wuqu' Ajpub'. 1998. *The life of our language: Kaqchikel Maya maintenance, shift, and revitalization.* Austin: University of Texas Press.
Geertz, Clifford. 1973. *The interpretation of cultures.* New York: Harper Collins.
Gillespie, Susan D. 2000. Maya "nested houses." In Rosemary A. Joyce and Susan D. Gillespie (eds.) *Beyond kinship: Social and material reproduction in house societies,* 135–160.
Goddard, Cliff. 2002. Ethnosyntax, ethnopragmatics, sign-functions, and culture. In Nick J. Enfield (ed.) *Ethnosyntax: Explorations in grammar and culture,* 52–73. Oxford: Oxford University Press.
Godfrey, Thomas James. 1981. Grammatical cateories for spatial reference in the western Mam dialect of Tacaná. Ph.D. dissertation. University of Texas at Austin.
Godfrey, Thomas James, and Wesley M. Collins. 1987. *Una encuesta dialectal en el area mam de Guatemala.* Guatemala City: Instituto Lingüístico de Verano.

Gossen, Gary. 1986. Mesoamerican ideas as a foundation for regional synthesis. In Gary Gossen (ed.), *Symbol and meaning beyond the closed community: Essays in Mesoamerican ideas*, 1–8. Albany: Institute for Mesoamerican Studies Press.

Hale, Kenneth L. 1986. Notes on world view and semantic categories: some Walpiri examples. In Pieter Muysken and Henk van Riemsdijk (eds.), *Features and projections*, 233–254. Dorcrecht: Foris Publications.

Halliday, M. A. K., and Ruqaiya Hasan. 1976. *Cohesion in English*. Essex, England: Longman.

Hammersly, Martyn, and Paul Atkinson. 1986. *Ethnography: Principles in practice*. London: Routledge.

Hanks, William F. 1990. *Referential practice: Language and lived space among the Maya*. Chicago: University of Chicago Press.

Haviland, John. 1996. Projections, transpositions, and relativity. In John J. Gumperz and Stephen C. Levinson (eds.), *Rethinking linguistic relativity*, 271–323. Cambridge: Cambridge University Press.

Headland, Thomas, Kenneth Pike, and Marvin Harris, eds. 1990. *Emics and etics: The insider/outsider debate*. Thousand Oaks, Calif.: Sage

Hendrickson, Carol. 1995. *Weaving identities: Construction of dress and self in a highland Guatemalan town*. Austin: University of Texas Press.

Hockett, Charles F. Chinese versus English: An exploration of the Whorfian thesis. 1954. In Harry Hoijer (ed.), *Language in culture: Conference on the inter-relations of language and other aspects of culture*, 106–123. Chicago: University of Chicago Press.

Hoijer, Harry, ed. 1954. *Language in culture: Conference on the interrelations of language and other aspects of culture*. Chicago: University of Chicago Press.

Hoijer, Harry. 1954. The Sapir-Whorf hypothesis. In Harry Hoijer (ed.), *Language in culture: Conference on the inter-relations of language and other aspects of culture*, 92–105. Chicago: University of Chicago Press.

Hopper, Paul J., and Elizabeth Closs Traugott. 1993. *Grammaticalization*. Cambridge: Cambridge University Press.

Hymes, Dell. 1974. *Foundations of sociolinguistics: An ethnographic approach*. Philadelphia: University of Pennsylvania Press.

Hymes, Dell. 1966. Two types of linguistic relativity. In William Bright (ed.), *Sociolinguistics, proceedings of the UCLA sociolinguistics conference*, 1964 (Janua Linguarum, series maior, 20), 114–165. The Hague: Mouton.

Itkonen, Esa. 1978. *Grammatical theory and metascience: A critical investigation into the methodological and philosophical foundations of "autonomous" linguistics*. Amsterdam: John Benjamins.

Johnston, Kevin J. 2001. Broken fingers: Classic Maya scribe capture and polity consolidation. *Antiquity* 75(288):373–381.

Kunow, Marianna Appel. 2003. *Maya medicine: Traditional healing in Yucatan*. Albuquerque: University of New Mexico Press.

Labov, William. 1972. *Sociolinguistic patterns.* Philadelphia: University of Pennsylvania Press.
Lakoff, George. 1987. *Women, fire, and dangerous things.* Chicago: University of Chicago Press.
Lakoff, George, and Mark Johnson. 1980. *Metaphors we live by.* Chicago: University of Chicago Press.
Landa, Diego de. 1566. *Relación de las cosas de Yucatán.* Translated by William Gates as *Yucatan before and after the conquest.* (New York: Dover Publications, 1978).
Lefebvre, Henri. 1997. The production of space (extracts). In Neil Leach (ed.), *Rethinking architecture: A reader in cultural theory,* 138–146. London: Routledge.
Levinson, Stephen C. 1983. *Pragmatics.* Cambridge: Cambridge University Press.
Low, Setha M., and Denise Lawrence-Zúñiga. 2003. *The anthropology of space and place: Locating culture.* Oxford: Blackwell.
Low, Setha M. 2000. *On the plaza: The politics of public space and culture.* Austin: University of Texas Press.
Low, Setha M. 1997. Public space as art and commodity. In Seymour Wapner, Jack Demick, Takiji Yamamoto, and Takashi Takahashi (eds.), *Handbook of Japan-United States environment-behavior research: Toward a transactional approach,* 313–324. New York: Plenum Press.
Low, Setha M. 1996. Constructing difference: spatial boundaries and social change in two Costa Rican plazas. In Deborah Pellow (ed.), *Setting boundaries: The anthropology of spatial and social organization,* 161–177. Westport, Conn.: Bergin and Garvey.
Low, Setha M. 1993. Cultural meaning of the plaza: the history of the Spanish-American gridplan-plaza urban design. In Robert Rotenberg and Gary McDonough (eds.), *The cultural meaning of urban space,* 75–93. Westport, Conn.: Bergin and Garvey.
Lucy, John A. 1992. *Grammatical categories: A case study of the linguistic relativity hypothesis.* Cambridge: Cambridge University Press.
Lyons, John. 1977. *Semantics,* Volume 2. Cambridge: Cambridge University Press.
Malinowski, Bronislaw. 1922. *Argonauts of the Western Pacific.* New York: Dutton.
Mandelbaum, David G. 1949. *Selected writings of Edward Sapir.* Berkeley: University of California Press.
Manderson, Lenore. 1987. Hot-cold food and medical theories: Overview and introduction. *Social Science and Medicine* 25(4):329–330.
Martin, Laura. 1986. "Eskimo words for snow": A case study in the genesis and decay of an anthropological example. *American Anthropologist* 88:418–423.
Martin, Laura. 1977. Positional roots in Kanjobal (Mayan). Ph.D. dissertation. University of Florida.

McArthur, Harry S. 1979. The role of the ancestors in the daily life of the Aguacatec (Maya). Paper presented at the XLIII International Congress of Americanists. University of British Columbia, Vancouver, Canada, August 10–17, 1979.

Messer, Ellen. 1981. Hot-cold classification: theoretical and practical implications of a Mexican study. *Social Science and Medicine* 15(B):133–145.

Morley, Sylvanus Griswold. 1956. *The ancient Maya,* Third edition, revised by George W. Brainerd. Stanford: Stanford University Press.

Mufwene, Salikoko S. 2002. Colonization, globalization and the plight of 'weak' languages. *Journal of Linguistics* 38:375–395.

Nájera, Martha Ilia. 1987. *El don de la sangre en el equilibrio cósmico: el sacrificio y el autosacrificio sangriente entre los antiguos mayas.* México: Universidad Nacional Autónoma de México.

Neuenswander, Helen L., and Shirley D. Souder. 1977. The hot-cold wet-dry syndrome among the Quiché of Joyabaj. In Helen L. Neuenswander and Dean E. Arnold (eds.), *Cognitive studies of southern Mesoamerica,* 96–125. Dallas: Summer Institute of Linguistics.

Neuenswander, Helen L. 1986. *El dualismo: un fenómeno lingüístico y cultural entre el pueblo Cubulco Achí (Maya).* Guatemala City: Summer Institute of Linguistics.

Orellana, Sandra L. 1987. *Indian medicine in highland Guatemala: The pre-Hispanic and colonial periods.* Albuquerque: University of New Mexico Press.

Osborne, Lilly de Jongh. 1965. *Indian crafts of Guatemala and El Salvador.* Norman: University of Oklahoma Press.

Pinker, Steven. 2007. *The stuff of thought: Language as a window into human nature.* New York: Penguin Group.

Preuss, Mary. 1988. *Gods of the Popol Vuh: Xmukane', K'ucumatz, Tojil, and Jurakan.* Culver City, Calif.: Labyrinthos.

Redfield, Robert. 1941. *The folk culture of Yucatan.* Chicago. University of Chicago Press.

Redfield, Robert, and Alfonso Villa Rojas. 1962. *Chan Kom: a Maya village,* Revised edition. Chicago: University of Chicago Press.

Reynoso, Fray Diego de. 1916 [1644]. *Vocabulario de la lengua Mame,* printed by Francisco Robledo and recopied by Alberto María Carreño. México: Departamento de Imprenta de la Secretaria de Fomento.

Richardson, Don. 1977. *Lords of the earth.* Ventura, Calif.: Regal.

Robinson, Julia W. 1989. Architecture as a medium for culture: public institution and private house. In Setha M. Low and Erve Chambers (eds.), *Housing, culture, and design: A comparative perspective,* 253–279. Philadelphia: University of Pennsylvania Press.

Rymer, Russ. 2012. Vanishing voices. *National Geographic* July 60–93.

Said, Edward. 1989. Representing the colonized: anthropology's interlocutors. *Critical Inquiry* 15:205–225.

Sanders, Ted J. M., Wilbert P. M. Spooren, and Leo G. M. Noordman. 1992. Toward a taxonomy of coherence relations. *Discourse processes* 15:1–35.
Sanders, Ted, and Wilbert Spooren. 2001. Text representation as an interface between language and its users. In Ted Sanders, Joost Schilperoord, and Wilbert Spooren (eds.), *Text representation: Linguistic and psycholinguistic aspects,* 1–25. Amsterdam: John Benjamins.
Sapir, Edward. 1921. *Language.* New York: Harcourt, Brace and Company.
Schaengold, Charlotte. 2004. Bilingual Navajo: Mixed codes, bilingualism, and language maintenance. Ph.D. dissertation. The Ohio State University.
Schlesinger, I. M. 1991. The wax and wane of Whorfian views. In Robert L. Cooper and Bernard Spolsky (eds.), *The influence of language on culture: Essays in honor of Joshua A. Fishman's 65th birthday,* 7–44. Berlin: Mouton de Gruyer.
Scotchmer, David. 1993. Life of the heart: A Maya Protestant spirituality. In Gary H. Gossen in collaboration with Miguel León-Portilla (eds.) *South and Meso-American native spirituality: From the cult of the feathered serpent to the theology of liberation,* 496–525. New York: Crossroad Publishing Company.
Scotchmer, David. 1989. Symbols of salvation: a local Mayan Protestant theology. *Missiology: An international review.* XVII(3)293–310.
Scotchmer, David G. 1978. Grammatical and semantic components of Ostuncalco Mam -*c'u'j* terms. University of New York at Albany. Ms.
Sexton, James D., ed. 1981. *Son of Tecún Umán: A Mayan Indian tells his life story.* Tucson: University of Arizona Press.
Slobin, Dan. 1996. From "thought and language" to "thinking for speaking." In John J. Gumperz and Stephen C. Levinson (eds.), *Rethinking linguistic relativity,* 70–96. Cambridge: Cambridge University Press.
Suárez, Jorge. 1982. *Mesoamerican Indian languages.* Cambridge: Cambridge University Press.
Tedlock, Dennis. 1996. *Popol Vuh: The definitive edition of the Mayan book of the dawn of life and the glories of gods and kings,* Revised edition. New York: Simon and Schuster.
Thompson, J. Eric S. 1966. *The rise and fall of Maya civilization,* Second edition. Norman: University of Oklahoma Press.
Townsend, Paul. 1980. *Ritual rhetoric from Cotzal.* Guatemala City: Summer Institute of Linguistics.
Vogt, Evon Z. 1976. Tortillas for the gods: A symbolic analysis of Zinacanteco rituals. Cambridge, Mass.: Harvard University Press.
Vogt, Evon Z. 1969. *Zinacantan: A Maya community in the highlands of Chiapas.* Cambridge, Mass.: Harvard University Press.
Wauchope, Robert. 1938. *Modern Mayan houses: A study of their archaeological significance.* Washington, D.C.: Carnegie Institution of Washington

Whorf, Benjamin L. 1941. The relation of habitual thought and behavior to language. In Ben G. Blount (ed.), *Language, culture and society: A book of readings,* 64–84. Prospect Heights, Ill.: Waveland Press.
Whorf, Benjamin L. 1940. Science and Linguistics. *MIT Technology Review* 42:229–231.
Wierzbicka, Anna. 2002. English causative constructions in an ethnosyntactic perspective: focusing on let. In Nick Enfield (ed.), *Ethnosyntax,* 162–203. Oxford: Oxford University Press.
Wierzbicka, Anna. 1997. *Understanding cultures through their key words: English, Russian, Polish, German, Japanese.* New York: Oxford University Press.
Wierzbicka, Anna. 1992. *Semantics, culture and cognition.* New York: Oxford University Press.
Wierzbicka, Anna. 1979. Ethno-syntax and the philosophy of grammar. *Studies in Language* 3(3):313–383.
Wisdom, Charles. 1940. The Chorti Indians of Guatemala. Chicago: University of Chicago Press.
Ximénez, Francisco. 1722 [2001]. *Popol Vuh.* Guatemala City: Editorial Atemis-Edinter.
Zaharlick, Amy. 1992. Ethnography in anthropology and its value for education. *Theory into Practice* 31(2):116–125.

Index

A

Aha! factor 23, 180
Annis, Sheldon 85, 98
anthropological linguistics 25; *see also* linguistic anthropology
anthropology 3, 5, 16, 17, 21, 23, 106, 133
Aphrodite 23
architectonics xv, 27, 65, 78
architecture 72, 75, 92
Atkinson, Paul 30
auxiliaries 146, 150, 152, 157, 155, 169; *see also* directional auxiliaries
Aztecs 66, 76, 78

B

balance 2, 32, 63, 69, 85, 96, 97, 110, 112, 172
b'a'n 'goodness' 2, 19, 107, 116, 121
Beach, Edgar 116
Becker, A. L. 31, 37, 105, 106
Berber 75, 80

Boas, Franz 5, 177
Boroditsky, Lera 5, 15, 178
Bourdieu, Pierre 18, 36, 80, 171, 178
Brewster, Elizabeth S. 28, 29
Burmese 105

C

centeredness 2, 18, 21, 23, 25, 34, 37, 52, 63, 68–70, 74, 76, 80, 85, 88, 93, 96, 114, 136, 138, 169, 171, 180
Centeredness as Cultural Theme 65
Central America 42, 60
Chafe, Wallace 23, 132
Chamula 79, 172
Chomsky, Noam 26, 35
cockfight 16, 31, 32, 104
coconut 96
Coe, Michael 57, 78, 176
cold *see* hot-cold syndrome
Collins, Wesley 56, 58, 124
Comitancillo 27, 36, 37, 41, 42, 44, 45, 48–50, 62, 79, 96, 107, 156
Costa Rica 79

couplets 90, 110, 112, 113, 175, 176
Cruz, Emiliana 61
cultural themes 13, 16, 20, 64, 65, 152, 171
culture 3, 4, 9, 11, 13, 19, 24, 36, 38, 64, 72, 85, 103, 105, 112, 133, 179, 180
Cyders, Robert 132

D

Danziger, Eve 161
deixis/deictic 20, 34, 138, 148, 150, 151, 161
democracy 9, 136
directional auxiliaries 140, 141, 145, 150, 153, 157, 169, 175; *see also* auxiliaries
discourse 20, 35, 64, 90, 110, 125, 136, 165, 169, 175, 176
  discourse analysis 27, 34
  discourse markers 161, 163, 164
  discourse particle 163
  discourse specifier 159
Dodsworth, Robin 25
"dogness" 135
Dos Pilas 92, 98
dualism 56, 57, 64, 90, 110, 112, 114, 169, 176
DuBois, John 18
Duranti, Alessandro 33, 102, 103, 167
Durkheim, Émile 23, 24

E

Edmonson, Munro 85, 87, 89, 111, 128
emic 17, 19, 30, 32, 75, 85
Enfield, Nick 19, 21, 136
England, Nora 2, 6, 18, 20, 37, 58, 61, 64, 136, 139, 140, 146, 166, 171
ethnography 3, 16, 22, 26, 27, 30, 31, 33, 37, 101, 103, 105, 130, 132
ethnophilosophy 136
ethnosyntax 6, 136

etic 17, 32, 75, 85
Eugenio 1, 26, 44, 90
Everett, Daniel L. 64, 178

F

faith; *see also* religion
  Catholicism 52, 94
  Evangelicalism 53, 96, 99, 121, 173
  Protestantism 52, 94, 95, 98
  traditional religion 52, 53, 61, 63, 85, 94, 95, 98
Fillmore, Charles 34, 141
four/"fourness" 2, 73, 89, 90, 114
Fraser, Bruce 164
Freidel, David 74

G

Garzon, Susan 60
Geertz, Clifford 13, 19, 31, 32, 37, 84, 85, 104
gesture 110
Gilberto 28, 69, 124
Gillespie, Susan 73, 81
Goddard, Cliff 136, 137
Godfrey, Thomas James 37, 58, 124, 139, 140, 141, 152
god's eye 74, 91
Gossen, Gary 6, 56, 57, 71, 92, 110, 176
grammar 2, 6, 23, 64, 135
grammatical categories 169
grammaticalization 154
grammaticalized xvi, 148, 154, 156, 168, 169, 174
grammatical theme 5, 11, 16, 21, 26, 64, 135, 136, 152
Guatemala 38, 44, 46, 48, 50, 60

H

habitus 18, 36, 178
Haiti 109
Hale, Ken 6, 136, 174
Halliday, M. A. K. 34, 161, 164

Hammersly, Martyn 30
Hanks, William F. 74, 166
Harris, Marvin 17
Hasan, Ruqaiya 34, 161, 164
Haviland, John 145, 152
Headland 17
heart 86, 87, 125
heart of earth 89, 92
heart of heaven 85, 89, 92, 94, 172
Hendrickson, Carol 99, 176
Herder, Johann 4
hermeneutic 22, 64
Hockett, Charles 12
Hoijer, Harry 4, 15
honorifics 7
Hopper, Paul J. 156
hot-cold syndrome xv, 43, 63, 66, 67, 71
  cold 67, 172
  hot/heat 47, 67–69, 71, 172
humors 66
Hymes, Dell 6, 18, 33, 38, 133, 178

I

imperative 10, 125
  stealth 10
  veiled 10
  whimperatives 10
interpretive anthropology 32, 64
intransitive 139, 152, 159, 169, 175
Inuit 8
Itkonen, Esa 16, 21, 64, 179

J

Japanese 7
jikyin/jikytzin 86, 174
Johnson, Mark 135
Johnston, Kevin J. 87, 89

K

key word 6, 125, 134
k'u'j see tk'u'j
Kunow, Marianna 69

L

Labov, Wiliam 30
Lakoff, George 135
Landa, Diego 86
Lawrence-Zúñiga, Denise 75
Lefebvre, Henri 75
Levinson, Stephen C. 138, 164
lexicon 3, 8, 133, 135, 152, 155, 169, 176, 180
linguistic anthropology 3, 27; *see also* anthropological linguistics
linguistic relativity 6, 15, 18, 19, 26
Low, Setha 73, 75, 76, 171
Lucy, John 15
Lyons, John 34, 138

M

Malinowski, Bronislaw 3, 101
Mam 18, 21, 27, 46, 56, 97, 180
Manderson, Lenore 66, 68
marriage 48, 104, 119, 129
Martin, Laura 2, 6, 8, 20, 25, 64, 92, 110, 171, 173
Mauer, Eugenio 53
Max 104, 115–117, 123
Maya/Mayan 19, 38, 53, 54, 56, 57, 63, 179
Maya-Achí 90, 110, 112
Maya-Ixil 113
Maya-Mam 33, 137
Mayanness 173
McArthur, Harry S. 116
Menchú, Rigoberta 61
Mesoamerica 38, 56, 57, 66, 76, 112, 179
Messer, Ellen 66, 67, 70, 71
meta-dialogue 37, 103, 132
metaphor 135, 150, 161, 173
microcosms 73, 75, 76, 80
Miguel 96
Morley, Sylvanus Griswold 74, 110, 176
morphology 3, 20, 135, 136, 155, 176
Mufwene, Salikoko 60

N

Nájera, Martha 86, 111, 128, 173
National Bilingual Education Program (PRONEBI) 45, 51, 61
Navajo 7, 8, 72
Neuenswander, Helen 66, 67, 98, 90, 111, 160, 176
nik'ul 121
niky'il 'to center, aim, understand' 126, 131, 174
niky'jin 'middle' 125, 126, 131, 174
niky'sil 'to split in half' 174
Noordman, Leo G. M. 35
nuk'b'il 'peace, order' 94, 121, 131, 174

O

Ohio State University, The xvii, 5, 45
Orellana, Sandra L. 66
origo 138, 144, 145, 152, 175
Oscar 156, 157, 163
Otzoy, Curruchiche 90, 113

P

participant observation 27, 30, 32, 102
pattern 33, 64, 133
Phillips, Webb 5, 15
Pike, Kenneth 17
Pinker, Steven 6, 10
place xv, 72, 75, 76, 93, 94
plaza 75, 76, 79, 80, 92, 171
politeness 118
Popol Vuh 63, 85, 86, 88–93, 110
positivistic (science) 16, 22
pragmatics 177

R

Rafael 107, 110, 114, 122, 129, 130
reciprocity 85, 86, 93, 115
Redfield, Robert 14, 65, 69, 172
relational nouns 166, 167, 169, 174
religion 52, 61, 85, 93, 95, 129, 173; *see also* faith
remittances 50, 83
Reynoso, Fray Diego de 126
Richardson, Don 71
Robinson, Julia 72, 75
Rodin, August 148
Russian 136, 137

S

sacrifice 86, 87, 88, 89, 97, 111, 173
Said, Edward 102
Sanders, Ted 35
Sapir, Edward 5, 12, 134, 177
Sapir-Whorf Hypothesis (SWH) 4, 6, 13–15, 26, 134
  strong version 14
  weak version 14
Schaengold, Charlotte 7
Schmidt, Lauren 5, 15
Scotchmer, David 36, 93, 95, 124, 173
semantics 2, 156, 161, 177, 178
Slobin, Dan 152
sociolinguistics 25, 38, 54
solar market system 49
Souder, Shirley 66, 67, 176
space 34, 75, 78, 92, 136, 161
Spanish 8, 27, 28, 44, 54, 60, 135
Spooren, Wilbert 35
strangemaking 17
Suárez, Jorge 58
susto 67
syncretism 53, 56
syntax 3, 135, 136, 155, 169, 176

T

tanmin 'one's heart' 128, 174
Tedlock, Dennis 91, 93, 99
Tektitek 116
Tenochtitlán 76
Teotihuacán 78
thermometer effect 30, 102
thick description 31, 32, 104, 105
thin description 104, 107
Tikal 76, 78, 97

Index

Timo 24, 81, 84, 85, 180
tk'u'j 'one's stomach, center' 25, 36, 63, 124, 126, 127, 131, 134, 138, 174
tourism 54, 62
Townsend, Paul 89, 112, 116
transitive 169
Traugott, Elizabeth Closs 156
triangulation 23, 33
tumil 'one's direction or ethic' 86, 96, 121, 122, 174
Tuvan 9
twitch 2, 13, 17, 106; *see also* wink
t-xilin 'one's essence' 122, 131, 174
txolil 'to order, line up' 121
tz'aqsin 'adjust' 86
Tzotzil 79, 171

V

vagrancy laws 46, 55
Vogt, Evon 18, 73, 92

W

Whorf, Benjamin 4, 5, 13, 134, 135, 178
Wierzbicka, Anna 6, 9, 11, 102, 125, 134, 136, 178
wink 13, 17, 106; *see also* twitch
Wisdom, Charles 73
world tree 87
worldview 7, 18
World View-1 6, 7, 12, 19
World View-2 6, 7, 12, 19

X

Ximénez, Francisco 90, 92, 99

Y

Yali 71

Z

Zaharlick, Amy 5, 23, 101, 130, 160, 180
Zapotec 66
Zinacantán 74, 92

SIL International Publications
Additional Releases in the
Publications in Ethnology Series

43. African friends and money matters, second edition, by David E. Maranz, 2015, 309 pp., ISBN 978-1-55671-277-7.
42. Ensnared by AIDS, by David K. Beine, 2014, 357 pp., ISBN 978-1-55671-350-7.
41. The Norsk Høstfest: A celebration of ethnic food and ethnic identity, by Paul Thomas Emch, 2011, 121 pp., ISBN 978-1-55671-265-4.
40. Our company increases apace: History, language, and social identity in early colonial Andover, Massachucetts, by Elinor Abbot, 2007, 279 pp., ISBN 978-1-55671-169-5.
39. What place for hunters-gatherers in millenium three? by Thomas N. Headland and Doris E. Blood, eds. 2002, 130 pp., ISBN 978-1-55671-132-9.
38. A tale of Pudicho's people, by Richard Montag. 2002, 181 pp., ISBN 978-1-55671-131-2.
37. African friends and money matters, by David E. Maranz, 2001, 237 pp., ISBN 1-55671-117-4.
36. The value of the person in the Guahibo culture, by Marcelino Sosa, translated by Walter del Aguila, 1999, 158 pp., ISBN 978-1-55671-085-8.
35. People of the drum of God—Come!, by Paul Neeley, 1999, 310 pp., ISBN 978-1-55671-013-1.
34. Cashibo folklore and culture: Prose, poetry, and historical background, by Lila Wistrand-Robinson, 1998, 196 pp., ISBN 978-1-55671-048-3.

SIL International Publications
7500 W. Camp Wisdom Road
Dallas, TX 75236-5629 USA

General inquiry: publications_intl@sil.org
Pending order inquiry: sales_intl@sil.org
www.sil.org/resources/publications

www.ingramcontent.com/pod-product-compliance
Lightning Source LLC
Chambersburg PA
CBHW070254230426
43664CB00014B/2536